THE
PROFESSIONAL LGV DRIVER'S HANDBOOK

THE PROFESSIONAL LGV DRIVER'S HANDBOOK

A COMPLETE GUIDE TO THE DRIVER CPC

2nd edition

David Lowe

The Chartered Institute of
Logistics and Transport (UK)

**KOGAN
PAGE**

It is important for readers to note that although this *Handbook* is intended to cover the full EU Driver CPC Syllabus to aid revision of the subject material, study of this alone is not sufficient to obtain a Driver CPC.

Unlike the Manager's CPC which can be studied at home and the examinations taken independently, approved centres for driver training and certification for the new Driver CPC have been established by the DSA. Attendance at these is necessary to qualify.

This book is intended to provide a practical interpretation of the law for the LGV driver. It is not a definitive legal text and should not be used as such.

Publisher's note
Every possible effort has been made to ensure that the information contained in this book is accurate at the time of going to press, and the publishers and authors cannot accept responsibility for any errors or omissions, however caused. No responsibility for loss or damage occasioned to any person acting, or refraining from action, as a result of the material in this publication can be accepted by the editor, the publisher or any of the authors.

First published in Great Britain in 2004 by Kogan Page Ltd
Reprinted in 2007
Second edition published 2008

120 Pentonville Road
London N1 9JN
United Kingdom
www.koganpage.com

© David Lowe, 2004, 2008

The right of David Lowe to be identified as the author of this work has been asserted by him in accordance with the Copyright, Designs and Patents Act 1988.

ISBN: 978 0 7494 5118 9

British Library Cataloguing in Publication Data

A CIP record for this book is available from the British Library.

Typeset by Jean Cussons Typesetting, Diss, Norfolk
Printed and bound in India by Replika Press Pvt Ltd

Contents

Preface to the second edition

This second edition of *The Professional LGV Driver's Handbook* has been published in large part because of the enactment of a new EU Directive on compulsory training for goods and passenger vehicle drivers.

The new Directive (2003/59/EC) on the training of such drivers, which came into effect on 10 September 2006, applies to bus and coach drivers from 10 September 2008 and to goods vehicle drivers from 10 September 2009. While this *Handbook* deals primarily with matters relating to goods vehicle driving, certain aspects of the text are, in fact, relevant to both goods and passenger vehicle operation.

Additions have been made to the content for this new edition of the *Handbook*, to include the detailed information now available on the new UK scheme. The original content of the *Handbook* has also been updated to provide the reader with the latest information needed to meet the new EU Driver CPC requirements, and to provide wider background knowledge of the legislative controls on the road haulage industry.

In the new Part 1 the provisions of the Directive are fully described, particularly in regard to those who need to hold a Driver CPC and those who are exempt, when it is needed and how it may be obtained. It explains the initial and periodic training regime set out by the Driving Standards Agency (DSA), which is the body responsible in the UK for establishing the EU scheme.

This part of the *Handbook* also sets out the 'List of Subjects' as per Annex I to the EU Directive. The reader will observe that while the Contents list for this *Handbook* differs from the 'List of Subjects', all the relevant topics are included with the proviso that:

1. individual topics are separated by sub-headings to make the text more readily understandable and suitable for study; and

2. additional subjects have been added to provide the wider background knowledge referred to above.

From Part 2 onwards the *Handbook* contains text covering all the topics listed in the EU syllabus, with the additional topics referred to above being included where relevant.

The reader should be aware that nothing in this book is superfluous; every line of text is intended to provide both the newcomer to LGV driving and the experienced driver alike with information they need to obtain and retain their LGV driving licences and their new Driver CPC. They will be doing themselves a great favour if they read it all carefully and ensure that the information has been fully understood at the time of reading and mentally retained for future reference.

Good luck in obtaining your Driver CPC.

The author

In a 50-year transport career, David Lowe has owned, driven and repaired heavy trucks, managed fleets, and written about all aspects of road haulage and road transport law, so he knows the business inside-out. He is best known for turning the legal gobbledegook of complex transport regulations into plain and under-standable English, particularly in the *Transport Manager's and Operator's Handbook*, published annually since 1970 by Kogan Page, but also in many other books and magazine articles for drivers and transport operators.

He is also well-known as a CPC trainer for transport managers, so he brings to this book not only a sound knowledge of road transport theory and practice, but wide experience in conveying, in an easy to understand manner, complex legal issues to industry newcomers, transport students and to those LGV licence holders who need to brush up on and add new theoretical knowledge to their existing practical experience for the Driver CPC.

Acknowledgements

The official publications and internet websites of the Driving Standards Agency (DSA) and the Driver and Vehicle Licensing Agency (DVLA) have been referred to in compiling this *Handbook*, for which acknowledgement is hereby given. Particular thanks are due to individual staff members of the DSA who provided helpful advice for the original edition.

I am grateful to long-time friend and former *Commercial Motor* colleague, Gibb Grace, for his invaluable help on technical matters; to Ian Hetherington, Chief Executive of the Road Haulage and Distribution Training Council (RHDTC) – now known as Skills for Logistics – for general advice, for commenting on parts of the text and for kindly writing the Foreword to the original edition; and to transport consultant and author, Alan Slater, who missed nothing in vetting the original manuscript.

Introduction

Today's professional large goods vehicle (LGV) driver has four important responsibilities:

- to act and drive with the utmost safety;
- to comply fully with the law on driving and the use of his vehicle on the road;
- to safeguard the valuable vehicle and loads entrusted to his care; and
- to carry out his employer's delivery instructions.

Fulfilling these responsibilities requires him to take great care in everything he does and to utilize all his experience and knowledge to ensure safety in his work. It requires clear thinking and caution, acute observation, sharp awareness, tact and diplomacy, a smart appearance and a polite manner. He must also understand:

- the law – how it applies to him and his vehicle and how to apply it in his work;
- the characteristics of his vehicle, the loads carried, the roads over which he travels and the potentially adverse effects of weather conditions;
- the implications of health and safety law on his own and his employer's activities;
- what to do in the event of an accident on the road or while loading or unloading;
- how to recognize mechanical defects in his vehicle;
- how to deal with the paperwork (eg, tachograph charts, consignments notes, transit documents and so on); and
- how to know when he is fit to drive and, more significantly, when he is not fit through drinking, drug taking, illness or undue stress.

In other words, he must be a professional. This means acquiring the skills, experience and knowledge needed to carry out an LGV driving job in an effective and efficient manner. It means no slip-ups, no silly mistakes, no stupid errors, not forgetting important instructions and no accidents. It also means having no need for pathetic excuses or feeble lies to cover up shortcomings due to lack of forethought or attention. A professional is easily recognizable; people know one when they see one, and everybody admires a person who does his job in a professional manner; it instils confidence.

Skills come from training and constant practice, while experience comes from doing the job well, times over, making mistakes occasionally, but learning from your own mistakes and those of others. Neither skills nor experience can be learned from a book. But a book can provide knowledge and this *Handbook* provides the essential knowledge needed by the professional LGV driver, the owner-driver haulier, and those who aspire to become Driver CPC holders.

Readers please note:

1. The masculine pronoun has been used to avoid cumbersome language and save space. No discrimination, prejudice or bias is intended against the female reader. Indeed, the author fully recognizes the key role played by many female LGV drivers on the road today, and by female staff in other transport roles.

2. Readers should take the word 'must' as used in the *Handbook* to mean that the law specifically requires the action described.

3. The information in this *Handbook* relates solely to that of concern to the LGV driver. Any reader interested in a more comprehensive study of road transport legislation, especially from the employer's or vehicle operator's perspective, should refer to *The Transport Manager's and Operator's Handbook* by David Lowe, published annually by Kogan Page.

4. This book is intended to provide a practical interpretation of the law for the LGV driver. It is not a definitive legal text and should not be used as such; nor is it relevant to bus and coach drivers apart from the indicated sections of the EU syllabus shown on pages 12–16.

5. Road traffic and directional signs are not illustrated in the *Handbook*; they are much more effectively reproduced, in colour, in the official *Highway Code*, a copy of which both learner and experienced drivers should always have readily to hand – it currently costs £2.50 for the 2007 15th edition.

Part 1

EU Driver CPC requirements and EU training syllabus

1.1

EU CPC requirements for LGV drivers

The European Commission is intent upon raising the standards of professionalism among LGV drivers by means of extended study/training periods and tough theory and practical testing leading to a Certificate of Professional Competence (CPC).

A draft Directive on the qualification and training requirements for LGV drivers sent out for consultation in 2001 was followed by publication of a revised version in April 2002, and a further version on 5 December 2002 amending certain aspects of the original proposals. A final version of the Directive (2003/59/EC) came into effect from 10 September 2006 and was to apply to bus and coach drivers from 10 September 2008 and to goods vehicle drivers from 10 September 2009. Despite the amendments, the principal objectives remain the same, namely to improve road safety and the safety of the driver, to reduce road casualties, to 'arouse young people's interest in the profession which is thought will contribute to the recruitment of new drivers at a time of shortage' and to bring an improved professional and positive image to the profession.

The aim has been to establish a system for the Certification of Professional Competence (CPC) for drivers who satisfy the training requirements for 'initial' training, which new drivers must complete before they can drive LGVs professionally, and 'periodic' training which all existing LGV drivers must undertake. An approved-design EU-wide certificate to be called a 'Driver Qualification Card' will be issued to successful candidates. This will confirm the individual's personal details and his/her driving qualifications and carry a photograph of the holder.

Pre-existing drivers who already hold a category C1, C1+E, C or C+E licence at the time the new scheme comes into operation will not need an 'initial' qualification, but they will have to undergo the 35-hour periodic training every five years. This means that all pre-existing drivers (i.e. as at 10 September 2009) must complete their first 35 hours of periodic training by 10 September 2014.

EXEMPTIONS

While the new rules will apply to most haulage drivers, there will be exemptions for drivers of certain specialized vehicles.

Drivers of the following vehicles *will not* need to hold a Driver CPC:

- vehicles with a maximum authorized speed not exceeding 45 km/h (approximately 28 mph);
- vehicles used by or under the control of the armed forces, a police force or a fire and rescue authority;
- vehicles undergoing road tests for technical development, repair or maintenance purposes, or of new or rebuilt vehicles which have not yet been put into service;
- vehicles used in a state of emergency or assigned to a rescue mission;
- vehicles used in the course of driving lessons for the purpose of enabling that person to obtain a driving licence or a Driver CPC;
- vehicles used for non-commercial carriage of passengers or goods for personal use;
- vehicles carrying material or equipment to be used by that person in the course of his or her work, provided that driving that vehicle is not that person's principal activity.

An example given by the Department for Transport (DfT) of a driver under the last exemption above (also known as an 'incidental driver'), would be a bricklayer who drives a load of bricks from the builder's yard to the building site and then spends his working day laying bricks. In this case, driving a lorry is incidental to his main occupation.

However, drivers can move in and out of an exemption, depending on the circumstances in which they are driving. For example, a lorry mechanic would be exempt while driving a lorry to check that it had been repaired correctly, but would need to hold a Driver CPC if he also drove a lorry to make a delivery of goods.

NB: This example is similar to one provided by the DfT for passenger vehicle operations.

INITIAL TRAINING

The Driving Standards Agency (DSA) is responsible, on behalf of the UK government, for implementing the EU Driver Training Directive (2003/59/EC) and, in conjunction with Skills for Logistics (and GoSkills representing the passenger transport industry), has established the regime for CPC training to comply with the Directive. Two levels of training requirement must be met by professional LGV drivers, namely;

- initial training (set at the level of NVQ 2) for newcomers to LGV driving from 10 September 2009; and
- periodic training which will need to be undertaken by pre-existing LGV drivers who held their vocational entitlement prior to 10 September 2009.

Initial training which will apply to new drivers who acquire their entitlement to drive vehicles in categories C1, C1+E, C or C+E from 10 September 2009. These drivers will need to complete the initial training *in addition* to obtaining their vocational licence before they will be allowed to drive LGVs on the public highway.

This initial training will involve additional theory and practical testing beyond that required to obtain the LGV vocational licence as follows:

- basic licence theory test of 1½ hours plus 2½ hours of extra theory testing for CPC – making 4 hours in total,
- basic driving test of 1½ hours plus half-an-hour of extra practical testing for CPC – making two hours total.

The basic theory test mentioned above will be in two parts comprising:

- 100 multiple choice questions (85 per cent pass mark required) and a 20-video clip hazard perception test, and
- a number of case studies using diagrams, pictures and graphics as well as text, in which the candidate is presented with a defined scenario on which questions will be based.

Where appropriate, the test presentation will be screen-based and will be undertaken at existing DSA driving theory test centres (see pages 112–13).

INITIAL TRAINING FOR YOUNG DRIVERS

The pre-existing Young LGV Driver scheme operated on behalf of the DfT by Skills for Logistics and the transport associations (RHA, FTA, etc) will be superceded by the new Driver CPC scheme. Consequently, the standard minimum age for professional LGV drivers will reduce to 18 years, and on gaining an 'accelerated initial qualification' such drivers will be allowed to drive goods vehicles in licence categories C1 and C1+E.

This 'accelerated' qualification must include studying all subjects in the syllabus over a minimum period, including a specified number of hours driving in a relevant approved test vehicle, followed by tests as described above.

PERIODIC TRAINING

All existing LGV driving licence holders at the commencement of the new scheme (10 September 2009) will be required to undergo approved periodic training sessions amounting to 35 hours in total within the first five years and in each subsequent five-year period. The training periods must be organized by an approved training centre, and each one must be of at least seven hours' duration – this means seven hours of actual direct contact with the trainer within 24 hours. So to achieve this training requirement, drivers could undertake one day of training each year or a week's training once every fifth year, either way amounting to 35 hours in total within the five years. The training objective could be to provide 'up-skilling' in general to improve overall driver performance and safety awareness, or specific training to account for new technological developments in vehicle design, for example.

TRAINING, TESTING AND CERTIFICATION

The whole of the new Driver CPC scheme is based on a system of approved methods of training, and certification is provided by approved trainers working within approved training centres (a list of these is to be found in Appendix I). Approval for trainers, training centres and training courses is given only by the Joint Approvals Unit for Periodic Training (JAUPT) -- see Appendix II for contact details.

For these purposes, the JAUPT falls within the auspices of the Driving Standards Agency (DSA) and the Driver Vehicles Testing Agency, and the schemes are managed by the Sector Skills Councils, namely, Skills for Logistics for the goods vehicle operating sector and GoSkills for the passenger vehicle operating sector.

What should be made clear here is that the Driver CPC qualification cannot be acquired by any means other than via these approved training methods. There are no facilities within the scheme for distance learning, study by correspondence course or other type of home study.

However, readers of this *Handbook* should understand that a great deal of knowledge of transport law and operating methods is needed to meet the CPC qualifying standard. Much of this can, of course, be obtained through hands-on experience and practical tuition such as that provided by the approved trainers. But nevertheless, it is also clearly necessary to spend some time studying subjects that cannot necessarily be demonstrated adequately in a practical setting. This is where, in opportune moments, quiet reading of a suitable text such as this *Handbook* will help.

Minimum age for driving LGVs

Under the new Driver CPC scheme, from 10 September 2009 the minimum age for driving LGVs will reduce to 18 years, but this will apply only to drivers holding a Driver Qualification Card having completed the requisite period of initial training.

Driving tests

The established system of driver testing will continue with the exception that from April 2008 the number of theory test questions will increase to 100 (85 pass mark), and the hazard perception test to 20 video clips. The practical driving test remains at 1½ hours duration, but this will be supplemented by a series of questions which require the candidate to demonstrate their knowledge of vehicle safety matters.

Availability of training

At the time of writing this *Handbook* quite a number of training centres have received the necessary approval to offer Driver CPC training (the current list of some 75 centres are to be found in Appendix I), but it is anticipated that in the fullness of time more may join the list, certainly by the time that the LGV scheme comes into operation in September 2009. A current list of approved training centres can be found on the JAUPT website at: www.drivercpc.org.

Testing and certification

Pre-existing LGV driving licence holders at the date when the new scheme comes into operation (i.e. 10 September 2009) will not be required to undertake any tests to acquire a Driver CPC, they will have what is known as 'acquired rights' and therefore will be deemed to be a 'professionally competent' driver albeit without an actual CPC document (a Driver Qualification Card – DQC) to prove the fact. Their CPC qualification will be evidenced, if such proof is required, by the date on their driving licence which shows when their entitlement to drive LGVs came into effect.

NB: This is a further reason why drivers should carry their vocational licences with them at all times when driving – they may be asked for such evidence (see also below).

Such pre-existing LGV licence holders will eventually obtain the Driver CPC on completion of their first (35-hour) spell of periodic training. This will then be renewed on completion of each subsequent 5-yearly session of periodic training.

New drivers who have not held an LGV driving entitlement prior to 10 September 2009 will need to complete the Driver CPC initial training, as described above, at the time of undertaking their LGV driving test. Without this extra qualification it will be illegal for them to drive goods vehicles professionally (ie for payment) unless the vehicle is one which falls into an exempt category (see page 6).

Certification of holding the CPC qualification will be by holding a Driver Qualification Card, issued by the Driver and Vehicle Licensing Agency (DVLA). A record of all driver training undertaken at approved centres will be held on a central database by DSA and it is on the basis of this record of training hours achieved that the DSA will notify the DVLA when to send the candidate his or her Driver Qualification Card. Drivers themselves may also check up on their own personal accumulated training hours by enquiry to the DSA, as may employers (provided they have the individual's permission to do so).

ENFORCEMENT, OFFENCES AND PENALTIES

Strict enforcement of the new Driver CPC scheme is promised by the authorities, with tough penalties for failure to comply with the legal requirements.

Enforcing authorities

The enforcing authorities are the police and VOSA, both of which will have direct access to the centrally-held data at the DVLA, enabling them to check instantly any dubious claims or records.

Offences and penalties

Once the scheme is in operation all such drivers must carry evidence of their Driver CPC qualification and may be asked to produce this at the time of a roadside check.

- For pre-September 2009 LGV licence holders the evidence will be the date on their vocational licence – so the message here is clear, LGV drivers must carry their driving licence at all times when doing any work that may involve LGV driving.
- For new LGV drivers from 10 September 2009, the evidence will be their Driver Qualification Card. This card must also be carried at all times when driving as described above.

Failure by a driver to produce their DQC (or driving licence with date evidence) on request by a VOSA enforcement officer or policeman carries a fixed penalty fine of £30.

The more serious offence that drivers are at risk of committing is failure to have undergone the mandatory 35 hours of periodic training within the preceding five years. Whether through forgetfulness or deliberate avoidance of the training regime, an offending driver could be fined up to £1,000 on conviction.

Because the Driver CPC scheme applies throughout the whole EU commu-nity, British drivers must, when driving abroad, carry with them their DQC or driving licence showing evidence of a pre-September 2009 driving qualification. They risk an on-the-spot penalty if found in breach of this requirement. Similarly, foreign LGV drivers operating in the UK face the prospect of a £30 fixed penalty fine if found not to have the requisite documentation with them, but there is an anomaly in the case of the more serious offence mentioned above. Due to the current inadequacy of the DVLA database in not carrying training records for non-UK drivers, such drivers will avoid the £1,000 fine for having failed to undergo or complete the periodic training requirement.

1.2

The EU training syllabus

The official EU training syllabus as set out in EU Directive 2003/59/EC (Annex I, Section 1, List of Subjects) indicates the knowledge to be taken into account by Member States when establishing the driver's initial qualification and periodic training regimes, which must include *at least* the subjects in this list. Trainee drivers must reach the level of knowledge and practical competence necessary to drive safely in all vehicles of the relevant licence category.

The syllabus is divided into three key subject area headings, namely:

1. advanced training in rational driving based on safety regulations;
2. application of regulations;
3. health, road and environmental safety, service, logistics.

The syllabus is reproduced here:

1. ADVANCED TRAINING IN RATIONAL DRIVING BASED ON SAFETY REGULATIONS

All licences

1.1. Objective: to know the characteristics of the transmission system in order to make the best possible use of it:
curves relating to torque, power, and specific consumption of an engine, area of optimum use of revolution counter, gearbox-ratio cover diagrams.

1.2. Objective: to know the technical characteristics and operation of the safety controls in order to control the vehicle, minimize wear and tear and prevent disfunctioning:
specific features of hydraulic vacuum servo-brake circuit, limits to the use of brakes and retarder, combined use of brakes and retarder, making better use of speed and gear ratio, making use of vehicle inertia, using ways of slowing down and braking on downhill stretches, action in the event of failure.

1.3. Objective: ability to optimize fuel consumption:
optimization of fuel consumption by applying know-how as regards points 1.1 and 1.2.

Licences C, C+E, C1, C1+E

1.4. Objective: ability to load the vehicle with due regard for safety rules and proper vehicle use:
forces affecting vehicles in motion, use of gearbox ratios according to vehicle load and road profile, calculation of payload of vehicle or assembly, calculation of total volume, load distribution, consequences of overloading the axle, vehicle stability and centre of gravity, types of packaging and pallets; main categories of goods needing securing, clamping and securing techniques, use of securing straps, checking of securing devices, use of handling equipment, placing and removal of tarpaulins.

Licences D, D+E, D1, D1+E

1.5. Objective: ability to ensure passenger comfort and safety:
adjusting longitudinal and sideways movements, road sharing, position on the road, smooth braking, overhang operation, using specific infrastructures (public areas, dedicated lanes), managing conflicts between safe driving and other roles as a driver, interacting with passengers, peculiarities of certain groups of passengers (disabled persons, children).

1.6. Objective: ability to load the vehicle with due regard for safety rules and proper vehicle use:
forces affecting vehicles in motion, use of gearbox-ratios according to vehicle load and road profile, calculation of payload of vehicle or assembly, load distribution, consequences of overloading the axle, vehicle stability and centre of gravity.

2. APPLICATION OF REGULATIONS

All licences

2.1.   Objective: to know the social environment of road transport and the rules governing it:

maximum working periods specific to the transport industry; principles, application and consequences of Regulations (EEC) No 3820/85 and (EEC) No 3821/85; penalties for failure to use, improper use of and tampering with the tachograph; knowledge of the social environment of road transport: rights and duties of drivers as regards initial qualification and periodic training.

Licences C, C+E, C1, C1+E

2.2.   Objective: to know the regulations governing the carriage of goods: transport operating licences, obligations under standard contracts for the carriage of goods, drafting of documents which form the transport contract, international transport permits, obligations under the Convention on the Contract for the International Carriage of Goods by Road, drafting of the international consignment note, crossing borders, freight forwarders, special documents accompanying goods.

Licences D, D+E, D1, D1+E

2.3.   Objective: to know the regulations governing the carriage of passengers:

carriage of specific groups of passengers, safety equipment on board buses, safety belts, vehicle load.

3. HEALTH, ROAD AND ENVIRONMENTAL SAFETY, SERVICE, LOGISTICS

All licences

3.1.   Objective: to make drivers aware of the risks of the road and of accidents at work:

types of accidents at work in the transport sector, road accident statistics, involvement of lorries/coaches, human, material and financial consequences.

3.2. Objective: ability to prevent criminality and trafficking in illegal immigrants:

general information, implications for drivers, preventive measures, check list, legislation on transport operator liability.

3.3. Objective: ability to prevent physical risks:

ergonomic principles; movements and postures which pose a risk, physical fitness, handling exercises, personal protection.

3.4. Objective: awareness of the importance of physical and mental ability:

principles of healthy, balanced eating, effects of alcohol, drugs or any other substance likely to affect behaviour, symptoms, causes, effects of fatigue and stress, fundamental role of the basic work/rest cycle.

3.5. Objective: ability to assess emergency situations:

behaviour in an emergency situation: assessment of the situation, avoiding complications of an accident, summoning assistance, assisting casualties and giving first aid, reaction in the event of fire, evacuation of occupants of a lorry/bus passengers, ensuring the safety of all passengers, reaction in the event of aggression; basic principles for the drafting of an accident report.

3.6. Objective: ability to adopt behaviour to help enhance the image of the company:

behaviour of the driver and company image: importance for the company of the standard of service provided by the driver, the roles of the driver, people with whom the driver will be dealing, vehicle maintenance, work organization, commercial and financial effects of a dispute.

Licences C, C+E, C1, C1+E

3.7. Objective: to know the economic environment of road haulage and the organization of the market:

road transport in relation to other modes of transport (competition, shippers), different road transport activities (transport for hire or reward, own account, auxiliary transport activities), organization of the main types of transport company and auxiliary transport activities, different transport specializations (road tanker, controlled temperature, etc.), changes in the industry (diversification of services provided, rail-road, subcontracting, etc.).

Licences D, D+E, D1, D1+E

3.8. Objective: to know the economic environment of the carriage of passengers by road and the organization of the market: carriage of passengers by road in relation to other modes of passenger transport (rail, private car), different activities involving the carriage of passengers by road, crossing borders (international transport), organization of the main types of companies for the carriage of passengers by road.

This syllabus is reproduced here (with typesetting amendments for style purposes only) with acknowledgement to the European Parliament and Council in whose Directive 2003/59/EC it is published.

Readers please note:

1. Subjects relating to passenger vehicle driving have been left in this syllabus in case they are of interest to readers.
2. Certain legislative items have been updated since publication of this syllabus in 2003. In particular, under section 2.1 above, Regulation (EEC) No 3820/85 has now been superceded by Regulation (EC) 561/2006 of 15 March 2006, effective, in so far as the driver's hours law is concerned, from 11 April 2007 while Regulation (EEC) 3821/85 relating to tachograph use has been amended by this same Regulation, but effective from the earlier date of 1 May 2006 (when the fitment and use of digital tachographs first became mandatory in certain cases). Further information on these issues can be found in Section 3.1 of this *Handbook.*

Part 2

Vehicle characteristics and heavy vehicle driving skills

2.1

Technical characteristics of heavy vehicles

Large goods vehicles are complex machines, varying considerably in construction, size, carrying capacity and wheelbase length. Many have specialized bodywork and/or components to handle particular types of load. Due to the nature of their employment, most drivers tend to confine their experience to just one vehicle type, but professional LGV drivers, ideally, should have a broad understanding of the differing technical characteristics of other vehicle types in different weight categories and especially those operating at the maximum legal weight. It is important to recognize that driving one lorry is not necessarily like driving any other lorry.

Stability is a key factor, as many LGV drivers will testify when they have driven a high-sided vehicle in high winds or a tanker driver who has experienced the surge of a fluid load when negotiating a roundabout. It is a fact that box vans handle differently from flat-bed vehicles, that driving articulated trucks is a world away from driving rigid vehicles and that lorry and trailer combinations require yet another, quite different, range of skills and experience.

The point about vehicle stability is that it introduces a series of complex technological issues – mainly concerned with various types of force – of which the professional LGV driver should at least have a basic understanding if he is to carry out his job safely.

MAIN TYPES OF GOODS VEHICLE

Goods vehicles are mainly of the types listed below although there are many non-standard vehicles used for special purposes that do not fall into these categories:

- rigid vehicles;
- rigid vehicles drawing trailers (referred to as drawbar combinations or road-trains);
- articulated vehicles comprising a tractive unit and a semi-trailer.

Vehicles are fitted with many types of bodywork as follows:

- flat platforms:
  - drop-side vehicles;
  - skeletal vehicles for carrying ISO-type shipping containers;
- closed vehicles:
  - vans;
  - curtain-sided;
  - refrigerated (or reefer) vans;
- tipping vehicles;
- tankers:
  - for bulk liquids;
  - for bulk powders/granular materials (these tankers often tip when discharging).

Some vehicles are used for carrying unit load devices such as:

- dry cargo containers (ISO-type);
- tank containers;
- demountable body systems;
- swap-bodies (for use in combined road–rail transport).

FORCES THAT AFFECT VEHICLE CONTROL AND STABILITY

Control

A moving vehicle is subject to a variety of forces over which the driver, largely, has no control. Such forces as friction, centrifugal force, gravity and momentum can be exerted on his vehicle in a manner that may result in loss of control and, in unfortunate circumstances, an accident – the vehicle skidding, turning over or running away being classic examples where driver control is subverted by such forces.

The study of these forces involves complex subject areas of physics, mechanics and motor vehicle technology, and is not our purpose here. However, the professional LGV driver should be aware of these phenomena and have an understanding of their potential effects on his control of his vehicle.

It is essential that the driver has full control over his vehicle at all times – and this means not being distracted by talking passengers, taking calls on mobile phones, fiddling with sat-nav devices or even lighting cigarettes. He should be observing the road ahead and planning his actions and manoeuvres according to the prevailing traffic and road conditions, being at all times aware of the antics of other road users and pedestrians.

Traction

Traction – the grip of the driving wheels on the road surface – is a key aspect of vehicle stability. Without grip the driver has virtually no control either on forward motion or on lateral or directional movement. For example, on ice-covered roads a vehicle may be just as likely to slide sideways as to go forward when the driver lets the clutch up. Similarly, a vehicle moving forward on ice may not stop when the brakes are applied, being carried forward by its own momentum (see below).

Energy

Energy is the power derived from physical resources, such as that produced by an engine to drive a vehicle. A moving vehicle produces kinetic energy, which can be harnessed to good effect (ie, to propel the vehicle) or which, conversely, can be disastrous where a vehicle is not under the control of the driver (ie, in a runaway situation).

Force

Force means physical strength or energy in relation to movement: for example, the action that changes the motion of a body. This is all to do with Newton's (ie, Sir Isaac Newton's) three laws of motion, which state that:

1. A body continues in its state of rest or motion in a straight line unless acted upon by an external force.
2. The rate of change of momentum of a body is proportional to the external forces acting upon it – the change of momentum being in the direction in which the applied force acts.
3. For every force there is always an equal force (reaction) acting in the opposite direction.

Force is measured in newtons (N) – a term that crops up regularly in connection with heavy goods vehicles – 1 kilonewton (kN) being equal to 1000 newtons (N). Many forces affect heavy vehicles, particularly lateral ones that can cause the driver to lose directional control.

Centrifugal force

Centrifugal force is the outward pull that occurs when a mass (ie, a vehicle) is rotated or turned. In other words, when a vehicle travels quickly around a traffic island, while the driver is turning the steering wheel to make it go in one direction, a hidden force (centrifugal force) is tending to make it go in another direction, namely, to fly off at a tangent and continue straight on. The faster the speed, the greater the centrifugal force.

Momentum

A moving vehicle has momentum. It is the force of the body (eg, a vehicle) in motion and the strength of that force is dependent upon the mass (ie, weight) and velocity (ie, speed) of the body in motion. Mass is the measure of quantity of matter that a body (eg, a vehicle) contains and is measured in kilograms (kg). The term 'mass' is often used to describe the weight of a vehicle. Momentum is best illustrated when the clutch is depressed so the engine is no longer powering the vehicle, but the momentum keeps it going for some considerable distance.

Gravity

According to Newton's law of gravity, as we all well know, everything is pulled downwards towards the ground – towards the centre of the earth. This 'pull' or force is proportional to the mass of the body and is what gives the body its weight. With heavy vehicles, the main force of gravity, while they are stationary, is downwards. However, once on the move this can change and the pull of gravity may be forwards or backwards, when travelling downhill or uphill, for example, or it may be to the side when negotiating a curve or bend in the road. The driver should be aware of these effects and counteract them in his driving by adjusting his speed accordingly.

Centre of gravity is defined as the point at which the weight of a body (eg, a vehicle) pivots. The nearer that point is to the ground the less likely the body is to pivot and become unstable. Therefore, a vehicle loaded with the predominance of weight located high up would be top heavy and therefore unstable, making it more difficult for the driver to control, especially when negotiating turns or when affected by side-winds. Similarly, when tipper vehicles are discharging, if the load – or part of it – sticks in the top end of the raised body, that becomes top heavy and is liable to topple over because the centre of gravity has been raised to an unsafe height above the ground. This situation is made worse if the vehicle is not standing on firm and level ground – a scenario that tipper drivers are regularly warned against.

Friction

Friction is the force that opposes the movement of one surface against another when they are in contact. The magnitude of the frictional force is dependent on the roughness of the two surfaces (what, in fact, may appear as very smooth surfaces still present a degree of frictional resistance), the nature of the materials and the pressure between the two surfaces. Once a sliding motion between the two surfaces has commenced, less force is required to maintain the movement. Conversely, more force is needed to stop the movement (eg, as with a skidding vehicle).

In the transport environment, friction is a major player, having a considerable bearing on safety issues. It includes the friction between a vehicle's tyres and the varying road surfaces on which it runs, and between the load on a vehicle and the load platform on which it sits. The driver should take account, constantly, of the road surface on which he is driving, noting whether it is wet – icy even, or covered in wet leaves – or dry, but covered in loose grit. These surfaces spell danger because they indicate potential lack of grip (friction) between the tyres and the road surface, which may result in a skid, loss of directional control or stability and therefore loss of control.

With regard to the frictional effect between a load and the vehicle load platform, it should never be assumed that a load will not move on account of its weight alone. The forces generated by heavy braking, particularly from speed, can be sufficient to dislodge the heaviest load, overcoming the frictional effect of the load-platform surface. For this reason, loads should always be secured by adequate means (eg, by chains or approved lashings). Shipping containers are typical of heavy loads often carried without adequate securing devices in place, but a number of tragic accidents have shown that the heaviest of loads such as these can move forwards under heavy braking forces – and once moving, vehicle headboards and driver cabs may not be strong enough to stop them!

Kinetic energy

Kinetic energy relates to the 'work' done (ie, energy applied) in accelerating a body from one velocity to another. The rate of acceleration is in relation to the change in the body's kinetic energy. In practical terms, a moving vehicle contains kinetic energy, the amount depending on the weight of the load and the speed of the vehicle, the greater of either resulting in a greater amount of such energy. This energy has to be dissipated to bring the vehicle to a standstill. Progressive braking allows the kinetic energy – and the heat it generates – to be dissipated slowly and harmlessly, but when in an accident situation where a moving vehicle hits a stationary object, for example, a great deal of kinetic energy has to be dissipated almost instantly, hence the catastrophic damage that invariably occurs.

POWER

While power is not essentially a function of vehicle control and stability, there is no doubt that misuse of engine power can have a significant adverse effect by way of increasing accident risk. For this reason it is useful to consider the meaning of power in vehicular terms. Power is a measure of the amount of work done; work is expended whenever a force operates over a distance, so, for example, pushing a wheelbarrow up a slope or lifting water from a well requires a force to be exerted over a distance. A calculation of the amount of work done in a 10lb (4.5-kilogram) force being moved over a distance of 20 feet (6 metres) would be 10 lb × 20 ft, equalling 200 ft-lb (foot-pounds) of work. When it comes to power, which is the rate of doing work, this brings in a time element, and using the wheelbarrow analogy again, running with the wheelbarrow to get up the slope more quickly is harder and therefore needs more power than when just walking with it.

Horsepower

Power is usually stated in terms of horsepower, deriving from Victorian times when engineers thought in terms of the horse, which was strong and in everyday use. It is an imperial measure that is largely being replaced in terms of the measure of diesel engine output by the kilowatt (written as kW and representing 1,000 watts), which is an international measure, although in common parlance, engines are still described in brake horsepower (bhp) – today's average 44-tonne truck features an engine of some 380 to 500 bhp (eg, the 12.1-litre D12 engine in Volvo's FH heavy truck range can be specified with power outputs of 380 bhp (279 kW), 420 bhp (309 kW), 460 bhp (338 kW) and 500 bhp (360 kW)).

Torque

Torque is defined as a mechanical force that tends to cause rotation. Engine torque is the turning effort about the crankshaft's axis of rotation expressed in foot-pounds (ft-lb) or newton metres (N m). Average torque varies across the engine speed (ie, revolutions per minute – rpm) range, producing its maximum at about mid-speed and decreasing on either side of that speed. Characteristically, diesel engines produce their maximum torque at much lower engine speeds than petrol engines. For example, whereas a typical 1.8-litre car-type petrol engine produces its maximum torque of about 114 ft-lb at about 4,250 rpm, a typical 460-bhp diesel engine produces maximum torque of 2,000 N m (approximately 1,475 ft-lb) at around 1,200 rpm.

A torque converter is a device (commonly found on heavy construction plant, for example, instead of a conventional multi-ratio gearbox) that transmits or multiplies (ie, converts) torque generated by an engine to drive the road wheels. It is, in effect, a type of gearbox producing variable ratios without the need for physical gear changes by the driver.

Power v torque

While most vehicle engines are described by their power output (and this is what grabs the attention of aficionados, whether of heavy trucks or Ferrari super-cars – 500 bhp in either case being something to drool over), it is not out and out horsepower that is ultimately desirable; it is pulling power that really counts and this is more a function of the torque of an engine. Manufacturers invariably display engine performance by means of power/torque curves, which highlight at what level of engine revs (and therefore power) in each gear maximum torque is achieved. Ideally, high torque at low engine revs is the most desirable characteristic of a heavy truck engine since this epitomizes its low-speed pulling power or, in trucker's language, its 'low-down grunt'.

Minimizing wear and tear and malfunctioning

Harsh and violent use of a vehicle – and overloading – causes unnecessary wear and tear on its component parts, particularly to the braking system, trailer couplings, suspensions, tyres and so on and may well lead to a malfunction of key parts and systems. Careful driving, on the other hand, does not necessarily mean slower journeys or delayed deliveries, but it does save on fuel consumption, tyre wear and brake lining life among other things. This is good for the vehicle, good for saving running costs and good for the environment by way of reducing both noise and polluting exhaust emissions.

STABILITY

Having examined some of the forces at work while a goods vehicle is in motion, it becomes easier to understand how these forces may create instability and cause the driver to lose control of his vehicle. In many cases such instability and loss of control result in an accident for which the driver may be inclined to disclaim responsibility, saying, 'there was nothing I could do'. But in some cases, there probably was something he could have done; for example, he could have understood that the wind force was likely to blow his vehicle over and taken action against it (eg, by opening the side curtains on an empty curtain-sided vehicle, by not travelling on an exposed route, by not ignoring the danger signals and warnings given on the radio etc). He could have understood the risk of his tanker rolling over on a traffic island and avoided this critical scenario (eg, by travelling at a much lower speed). He could have understood the likelihood of his articulated vehicle jack-knifing and avoided the situation (eg, by being more observant of what was happening to the traffic ahead of him, or by braking more carefully if the surface was wet or potentially slippery).

The 'wave' effect

Tanker vehicle drivers should be aware of the so-called wave effect that can occur during braking when the motion of the fluid in the tank forces the vehicle forward. This surge is more likely to occur with tanks that have no baffle plates – generally food tankers, where baffles make tank cleaning difficult.

Precautions in high winds

When travelling in severe weather conditions it is sensible to listen to the latest weather forecast before setting out, and to local forecasts on the vehicle radio while *en route*. This advice applies especially to drivers of high-sided and curtain-sided vehicles/trailers, and those transporting high loads such as portable buildings, especially on high-level bridges and exposed stretches of motorway and viaducts.

GEAR RATIOS

With just a few exceptions, most vehicles need to have a gearbox providing a range of alternative gear ratios to allow speed to be progressively increased without undue stress on the engine. It is a technical fact that piston engines do not develop sufficient torque (ie, turning effort) to propel a vehicle from standstill to its top, or optimum cruising, speed. Even the greatest torque produced at high engine speed would not be sufficient to accelerate a vehicle at an acceptable rate, consequently a means is needed to multiply the engine torque and thereby increase the turning speed of the road wheels without an increase in engine speed. A gearbox matches engine output torque and speed to match the vehicle speed and load (ie, comprising the load carried and the road conditions – surface, gradient, wind resistance etc) and the rate of acceleration required. To achieve this a train of gears is devised to provide the progressive increase in speed desired.

Use of gears

Experienced drivers obviously fully understand the purpose and correct use of gears, particularly the concept of working up through the ratios to move a vehicle from a standstill up to its cruising speed, using all or most of the interim ratios between the lowest (ie, bottom gear) and the highest (ie, top gear). Modern heavy vehicles have a multiplicity of ratios, normally from 6 up to as many as 16 gears, these often being arranged in two ranges, high and low (hence the term 'range change' gearbox). Alternatively, some vehicles have a two-speed rear axle matched to a six- or eight-speed gearbox, effectively doubling the number of available ratios. These systems tend to be operated by compressed air, invariably without the aid of the clutch. The driver's skill is employed in selecting the right gear for the prevailing conditions, particularly when going uphill, he will need to gradually change down to each lower gear as he tries to maintain his road speed without allowing the engine to struggle. Secondly, when going downhill he may need to use progressively lower gears to provide a braking effect to relieve pressure on the brakes, thereby avoiding overheating of the drums or disks and loss of efficiency (ie, retardation and brake fade).

Weight, of course, also plays an important role in the driver's determination of which gears to use. A heavily laden vehicle will require him to make many more gear changes to maintain road speed than when driving one that is lightly loaded or even unladen when, with a multi-range gearbox, he would be able to eliminate many intermediate changes.

Correct use of gears also plays a key role in vehicle fuel consumption by avoiding both over-speeding and labouring of the engine, both of which result in excessive use of fuel. Modern vehicles are provided with dashboard instruments (ie, either a rev counter or separate gauges) that clearly show to the driver the optimum engine revs band for maximum fuel economy – usually marked in green, as opposed to the red band that indicates uneconomical driving.

Observing the rev counter

Most modern heavy vehicles are equipped with revolution (rev) counters or tachometers – an instrument formerly only encountered on a sports car dashboard or on so-called 'super' bikes. However, in the case of heavy vehicles their purpose is not to help the driver make the vehicle go faster but to enable him to drive with the optimum of efficiency to achieve maximum fuel economy. Most rev counters are colour-coded showing the optimum band (green) for economic driving and the worst or danger band (red) to be avoided at all times. Other colours are sometimes used to indicate fierce acceleration (usually amber) and engine braking (usually blue). The driver should ensure that he has read the vehicle handbook and knows in which colour band the rev counter needle should appear to indicate efficient use of the engine.

2.2

Vehicle braking and speed controls

BASICS OF HEAVY VEHICLE BRAKES

Drivers should understand the basics of the braking system on heavy vehicles and, where appropriate, the connections between vehicles and trailers. Heavy vehicle braking systems have progressed over the years from simple mechanically operated contraptions, through hydraulic and vacuum systems, to the highly efficient and technologically sophisticated air-brake systems that we have today. These use compressed air produced from an engine-mounted compressor to provide the operating force.

Additionally, most modern vehicles are fitted with anti-lock braking systems (ABS), which effectively prevent wheel locking under heavy braking, and retarders (or endurance brakes), which add to the braking effect by slowing the rotation of the transmission system with electro-magnetic devices or by exhaust gases diverted into an exhauster linked into the braking system. Retarders are best suited to slowing vehicles on long downhill runs where the main brakes may become overheated and begin to fade.

Heavy vehicles usually have three separate braking systems, comprising:

- service brakes;
- secondary brakes;
- parking brakes (on the vehicle and also on the trailer or semi-trailer).

The service brake is the principal braking system used and is operated via the foot pedal on the wheel brakes (usually drum-type brakes, but increasingly these days, disc brakes). This brake is used to control the speed of the vehicle and to stop it safely when required. The secondary brake is usually combined with either the foot brake or the parking brake control. It is for use if the service brake fails and normally operates on fewer wheels than the service brake and therefore has a reduced level of performance. The parking brake is usually a hand control mounted on the steering column or the dashboard – it may also be the secondary braking system. Normally, the parking brake is used only when the vehicle is stationary to ensure it cannot move when the driver leaves the driving cab. It is an offence to leave a vehicle unattended without setting the parking brake.

Trailer connections

It is vital to understand the rules that apply to connecting and disconnecting brake lines on either an articulated vehicle or a rigid vehicle and drawbar trailer combination. Drivers are required to demonstrate this procedure during the practical driving test.

Two different brake configurations may be encountered – either a three-airline system or a two-airline system. A three-line system comprises the emergency line (coloured red), the auxiliary line (coloured blue) and the service line (coloured yellow) whereas a two-line system has only emergency and service airlines.

Connecting two-line vehicles and two-line trailers is not difficult because they appear clearly compatible, as are three-line vehicles and three-line trailers. However, a two-line tractive unit can be connected to a three-line trailer with the trailer auxiliary line being left *unconnected.* But caution is needed when connecting a three-line tractive unit to a two-line trailer – in this case it is important to follow the vehicle manufacturer's advice as to what to do with the third (blue) line. Failure to follow such instructions could result in a dangerous situation with the combination brakes not operating effectively.

Airlines

The function of the airline is to carry compressed air from the tractive unit to the semi-trailer for the purpose of braking. Nylon air-coils, commonly known as *susies*, are fitted to most tractive units – they overcome the disadvantages normally associated with the old rubber hose-type airlines. All airline coils are internationally colour coded (red, blue and yellow – see above) and are capable of extending to such a length that they remain fully operational even when the articulated vehicle is in a complete jack-knife position.

Safe procedure for stowing airlines

When disconnecting airlines, for the purposes of uncoupling the trailer, it is sensible to start with the one nearest and stow them away, one at a time. When connecting airlines, follow the opposite procedure, starting with the one furthest away. This practice reduces the risk of accidentally tripping over the coils, and helps to keep them from becoming tangled.

Brake line adaptors

Most articulated vehicles in the United Kingdom are equipped with standard male/female adaptors, which reduce the risk of wrong connection. Some, however, use 'palm-couplings', which are all alike, and great care must be exercised to ensure that incorrect connections are not made, which can render the trailer brakes inoperative. The colour coding is the reliable key.

Non-return valves and air taps

Modern braking systems have non-return valves located within the air-brake system allowing the air pressure to be immediately shut off, or automatically as the airlines are disconnected or reconnected. On older braking systems manual air taps are fitted, which the driver must operate himself when connecting and disconnecting the brakes. Where such taps are fitted into the airlines, it is important that they are turned off before disconnecting the airlines. If this is not done, it will result in an immediate air loss from the red emergency line and will render the yellow service line and the blue auxiliary line ineffective when the brakes are applied. It is equally important that the air taps are turned on again after airlines have been connected. If this is not done, the trailer brakes will be totally inoperable.

ANTI-LOCK (ABS) BRAKES

ABS is the registered trademark of German firm Bosch and stands for Anti-Blockiersystem (ie, anti-lock braking system). Many modern heavy vehicles (and cars too) are equipped with anti-lock braking systems – some are compulsorily fitted by law.* These systems use electrically powered speed sensors (with multi-pin connectors and cables carrying the electrical supply to the trailer brakes) to anticipate when a wheel is about to lock up under braking (eg, especially on wet or slippery surfaces). Just before lock-up happens the system releases the brake and then reapplies it rapidly many times in quick succession. This provides virtually continuous braking to the wheel without the dangers of skidding that would result if the wheel locked. Preventing the wheels from locking also means that the driver is still able to steer the vehicle during braking.

Note: ABS fitment is legally required for goods vehicles over 16 tonnes gross weight first used since April 1992, for goods vehicles over 3.5 tonnes gross weight first registered from April 2002 and for goods-carrying trailers over 3.5 tonnes gross weight first used since this date.

Checking the ABS

The driver should ensure that the ABS on his vehicle/trailer is functioning correctly before setting out on a journey. Driving with a defective ABS is illegal.

Satisfactory operation of the ABS can be checked via the warning instrument/light on the vehicle dashboard with a separate warning instrument/light signal for the trailer mounted either on the vehicle dashboard or, in some cases, on the trailer headboard. Warning light signals operate differently between manufacturers, but in all cases the signal should be displayed when the ignition is switched on and should go out no later than when the vehicle has reached a road speed of about 10 kph (6 mph).

Technique for driving with ABS

ABS is only an aid to the driver; it does not replace good driving techniques and is not provided to allow last-minute braking as a regular practice. The driver should still anticipate what is happening on the road ahead and should assess traffic flow and road surface condition to allow plenty of time for normal braking. However, when it is necessary to exert greater pressure on the brakes for a quick stop the driver will feel the cadence (hammering) effect through the brake pedal as the system pumps the brakes on and off very rapidly. He should ignore this and continue to press the pedal in the normal way, allowing the ABS to work effectively.

ENDURANCE BRAKES – RETARDERS

Endurance brakes are commonly referred to as 'retarders'. These are braking systems that enable vehicle speed to be controlled without using the normal wheel brakes. They are especially useful when descending long gradients, saving wear on the service brakes as well as avoiding the risk of reduced braking performance due to brake fade – caused by overheating of the drums and linings. The use of a retarder allows the service brakes to remain cool ready for when they are needed.

Use of brakes and retarders

Skilled drivers can combine the use of the footbrake and retarder on the vehicle to provide smooth driving – particularly essential when driving a coachload of passengers or a load of livestock, but equally commendable when driving goods vehicles. Significantly, too, such use can save considerably on the costs of brake and tyre wear and in fuel consumption. The skill is that of being aware of the road and traffic conditions ahead and adjusting the vehicle speed accordingly by judicious use of the retarder in good time, not leaving it until the last minute when approaching an obstacle, a bend in the road or a traffic sign, which may result in the need for heavy braking. Looking and being aware of what is ahead is the sign of a skilful LGV driver.

LOW-PRESSURE WARNINGS

Air-brake systems are fitted with warning devices (lights and buzzers) that are activated when air pressure in the system falls below a predetermined level. No attempt should be made to move a vehicle when the brake pressure warning system is operating. Similarly, if the warning activates while the vehicle is moving, it should be brought to a standstill quickly and safely, and not be moved again until the defect is rectified. Driving with a warning device operating is very dangerous and is an offence.

Brake failure – what to do

Only in the rarest of circumstances do modern heavy vehicle air-braking systems fail completely leaving the vehicle totally uncontrollable. It is to ensure against this that vehicles are equipped with three types of brakes: service brakes providing a minimum of 50% braking efficiency, secondary brakes providing a minimum of 25% braking efficiency and a parking brake. Should one part of the system fail (ie through loss of air pressure), besides being given an audible or visual warning in the cab, the driver would have an adequate reserve of air pressure in the secondary system to enable him to stop the vehicle safely.

DRIVER CHECKS

Drivers must check that the braking system of their vehicle is working satisfactorily before driving on the road – no matter how short the journey. Before each journey they should make sure that all warning systems are working correctly and should note whether brake pressure warning signals activate automatically when the ignition is turned on (as for the ABS), or whether a switch on the dashboard has to be operated to check the system.

Draining the air tanks

Where necessary the driver should also use the manual drain valves on the air tanks (reservoirs) to release any moisture that has been drawn into the system and that may freeze on frosty mornings forming ice in valves and pipework. This may result in loss of air pressure or even system failure. Some air systems have automatic drain valves to remove moisture, making this task unnecessary.

Warning – don't forget the hand brake!

When uncoupling a trailer and *before* disconnecting any of the brake lines the driver must ensure that the trailer parking brake has been correctly applied. Without this safety step being carried out, the trailer could move when the airlines are disconnected.

SPEED LIMITERS

The law requires speed limiters to be fitted to certain heavy goods vehicles to prevent over-speeding and thereby help to reduce road accidents. Also, driving at a reduced speed (ie, within the legal limits set for speed limiters) means considerable benefit will accrue to operators in terms of fuel economy, saving as much as 150 million litres annually according to the UK government, and helping the environment by an annual reduction of some 0.5 million tonnes of carbon monoxide (CO) from exhaust emissions pumped into the atmosphere.

UK regulations limit all new goods vehicles over 7.5 tonnes maximum gross weight (with certain special exceptions) to a maximum speed of 60 mph (96 kph). The speed limiter must be maintained in good working order, but where a vehicle is driven with a defective limiter, it is a defence to show that the defect occurred during that journey or that at the time it was being driven to a place for the limiter to be repaired.

EU requirements

EU regulations require over-12-tonne goods vehicles to have their speed limiter set to a maximum speed of not more than 85 kph (53 mph), allowing a stabilized speed of not more than 90 kph (56 mph).

The only other exemptions are where a speed limiter has failed on a journey and the journey is being completed or when the vehicle is being taken to a place for the speed limiter to be repaired or replaced.

Speed limiter plates

Vehicles covered by the above-mentioned regulations must be fitted with a speed limiter plate fitted in a conspicuous and readily accessible position in the vehicle cab.

2.3

Vehicle suspensions and trailer couplings

Among the many key components that affect the safe operation of heavy goods vehicles, both suspension and trailer coupling systems are particularly important – the former because of the effect that the suspension system has on the handling and stability of the vehicle and the latter because of the considerable risks that arise if trailer couplings, and the associated brake and lighting systems, are not properly connected. Statistics highlight the many tragic accidents that have occurred through drivers failing to ensure that trailer coupling and uncoupling procedures and safety measures have been strictly followed.

HEAVY VEHICLE SUSPENSIONS

At its most basic, a vehicle suspension system is no more than an arrangement of springs and dampers located between the wheels and axles and the chassis to reduce shocks and vibration from irregularities and undulations in the road surface being transmitted to the main structure of the vehicle, where they would cause fatigue damage to components and the load, and discomfort to the driver and passengers. It is important that the suspension should work effectively without impairing either the stability or the steering control and handling of the vehicle. In fact, modern vehicles have highly efficient suspensions, achieved by combinations of springs of various types, shock absorbers, anti-roll bars and mechanical linkages controlling the relative motion between the unsprung masses (eg, the axles and wheels) and the sprung mass of the chassis and superstructure.

In practice, suspension systems need to satisfy a number of conflicting requirements due to differing operating requirements and conditions. For example, they must accommodate:

- the forces generated during vehicle acceleration and deceleration;
- the differing weight-carrying and ride performance requirements when the vehicle is laden and so as to ensure the vehicle itself and its occupants are not shaken and jolted to pieces when it is unladen;
- the effects of being driven slowly or at speed, in a straight line or when cornering, on smooth roads or over uneven surfaces.

Above all, the suspension must not impair the vehicle's stability, but it must provide good road holding and handling characteristics, allowing the driver full control under all prevailing conditions.

Road-friendly suspensions

Many vehicles these days are fitted with so-called 'road-friendly' suspensions that have the benefit of reducing damage to loads in transit and damage to road surfaces and under-surface services (eg, gas, water and sewerage pipes and electricity and telephone cables) – hence the reason why the law permits higher weights on such vehicles in some instances.

Generally, these suspension systems comprise air bags in place of traditional steel multi-leaf springs, and can often be controlled by the driver (by reducing the air pressure via release valves or increasing it by means of the engine-powered air compressor) as to the relative height for loading and travel.

TRAILER COUPLINGS

In this section we are concerned with two distinct types of coupling: fifth-wheel couplings connecting articulated tractive units and semi-trailers, and drawbar couplings connecting rigid vehicles and drawbar trailers.

Candidates taking the LGV driving test in an articulated vehicle will be expected to know all about the coupling and uncoupling procedures, and the various safety checks that are involved in connecting and disconnecting the tractive unit and semi-trailer. Additionally, it is important for drivers who may need to drive drawbar combinations (sometimes also referred to as lorry and trailer combinations or road-trains) to understand the procedures for coupling and uncoupling these types of unit.

Fifth-wheel couplings

The fifth-wheel coupling is so described because the point of contact between the tractive unit and the semi-trailer is a fifth-wheel plate, a heavy metal plate (turntable) mounted on the rear of the tractive unit. This matches up with a matching flat plate on the underside of the semi-trailer, which also has a steel kingpin that locates into a slot in the turntable and locks into position. The actual locking mechanism is located inside the fifth wheel, and to ensure proper connection it is important for the driver to check the relative height between tractive unit and trailer before coupling commences.

If the trailer is too high, not only is it possible for the kingpin to damage the turntable, but also, and even more important, a false coupling could take place. The locking jaws in the fifth wheel may have only partly gripped the kingpin and although the trailer will move away with the unit, it is liable to disengage at any time without warning. As a safeguard against false coupling, the fifth wheel is equipped with a locking bar and a safety catch – it is important that these function correctly and that the driver checks to ensure they are fully engaged.

Trailer parking brakes

Trailer parking brakes are usually located on the nearside (left-hand) of the semi-trailer close to but forward of the trailer wheels. A trailer parking brake is a mechanical cable brake that is applied manually and secures the trailer wheels. It is essential that it is put in the 'on' position whenever uncoupling takes place and, just as important, it must be set in the 'off' position immediately after coupling. It can also be used as an additional safety factor for overnight parking, or when leaving the vehicle on steep gradients.

Landing gear

The trailer landing gear, commonly referred to as the landing legs, is the one component that is misused more than any other, and care should be taken when lowering the landing legs that they are stopped just short of the ground (about 1 inch or 2.5 centimetres). If the landing gear is forced hard down to the ground, strain and possibly damage may occur when recoupling, as the trailer is tugged. Many landing gears are of a two-speed design. The high-speed ratio is normally used for coupling and uncoupling purposes, but in exceptional circumstances it may be found necessary to lift or lower a detached trailer, which would necessitate using the low ratio. The locking mechanism used to connect semi-trailers to tractor units is a combination affixed to both tractor and trailer.

These components must be checked immediately after coupling to ensure the trailer is connected properly to the tractive unit. The final action to be carried out to ensure a properly connected articulated vehicle is to select a low forward gear and, with the trailer brake still *on*, tug forward.

Correct procedure for coupling a semi-trailer

- Check that the trailer brake is on.
- Reverse slowly, checking relative heights of tractive unit and semi-trailer and making sure that the unit is in line with the trailer.
- Continue reversing until the coupling engages.
- Select a low forward gear and move the tractive unit forward.

- When satisfied that the fifth wheel is connected, secure the tractive unit with the parking brake.
- Carry out a visual check on the fifth-wheel coupling and ensure that the safety catch is locked on.
- Connect the airlines to their matching colours (turn on the air taps if fitted) and connect the electrical line.
- Raise landing gear and stow away the handle.
- Release the trailer parking brake.
- Fix the rear number plate in position.
- Switch on lights and check round the vehicle, making sure they are all correctly illuminated.
- Check that the vehicle is safe to travel on the road.

Correct procedure for uncoupling a semi-trailer

- Check that the ground where the trailer is to be uncoupled is firm, level and that the trailer will be left in a safe position.
- Apply the trailer parking brake.
- Lower the landing gear and stow the handle away.
- Turn off the air taps (if fitted) and disconnect the airlines and electrics; stow these away.
- Remove the safety catch on the fifth wheel and disconnect the fifth-wheel lock.
- Retrieve the rear number plate from the trailer and stow it in the cab.
- Drive the tractive unit away, slowly, making sure that the trailer causes no damage as it settles.

Coupling and uncoupling drawbar trailers

A freestanding drawbar requires a second person to help ensure correct alignment when coupling to the drawing vehicle, whereas a preset, aligning, drawbar can be safely operated by the driver alone.

Correct procedure for coupling drawbar trailers

Before coupling:

- Ensure that trailer parking brake is on.
- Ensure that wheel chocks are in place.
- Ensure that drawbar is in the straight-ahead position.

Coupling (two-man operation)

Driver – action:

- Reverse slowly – check to see exactly where the assistant is positioned.
- Keep engine noise to a minimum – it is necessary to hear the assistant's instructions.

Assistant – action:

- As vehicle is reversed make sure that its coupling box is in line with the drawbar.
- Tell the driver to stop as soon as the coupling connection is made.
- Lock the coupling mechanism – *stand clear.*

Driver – action:

- When certain that the assistant is clear of the vehicle select a low gear and tug forward to test the coupling.
- Stop – apply handbrake.

Assistant – action:

- Connect air and electrical lines.
- Turn on air taps (if fitted).
- Attach number plate to rear of trailer.
- Remove wheel chocks.
- Release trailer brake.

After coupling:

- Check all tyres and lights (including indicators).
- Test brakes.

Correct procedure for uncoupling drawbar trailers
Before uncoupling:

- Select a safe and sensible position for the trailer to be left before starting.
- Make sure that the ground where the trailer is to be left is firm and level.

To uncouple:

- Apply trailer brake.
- Chock trailer wheels.
- Turn off air taps (if fitted).
- Disconnect air and electrical lines.

- Remove safety pin and disconnect drawbar.
- Retrieve trailer number plate and store in vehicle cab.
- Drive away slowly.

After uncoupling:

- Check trailer brake.
- Check trailer wheel chocks are secure.

2.4

Road traffic accidents and emergencies

It is an unfortunate fact of life that professional drivers who spend much of their lives on the road may inevitably encounter a road accident on their travels; they may even be involved in one themselves. When this occurs it is important to know what to do and what the legal requirements are for reporting an accident.

DUTY TO STOP

Any driver involved in a road accident in which personal injury is caused to any person other than himself, or damage is caused to any vehicle other than his own vehicle, or to any animal* other than animals carried on his own vehicle or to any roadside property**, *MUST STOP*. Failure to stop after an accident is an offence carrying a maximum fine of up to £5,000 on conviction.

AT THE SCENE OF AN ACCIDENT

Avoid panicking. Taking immediate and positive action at the scene can help to avoid further injury and damage, and even possibly save a life. The following general rules should be observed:

1. Make sure that you, your passengers and your own vehicle are safe before going to the aid of others.
2. Call the police immediately and an ambulance where necessary – or organize somebody else to do so quickly.
3. Take steps to safeguard the accident scene by:

-   getting witnesses and bystanders to stop the approach of other vehicles (use hazard warning lights, torches and warning triangles for this purpose) but taking care that they do not cause or become involved in further accidents;
-   switching off car ignitions to prevent fire;
-   preventing onlookers from actions that may cause further injury or damage (eg, by smoking at the scene, moving injured persons or moving crashed vehicles).

4. Check casualties to see if you can help to make them more comfortable (keep them warm and reassured that help is coming) and determine who needs the most urgent help. *Do not give (or even offer) food, drink or other substances (eg, medicines) to injured persons.*
5. If you are experienced in first aid, or an experienced first-aider makes themselves known, give what help you (or they) can to the casualties. *Remember, it is unwise to move people who are injured, or to attempt to treat them unless you have the proper training; you may exacerbate their injuries.*
6. Try to prevent injured, or even uninjured, persons from leaving the scene and ask witnesses to remain until the police arrive and have taken details. Ensure that other vehicles, even if only marginally involved, do not slip away from the scene (don't forget that people often do not wish to get involved, or may not wish others to know that they were in that place at that time).

INFORMATION TO BE GIVEN

The driver of a vehicle involved in a road accident must give to anybody having reasonable grounds for requiring it his own name and address, the name and address of the vehicle owner and the registration number of the vehicle.

WHAT NOT TO SAY AT THE SCENE OF AN ACCIDENT

The driver should NOT make any statement of guilt or responsibility at the scene of a road accident. Apologizing for a driving error, or admitting that you did not see the other vehicle, for example, are certain admissions of liability. Do not discuss, even in general terms, the sequence of events leading up to the accident or the consequences of the actual collision with any person (ie, involved parties, witnesses and bystanders) – what you say in this context may also be construed or misinterpreted as an admission of guilt.

If the police attend the scene they may ask you to make a statement – you are not obliged to do so at that time but you can offer to make a statement later with a solicitor or with another person present (eg, a union representative, a colleague, a representative of your employer or a relative).

REPORTING TO THE POLICE

If the accident results in injury or damage to any person other than the driver himself or to any other vehicle or to any reportable animal,* or to roadside property,** then the details of the accident must be reported to the police as soon as reasonably practicable afterwards, but in any case no later than 24 hours after the event. Failure to report an accident is an offence also carrying a maximum fine of £5,000.

*Note: for these purposes an animal means any horse, ass, mule, cattle, sheep, pig, goat, dog (in Northern Ireland only, a 'hinnie' is added to this list).

**Note: property 'constructed on, fixed to, growing on, or otherwise forming part of the land in which the road is situated or land adjacent thereto'.

PRODUCING EVIDENCE OF VEHICLE INSURANCE

When a road accident results in injury to any person other than the driver of the vehicle (ie, any person other than yourself), a certificate of insurance must be produced to the police (or to any other person who has reasonable grounds for requesting it) either at the time of the accident or when reporting the accident to the police within 24 hours. If the insurance certificate is not available at that time, it may be produced at a police station of your choice within seven days.

The police issue a small form (HO/RT 1) at the time of the initial request for the insurance document and this must be taken to the police station when producing the evidence of insurance. A temporary insurance cover note covering the vehicle and authorizing you to drive it during the period in question is acceptable if a full certificate of insurance is not available at that time.

PRODUCTION OF DRIVING LICENCE

The police will usually ask to see your driving licence at the same time that they want to see the vehicle insurance and if you do not have it with you it may be produced at the police station within seven days, along with the vehicle insurance. However, it is important to note that you must produce your driving licence personally (although the vehicle insurance may be produced on your behalf by somebody else – eg, your employer).

RECORDING ACCIDENT DETAILS

It is useful to record details of the accident while still at the scene for future reference rather than rely on memory for vital details that will be needed for completing the accident report. In particular, the following details should be noted:

- date, time and exact location of accident (eg, road names and/or numbers);
- volume and speed of traffic;
- weather conditions and visibility;
- condition of road surface and any obstructions;
- any traffic signs and signals relevant to the location or accident;
- any signals made by yourself or other parties prior to the accident.

You should also take a note of the following details:

- other drivers' names, addresses and telephone numbers;
- insurance details from the other parties involved;
- the make, model and registration number of other vehicles;
- details of the name and address of the vehicle owner/s if not owned by the driver;
- a description of the damage to the other vehicle/s;
- witness details (get these quickly as they may leave the scene):
  - names, addresses and telephone numbers;
  - their vehicle registration numbers.

It is useful to make a sketch map of the scene (even take photographs if possible) including road layouts with names, road widths, gradients, vehicle positions, approximate speeds and position of witnesses.

COMPLETING AN ACCIDENT REPORT

Insurance companies must be given immediate notice of an accident to any vehicle for which they provide cover, followed by a properly and fully completed accident report and claim form. A time limit of seven days is normally specified for this.

The driver should complete the insurance company's claim form giving as much detail of the accident as possible. In particular it will require details of the time, place, conditions of the weather and the road surface, the position of his vehicle on the road and its speed at the time of impact and prior to that, the direction of travel (his and that of the other vehicles involved) and the location of identifying objects. A description of events leading up to the accident and a sketch of the relative positions of the vehicles involved, both before and after the collision, should be given on the report form, together with an indication of the damage to vehicles and property.

It is also important to be able to give the names and addresses of other parties involved and of any witnesses to the accident. You should make a note of what any of these parties may have said at the scene, especially if any of them admit blame, say sorry or say they did not see your vehicle etc, or if a witness states who they think was to blame – these matters can be helpful to the insurance company in determining liability.

INSURANCE CLAIMS

The accident report is part of the claim made on the insurance company. Once the insurance company has received the claim it will decide where blame for the accident lies and how it should be apportioned (normally, no one party is completely to blame or completely innocent). It will arrange for one of its assessors to examine the damaged vehicle and give permission for the repairs to be carried out, if it is repairable and the repairer's estimate is acceptable. If the vehicle is beyond economical repair the assessor will authorize a 'write-off'.

Third parties injured in accidents who find that when making claims for damage the other vehicle was uninsured at the time, can make a claim for their personal injuries and for damage to their property to the Motor Insurers' Bureau (MIB).

EMERGENCY ACTION

Road traffic crashes are not the only accidents and incidents that the driver may have to deal with on a day-to-day basis. Other on-road or roadside incidents may occur which require the driver to take action: for example incidents involving other vehicles which may, morally if not essentially, require his participation or assistance – the occurrence of a vehicle fire or the need to render first aid to an injured person, for example.

Generally, the first priority in all such incidents is to telephone the emergency services (police, fire, ambulance) as appropriate. Secondly, there is a need to ensure that the incident itself does not result in further incidents causing harm to those involved (e.g. such as vehicles running into crashed vehicles or those standing nearby), and thirdly it may be necessary to render first aid and assistance to those injured – all as described in more detail on page 40 'At the scene of an accident'.

Dealing with fire

In the event of fire, either in his own or another vehicle, the driver should be prepared by having an extinguisher in his vehicle (highly recommended and essential when travelling abroad). Fire extinguishers are of different types (colour coded) for different purposes; for vehicle fires a dry powder extinguisher is required. It is important to know, or to have read before use, the purpose of a particular type of extinguisher: the few moments taken to read the label before use may avoid the unfortunate consequence of using, for example, a water-based extinguisher on an electrical hazard.

Besides having a fire extinguisher handy, the first priority in a vehicle fire is to try to get people out of and safely away from the vehicle. If the fire is in a car or van engine, bear in mind that opening the bonnet fully will cause it to flare up more violently, so the extinguisher should be aimed through just a small bonnet opening.

EMERGENCY AND FIRST AID EQUIPMENT

It is useful to carry emergency and first aid equipment in your vehicle in case of accident, particularly the following items:

- a blanket (and additional warm clothing, especially in winter);
- a first aid kit (a proprietary kit from a good chemist, or from the motoring organizations, will contain a supply of suitable items);
- a fire extinguisher (suitable for electrical and petrol fires);
- a good torch or an emergency lamp (ie, with a white beam, plus an amber and/or red flashing beacon);
- a warning triangle (this is mandatory equipment when travelling abroad);
- a tow rope (or webbing towing strap);
- a set of battery jump leads.

In winter, especially when travelling in remote areas, additional items should be carried in case of accident, breakdown or stranding, particularly a flask of coffee or hot soup and something to eat (or at least a chocolate bar). The proliferation of mobile phones (which most truck drivers carry these days) has helped to overcome the problems of communication when stranded due to breakdown or adverse weather conditions.

STOPPING ON MOTORWAYS

Stopping on a motorway without good reason is illegal and is the cause of many unnecessary accidents. However, it may be imperative to do so in the event of an accident or vehicle breakdown, in which case great care should be taken to pull as far to the left as possible and get any passengers out of and away from the vehicle to avoid further tragedy.

2.5

Safe driving

WHAT IS SAFE DRIVING?

Safe driving means driving with a strong emphasis on the exercise of care, attention and consideration for other road users, and strict observance of statutory speed limits and other legal requirements. You should never drive after having consumed alcohol, or when feeling tired or unwell. The *Highway Code* contains a wealth of advice and information for road users on good manners and safe driving. It is useful to obtain and read a copy as a reminder.

HOW TO AVOID ACCIDENTS

Good driving is the best way to avoid road accidents in which you the driver and other road users may be injured and vehicles and other property damaged. Accidents invariably cause considerable distress to the parties involved and to their loved ones; they also involve considerable hassle in making reports and lodging insurance claims for damage, and they cost time and money. What to do in the event of an accident is described in detail in Chapter 2.4.

ILLEGAL USE OF MOBILE PHONES

You should not drive while using hand-held telephones and microphones; this is unwise and could be illegal – if seen by the police you may be prosecuted for not exercising proper control of the vehicle. You should find a safe place to stop and make or take calls, but not on the hard shoulder of a motorway, except in an emergency.

SPEED AND BRAKING DISTANCES

You should always drive well within the limits of your forward vision, and leave plenty of space between your vehicle and the one in front, taking account of the speed and braking distance of your vehicle. In fog and poor visibility allow a greater distance. Typical minimum braking distances (in metres) for a car or light van in good condition and on a dry road are shown in Table 2.5. Loaded goods vehicles will obviously need much longer distances in which to stop safely and this should be allowed for.

Table 2.5 *Typical minimum braking distances*

Speed	Thinking distance (metres)	Braking distance (metres)	Total distance (metres)
30 mph (48 kph)	9 m	14 m	23 m
50 mph (80 kph)	15 m	38 m	53 m
70 mph (112 kph)	21 m	75 m	96 m

Acknowledgement: The *Highway Code*.

SAFE VEHICLES

Besides good driving, it is equally important to ensure that your vehicle is in a safe, roadworthy condition and that it complies in all respects with the law. Where appropriate, seat belts should be worn – note that on goods vehicles, if seat belts are fitted, they must be worn. Make sure that your tyres have adequate tread and are inflated to correct pressures.

When driving at night and in poor-visibility daytime conditions, the vehicle lights should be switched on in good time (having clean lights, reflectors, rear-view mirrors, windscreen and side windows is an important safety measure as well as a legal requirement). Remember the motto: see and be seen.

DAILY SAFETY CHECKS ON GOODS VEHICLES

If you are the driver of a goods vehicle covered by operator ('O') licensing – ie, most goods vehicles over 3.5 tonnes gross weight – you are required under these rules to carry out regular daily checks of your vehicle prior to driving it on the road and to make a written report of any defects that come to light at any time while the vehicle is in your charge – *you must do this, the law requires it.*

Besides any requirement that your employer may impose for carrying out such checks, it is in your own personal interest to do so. For one thing, your own personal safety is at risk should a vital component fail, and for another, a prosecution may result from being found driving a vehicle with defects that contravene the law. This could result in penalty points being endorsed on your driving licence or even loss of your LGV driving entitlement – and possibly your job.

Items to be checked

The daily check would typically include such items as:

- battery;
- fuel;
- engine oil;
- horn;
- indicators;
- lights;
- marker lights;
- mirrors;
- reflectors and markers;
- security of load;
- security of vehicle bodywork;
- steering;
- tyres (pressure and condition);
- water;
- wheels/wheel nuts;
- windscreen wipers and washers.

On articulated and drawbar combinations:

- brake hoses (susies);
- couplings/landing gear;
- electrical connections;
- rear number plate.

TIREDNESS CAN KILL

Tiredness has been established as the main cause in around 10 per cent of all road accidents and it is sensible to follow the DfT campaign to combat tiredness among both car and LGV drivers. The main points for drivers to observe are:

- Make sure you are fit to drive, particularly before undertaking any long journeys (over an hour) – avoid such journeys in the morning without a good night's sleep or in the evening after a full day's work.
- Avoid undertaking long journeys between midnight and 6 am, when natural alertness is at a minimum.

- Plan your journey to take sufficient breaks. A minimum break of at least 15 minutes after every two hours' driving is advised.
- If you feel at all sleepy, stop in a safe place and either take a nap for at least 15 minutes, or drink two cups of strong coffee.

THE 'WELL DRIVEN' CAMPAIGN

The 'Well Driven' labels (with a freephone number 0800 22 55 33; for mobile phone users the number is chargeable on 800 22 55 33) seen on many large goods vehicles indicates that they belong to operators who have signed up to observe the voluntary 'Good Lorry Code', which promotes high standards of driving, vehicle maintenance and consideration for other road users. The freephone number is an invitation for members of the public (and other drivers and transport operators) to have their say about the standard of driving (bad or good) or the condition of the vehicle. A help desk, manned round the clock, takes calls, which, provided sufficient information is given, are passed on to the operator concerned.

2.6

Professional driving – respect for other road users and the environment

DRIVER BEHAVIOUR

Being a professional driver does not mean having only the ability to control a vehicle well. It also means a driver taking responsibility for his actions in controlling his vehicle within the environment in which it works, particularly avoiding damage to the built-up and green environments and risk to pedestrians and other road users. It also means having the right attitude to driving and road use. Aggressive driving, for example, which is typical of the wrong attitude, is seen by others as the sign of a bully and a thoughtless driver and it is the sign of a person for whom an accident is invariably waiting to happen.

Drivers are invariably the most frequent point of direct contact between their firm and the customer – sometimes the only personal contact. As such they carry considerable responsibility for portraying a good image by being smart in appearance, well-mannered and courteous, helpful and aware of the customer's needs. How company drivers act and react when on the road and when making collections and deliveries may be taken to be a reflection of the service level their company aims to provide. If they are held up *en route* they should endeavour to let the customer know of the delay and a revised arrival time. If they have problems with their vehicle they should maintain close contact with their base so that any repairs or recovery can be arranged with a minimum loss of time and undue cost.

Efficiency and work organization

Although they may be inclined to think otherwise, drivers are part of a team and their collections and deliveries are part of a supply chain operation, the aim of which is to perform economically and efficiently. What a driver does and how he goes about his job can have a significant bearing on the success of those targets. Not meeting planned schedules, not following laid-down routes and delivery sequences, or spending undue amounts of time in lay-bys and roadside cafes are indicative of a driver who does not have the best interest of his employer's business at heart.

RESPECT FOR OTHER ROAD USERS

The *Highway Code* is based on the concept of consideration for other road users: for example, by suggesting that the driver should give way if it will help to avoid an accident. In particular it says (in section 147) that the driver should be careful of and considerate towards other road users in the following ways:

- Try to be understanding if other drivers cause problems; they may be inexperienced or not know the area well.
- Be patient; remember that anyone can make a mistake.
- Do not become agitated or involved if someone is behaving badly on the road. This will only make the situation worse. Pull over, calm down and, when feeling relaxed, then continue the journey.
- Slow down and hold back if a vehicle pulls out into your path at a junction. Allow it to get clear and do not overreact by driving too close behind it.

Tailgating (ie, driving very close to the rear of another vehicle or cyclist) and using a heavy and/or large vehicle to intimidate other road users, especially those who are slow or hesitant, is an unacceptable form of aggressive driving, which is likely to result in an accident. So, too, is the unnecessary sounding of a horn or flashing of headlights to incite other drivers to give way. The heavy vehicle driver should also be conscious of the way that spray from his vehicle on wet roads limits the visibility of other drivers, especially those of small cars and vans.

Making violent gestures such as shaking a fist or making other obscene signs (or shouting obscenities) at other road users is yet another form of unacceptable behaviour, as is, of course, actually getting out of the vehicle to accost, threaten or abuse other drivers in a so-called 'road rage' attack.

None of these actions is what is expected of a professional LGV driver and any driver who finds that he becomes unduly hyped-up and aggressive in this way due to the stresses of driving on our crowded road network should perhaps question not only his attitude, but also his personal health and fitness to drive, and consider whether he needs help in combating such aggressive tendencies.

There are so many vehicles on our roads these days, most of them just as entitled as you to be there, and most in an equal hurry to get to their destination, that being careful, considerate and respectful to other road users is the only sure

way to avoid the risk of accident and get to your destination safely, arriving in a
suitable (unstressed) frame of mind to carry out your duties when you get there.

RESPECT FOR THE ENVIRONMENT

One of the most important and widely discussed issues in transport over recent
years has been the impact of heavy lorries on the environment. So-called 'green'
issues feature in every aspect of transport operation from the siting of vehicle
depots, to the routeing of heavy goods traffic and the disposal of certain loads,
especially waste. Many firms' environmental policies have concentrated mainly
on fuel conservation, which has a direct benefit to them by way of cost savings
and an indirect benefit by way of improved company 'image', as well as
achieving actual reductions in the amount of oxides of carbon that their vehicles
discharge into the atmosphere. This in turn helps to reduce global warming,
which has been identified as being a problem of catastrophic proportions.

The professional LGV driver can, and should, play his part in this by being
aware of the environmental implications of his actions, particularly with regard
to noise, air pollution, visual intrusion, traffic congestion and damage to the
green environment. Useful preventive measures may be summarized as follows:

- not making undue noise from revving engines, from slamming cab and
  bodywork doors, by leaving radios playing loudly when the cab is vacated,
  and, in the case of tipper and skip lorries, by leaving chains and other
  restraining devices hanging loose;
- not leaving engines ticking over unnecessarily while loading/unloading,
  creating irritating noise and undue air pollution from exhaust emissions;
- not parking in front of private premises, blocking light from windows and
  suchlike (especially with high box van-type vehicles), leading to complaints
  of visual intrusion;
- not parking where the vehicle is likely to cause traffic congestion, bearing
  in mind that if an actual obstruction is caused this could be dangerous, lead
  to an accident and result in an offence being committed and likely prosecution;
- not driving on to and/or parking on verges, so damaging the green environment, unnecessarily mowing down hedges, bushes and plants (whether wild
  or cultivated) or damaging trees or even just the overhanging branches of
  trees.

The LGV driver who is socially conscious will be aware that actions such as
those described above, and many others like them, are antisocial and largely
unwarranted. They harm the environment, spoil the look of both urban and rural
roadside scenery, and cause damage to the health of people, animals and bird
life. Typically they are the actions of a 'yob' driver, not a trained professional.

2.7

Driving abroad

Travelling abroad by road, especially within the European Union, is now very easy, but the inexperienced driver will find himself burdened with additional responsibility when he sets out to drive goods vehicles into Europe and beyond. Many legal requirements have to be strictly observed, and official documents carried to avoid falling foul of foreign Customs, frontier officials or the local gendarmerie, resulting in extensive delays and the severe penalties that can be imposed. Heavy on-the-spot fines for breaking the law are a hazard and in certain cases vehicles can be impounded and drivers imprisoned until legal requirements are met or penalties are paid.

ROAD HAULAGE CONTROLS

International road haulage operations between EU member states are controlled by a system of Community Authorizations. UK standard international 'O' licence holders are issued with an Authorization and a set of certified copies so each vehicle on international work can carry one copy as required by law.

Road haulage operations to non-EU member states still (in most cases) require a bilateral road haulage permit. However, certain countries do not require permits and neither are they necessary for haulage or own-account vehicles up to 6 tonnes gross weight travelling to or through any European or Scandinavian country. Full details of all these requirements can be obtained from the International Road Freight Office.

Where applicable, vehicles must not leave the United Kingdom without a valid permit – inspectors at the port of exit may ask drivers to produce the permit. It is an offence to forge or alter permits, to make a false statement to obtain a permit or to allow one to be used by another person.

INTERNATIONAL CARRIAGE OF GOODS BY ROAD (CMR)

For loads other than furniture removals that are transported abroad, the haulier is controlled by the Convention on the Contract for the International Carriage of Goods by Road (CMR Convention) except for journeys between the United Kingdom and Eire and between the United Kingdom and Jersey. Under this convention, a CMR consignment note must accompany the load, and the carrier (or the driver) taking over the goods must check the accuracy of the consignment note regarding the number of packages, their marks and numbers, the apparent condition of the goods and their packaging.

CMR consignment notes for international haulage

Road hauliers carrying goods for hire and reward on international journeys under the provisions of the Convention on the Contract for the International Carriage of Goods by Road (CMR) must complete CMR notes to be carried on the vehicle. These consignment notes confirm that the carriage is being conducted under a contract subject to the terms of the CMR Convention, but even in the absence of a CMR note, the carriage will still be subject to the terms of the Convention under international law.

The consignment note is made out in three original copies, all of which should be signed by both the carrier and the consignor of the goods. One copy of the note with red lines is retained by the consignor, the second copy with blue lines is for the consignee, and the third copy with green lines is for the carrier and must travel forward with the vehicle and remain with it while the goods are on board. A fourth copy with black lines may be retained on file by the originator of the document.

The following details must be entered in the numbered and labelled boxes on CMR consignment notes where applicable:

- a statement that trans-shipment to another vehicle is not allowed;
- the charges which the sender undertakes to pay;
- the amount of 'cash on delivery' charges;
- a declaration of the value of the goods and the amount representing special interest in delivery;
- the sender's instructions to the carrier regarding insurance of the goods;
- the agreed time limit within which the carriage is to be carried out;
- a list of documents handed to the carrier.

The consignor or consignee can also add to the consignment note any other particulars which may be useful to the road haulier.

FREIGHT FORWARDERS

Many exporters/importers of goods, and even road haulage firms contracted to carry out international journeys, use the services of freight forwarders. Their role is to provide a complete transport service in connection with the export or import of goods (as well as for inland movements) covering some or all of the following aspects:

- advice on the best method of movement (ie road, sea, air);
- advice on legal/commercial requirements;
- advice on the best services;
- making necessary bookings with appropriate transport services;
- completing all documentation;
- advising on and arranging packing and labelling;
- arranging insurance cover as necessary;
- arranging for collection and following through until delivery is completed;
- arranging Customs clearance for export/import consignments;
- ensuring that all charges are reasonable and presenting comprehensive final account.

CUSTOMS PROCEDURES

Drivers normally would carry the documentation for one or other of the two Customs transit procedures, namely Community Transit and TIR (for journeys outside the EU).

Community Transit

Under the Community Transit System the driver may have copies of the Single Administrative Document (SAD) for Customs purposes connected with exports and imports within the EU.

TIR

The TIR system for journeys to destinations outside the EU enables goods in Customs-sealed vehicles to transit intermediate countries with the minimum of formality provided a TIR carnet is carried for the journey. The carnet is a recognized international Customs document intended purely to simplify Customs procedures.

Strict rules govern the use of carnets. Drivers should never leave TIR carnets with any Customs authority without first obtaining a signed, stamped and dated declaration quoting the carnet number and certifying that the goods on the vehicle conform with the details contained on the carnet. They should also ensure that the Customs at each departure office, transit office and arrival office take out a voucher from the carnet and stamp and sign the counterfoil accordingly. If a Customs seal on a TIR vehicle is broken during transit as a result of an accident or for any other reason, Customs or the police must be contacted immediately to endorse the carnet to this effect.

Goods may be sent outside the EU in vehicles without TIR cover and no carnet is required. In this case, however, it is necessary to comply with the individual Customs requirements of each country through which the vehicle passes.

Carnets de passage

Most European countries allow foreign *vehicles* to be temporarily imported (not be confused with the loads they carry) free of duty or deposit, but a 'Carnet de passage en douane' may be required for vehicles and trailers entering certain countries. Check with IRFO.

ATA carnets

Goods for temporary importation into Europe, such as samples and items for exhibitions and fairs to be returned to the United Kingdom, are moved under an ATA (acronym for Admission Temporaire) international Customs clearance document.

DANGEROUS GOODS (ADR)

The European ADR Agreement on the carriage of dangerous goods enables road haulage vehicles carrying such loads to cross international frontiers without hindrance provided they are packed, labelled and carried in compliance with the Agreement.

Tanker and other vehicles operating under ADR must be inspected and certified and the approval certificate must be carried on the vehicle. Vehicles must carry orange reflex reflecting markers and must carry tool kits for use in an emergency and at least two fire extinguishers and two amber flashing lights that operate independently of the vehicle. While on the continent, if the vehicle stops at night without lights the amber flashing lamps must be placed on the road 10 metres in front of and behind the vehicle. A wheel chock capable of holding the vehicle must also be carried.

Drivers must be properly trained (and carry certificates of training) and be briefed on parking, loading and unloading procedures and what to do in case of an emergency and should also have details of authorities to contact in the event of a dangerous situation arising.

PERISHABLE FOODSTUFFS (ATP)

Vehicles carrying perishable foodstuffs on journeys through most European countries and many others must conform to the strict requirements of the ATP

Agreement. Insulated or controlled-temperature vehicles must be used and the vehicle must carry an ATP certificate showing that it conforms to the requirements laid down for temperature control of the cargo.

EUROVIGNETTES

Motorway charges (ie, tax) must be paid for goods vehicles of 12 tonnes maximum weight and over, including those towing trailers where the combined maximum weight is 12 tonnes or more, when travelling in or through Germany, Holland, Belgium, Luxembourg, Denmark and Sweden*. The tax is charged in euros (€), payable in advance, and is based on a sliding scale according to the pollution emission rating of the vehicle engine (ie, Euro 1, 2, 3, 4 or 5 – see 'Euro exhaust emissions' page 163), the number of axles and the amount of time during which the motorways will be used (eg, per day, week, month etc). Payment covers journeys in all five countries.

Note: Germany launched its own new road toll system in early 2005.

FISCAL CHARGES

Drivers on the continent may find it necessary to pay a variety of taxes, duties and tolls. In some countries goods vehicles are subject to vehicle taxes based on tonne-kilometres or length of stay. Prices for diesel fuel on the continent include tax, as in the United Kingdom, but additional tax may be levied on fuel entering certain countries in the tanks of a vehicle if this exceeds 200 litres.

It is important for vehicle operators and their drivers to be aware of the current requirements for each country they intend travelling to and passing through to avoid unexpected expense and lack of funds. Drivers should always ensure they have sufficient local currency or acceptable credit cards (or pre-established credit arrangements) to meet these costs, otherwise they can expect considerable delays while money is telegraphed and matters are resolved.

INSURANCE FOR TRAVEL ABROAD

A Green Card, issued by an insurance company, should be carried to provide evidence of insurance against compulsory insurable liabilities. While these cards are not mandatory for British vehicles travelling within the EU they may be required as evidence of insurance when travelling to other European, Scandinavian and Eastern bloc countries. It is always advisable to carry one and usually when they are issued the insurance company also provides a European Accident Statement – a form to be completed if involved in a road accident in Europe, and signed by the parties concerned at the time as an agreed statement of facts of what happened, to save disputes and difficulty later.

MEDICAL AID FOR INTERNATIONAL TRAVEL

Medical aid for drivers on international journeys is available from a number of sources and is recommended. Usually cover is provided for payment of medical expenses arising from illness or accident abroad and includes the cost of repatriation where this is necessary by air ambulance or by regular air service with the provision of qualified medical attention during the journey. Without proper insurance cover drivers needing medical or dental treatment may have difficulty in obtaining assistance without payment of fees (usually in advance). State medical aid (ie, free or at reduced cost) is available in emergencies in the EU but drivers can only take advantage of this if they carry a European Health Insurance Card (EHIC), obtainable before departure from the Department of Health via its online service at www.dh.gov.uk.

TRAVEL DOCUMENTS

Passports and visas

Drivers and other crew members or passengers must carry a valid passport when travelling abroad. They should carry it at all times, even when out for meals in the evening. Full 10-year UK passports are obtainable from regional passport offices (London or Peterborough).

Certain countries such as Bulgaria, the CIS, Romania and the Ukraine require an entry or transit visa in addition to a passport. This does not apply in EU countries. Drivers travelling in these visa countries are advised, in their own interests, to contact the nearest British consulate on arrival in the country and provide details of their passport and home address. If they are staying for more than a few days they should maintain contact with the consulate and advise it when they leave the country.

Application for visas should be made to the consulate in the United Kingdom for the country concerned. Besides providing the visa it will also give information regarding any special regulations that must be observed in that country.

Driving licences and international driving permits

European Union member states and many other countries accept a current British driving licence valid for the type of vehicle being driven. For some other countries* an international driving permit is needed. These can be obtained from the AA, RAC, RSAC or the National Breakdown Recovery Club – a passport-type photograph is required for attachment to the permit. For Italy, an Italian translation of the old-type British green driving licence (but not for pink Euro-licences) is needed – available from the motoring organizations.

*Albania, Bulgaria, CIS, Estonia, Hungary, Latvia, Lithuania, Poland, Slovenia and Ukraine.

Vehicle registration document

The vehicle registration document (ie, the original, not a copy) should always be carried on the vehicle when travelling on international journeys. The driver should have written authority from his employer on company letter-headed paper showing that he is the authorized driver of the vehicle.

If a hired or borrowed vehicle is taken abroad (or any vehicle not registered in the operator's name), the driver must carry written authority from the owner permitting his use of the vehicle together with the vehicle registration document. Alternatively, a special registration certificate can be obtained from the motoring organizations, in which case there will be no need for the registration document to be carried. On all journeys abroad, British vehicles must display a valid vehicle excise disc in the windscreen.

Nationality sign

All UK registered vehicles must display the black-on-white British nationality sign – GB – when travelling outside the United Kingdom.

Operator's licence disc

An 'O' disc must be displayed in the vehicle windscreen during all international journeys.

CHECKLIST OF DOCUMENTS TO BE CARRIED

Drivers have to carry a mass of paperwork on a trip to Europe and it is essential to have the right documents and for them to be fully and correctly completed. If not, you could experience excessive delays, being turned back or having your vehicle impounded until satisfactory alternative arrangements have been made. This is both costly and frustrating, so proper attention before setting out is important. The following is a checklist of documents that may be needed:

- ADR certificate of training (for dangerous goods carriage);
- ATA carnet for temporary imports that are to return to country of origin;
- ATP vehicle approval certificate (for perishable goods in reefer vehicles);
- Carnet de passage (where necessary);
- Community Authorization (for operations within the EU);
- consignment note (CMR note for international haulage journeys);
- copies of vehicle test and plating certificates;
- driving licences/international driving permit;
- Eco-points stamps and COP document (for Austrian transit journeys only);
- Eurovignettes (where necessary);
- EHIC where State medical aid may be required abroad;
- insurance Green Card/European Accident Statement/Bail Bond (for Spain);

- medical vaccination certificates;
- 'O' licence and VED (tax) discs displayed in the windscreen;
- own-account document (confirming own goods where appropriate);
- passport/visa;
- road haulage permit (where applicable);
- SAD documents (for Community Transit operations where applicable);
- tachograph charts;
- TIR carnet (for operations outside the EU);
- TIR vehicle approval certificate (when operating under TIR plates);
- vehicle registration document;
- written authority to have charge of vehicle.

WEIGHING OF VEHICLES

Goods vehicles over 7.5 tonnes must be weighed before being loaded on to a roll-on/roll-off passenger ferry ship leaving a UK port.

DRIVERS' HOURS AND TACHOGRAPHS

Drivers of goods vehicles over 3.5 tonnes gross weight travelling to EU countries must observe the EU drivers' hours rules (see Chapter 3.3) and the vehicle must have a calibrated tachograph for record-keeping purposes (see Chapter 3.4).

DRIVING AND RULES OF THE ROAD

Driving in Europe is on the right side of the road. Special care is needed at road junctions and traffic islands where traffic approaching from the right mainly has priority, and when overtaking because of the difficulty of pulling out 'blind' from behind other big vehicles. When travelling on autobahns or autostradas the driver should remember that the speeds at which many continental cars are driven is far higher than on British motorways. Cars travelling at 100–120 mph (160–190 kph) are still common despite speed restrictions, so the goods vehicle driver must take great care to ensure that the road is clear for a long distance behind when pulling out to overtake.

Most traffic signs on the continent conform to international standards (as do those in Great Britain) and are instantly recognizable.

Drivers who infringe road traffic rules (and parking restrictions for example) or who infringe drivers' hours or tachograph rules may have to pay on-the-spot fines if they want to avoid returning to the country at a later date to appear in court.

Warning triangles, wheel chocks, snow chains

Many European countries require the use of warning triangles when vehicles break down. These should be placed on the road behind (also sometimes in front) of the vehicle to warn other road users of a danger ahead. *Check local rules.*

Dangerous goods-carrying vehicles must carry one wheel chock and two amber lights that operate independently from the vehicle electrics, but Austria requires vehicles over 3.5 tonnes gross weight to carry two wheel chocks for use in an emergency.

Snow chains are required for vehicles travelling from France and Italy into the Mont Blanc tunnel and for vehicles travelling in Switzerland between October and April.

Bans on goods vehicles

Many European countries prohibit goods vehicles from travelling at night, weekends or on public holidays. Drivers and operators should make detailed inquiries about these bans when planning journeys abroad because public holidays in Europe can vary from time to time.

ACCOMMODATION FOR DRIVERS

Drivers who travel regularly to Europe will know that a wide variety of accommodation is available and there are many eating places to choose from. Most are of a very good standard and are relatively cheap (so is the wine – but remember the tougher drink/driving rules that apply abroad, and that it will make you sleepy on a warm afternoon). Watch out for the renowned Les Routiers establishments, which provide a welcome to heavy goods vehicle drivers and excellent food and accommodation at reasonable prices.

MONEY FOR TRAVEL ABROAD

Drivers travelling abroad should take care in carrying and exchanging money. In Europe the euro (€) is the universal currency, apart from in the United Kingdom, Denmark and Sweden, which makes life for the international driver much easier. However, when travelling further afield local currencies will still be essential. For security reasons, while some local currency is essential (for food, tolls, parking and other incidental expenses), ideally money should be carried in the form of traveller's cheques.

It is important to note that fluctuating exchange rates and bank commission charges mean that considerable losses can be sustained by frequent changing of small amounts or by changing too much and having to change it back on leaving the country concerned. Recognized credit cards such as Access and Visa (where they are accepted) are a convenient way of paying for accommodation, meals and fuel for example.

International Road Freight Office
Eastgate House
Kings Manor
Newcastle upon Tyne NE1 6PB
Tel: 0191 2014090
Fax: 0191 2220224

Part 3

Transport regulations, offences and enforcement

3.1

Regulations governing transport

Road haulage in the United Kingdom is notoriously burdened with a mass of complex, restrictive and costly legislation in the form of EU Directives and Regulations and UK domestic legislation.

Domestic legislation is created through Acts of Parliament, following the publication of discussion documents (ie, Green Papers), consultation procedures and the publication of a Bill, which is debated by Parliament. Once passed by Parliament, the Bill becomes an Act and receives the Royal Assent and a date is set for its enactment.

An Act empowers the relevant Secretary of State (eg, for Transport) to create regulations in the form of Statutory Instruments (SIs) or Orders. Copies of Acts of Parliament, Statutory Instruments and Orders can be downloaded via the internet from: www.legislation.hmso.gov.uk or purchased from The Stationery Office and/or local HMSO stockists.

The professional LGV driver may think that he is not much concerned with legislation, but far from it. Almost everything he does is regulated by law from the licence he holds to the speed at which he drives, to say nothing of controls on the hours he works and his rest periods, on the mechanical condition of his vehicle and on requirements to ensure his health and safety at work, and on his employment rights, to name just a few random examples. He will need to ensure he knows all these legal provisions and the many others outlined in this *Handbook* if he is to avoid unwittingly breaching the law, which could cost him a heavy fine, lose him his driving licence or, in a worst-case scenario, even land him in prison.

It has often been said that an LGV driver needs to be as much a transport lawyer as a skilled heavy truck driver and reading through this text (which is by no means exhaustive) will certainly show just how much he really needs to know, but at least this *Handbook* provides him with a ready source of reference to all the important legal requirements.

Transport operations in the UK are primarily controlled by the Operator ('O') licensing system as outlined below. Drivers need to be aware of the fundamentals of the system because their actions can result in a breach of the law with consequent prosecution for themselves and for their employer (ie the 'O' licence holder), and potential loss of their LGV entitlement and their job if the employer loses his 'O' licence.

OPERATOR LICENSING

The 'O' licensing system is concerned with safety, and this is achieved by regulating the 'quality' of goods vehicle operators entering the industry (they must show that they have the ability and willingness to comply with the law and the funds to do so). It is administered by the Traffic Commissioner (TC) for each of the traffic areas covering England, Wales and Scotland.

Trade or business users of most goods vehicles over 3.5 tonnes maximum permissible weight must hold an 'O' licence for such vehicles, whether they are used for carrying goods in connection with the operator's main trade or business as an own-account operator (i.e. a trade or business other than that of carrying goods for hire or reward) or are used for hire or reward road haulage operations. Certain goods vehicles, including those used exclusively for private purposes, are exempt from the licensing requirements.

The vehicle user

An 'O' licence is required by the vehicle 'user' who is defined as the person who operates and drives the vehicle in the case of an owner-driver; the employer of a person who drives the vehicle for him in connection with his trade or business; and the driver himself. Ownership of the vehicle is *not* relevant in determining who the 'user' is.

Restricted 'O' licences

Own-account operators who only carry goods in connection with their trade or business (other than that of professional haulier) may hold a restricted 'O' licence which allows them to operate both within the United Kingdom and internationally. The licence does not permit them to carry any goods for hire or reward, or in connection with a trade or business other than their own.

Standard 'O' licences for national/international operations

Professional haulage operators and own-account operators who wish to carry goods for hire or reward in addition to their own goods, solely within the UK are required to hold a standard national 'O' licence. Professional hire and reward operators who wish to carry goods both nationally and internationally need to hold a standard national and international 'O' licence.

Conditions for the granting of restricted/standard 'O' licences

Applicants for restricted licences must be fit and proper persons and must be of appropriate financial standing. Applicants for standard 'O' licences must be of good repute, of appropriate financial standing and be professionally competent in either national or national and international transport operations.

Observing the legal requirements

It is a condition of 'O' licensing that the law must be observed on such matters as drivers' hours and records (including tachographs), use of vehicles, overloading, vehicle maintenance, roadworthiness, vehicle plating and testing, speed limits and traffic rules, driver licensing, and such other matters as the illegal use of rebated fuel oil, parking restrictions and prohibitions on loading/unloading. 'O' licensing conditions on the reporting of vehicle defects by drivers, safety inspections of vehicles and keeping maintenance records (driver defect reports, safety inspection reports and defect repair records) must be observed.

Declaration of intent

When applying for an 'O' licence, or variation of an 'O' licence, the applicant must make a declaration of intent – a legally binding promise that the law regarding all the above mentioned requirements will be strictly observed. This promise must be kept throughout the duration of the licence. Failure to fulfil promises made leaves the licence holder at risk of penalty against the licence by the Traffic Commissioner who has the power to curtail, suspend or revoke the licence where appropriate.

Maintenance

Operators must make proper arrangements, acceptable to the TC, for the maintenance and repair of their vehicles. These arrangements may be the use by the operator of his own workshop facilities or by the services of an outside repairer, in which case the TC would want to see a proper written agreement between the operator and the repairer. Although repairs may be carried out by other repairers, the licence holder remains fully and solely responsible for the mechanical condition of the vehicles on the road. Blame for faulty work cannot be transferred to the repairers.

Maintenance records, whether prepared in an operator's own workshop or supplied by an outside repairer, must be kept available for inspection for at least 15 months.

3.2

Goods vehicle weights and dimensions

Professional goods vehicle drivers should have a sound knowledge of the legal weights and dimensions of goods vehicles as follows:

CURRENT LEGAL MAXIMUM WEIGHTS

- two-axled rigid vehicles – 18 tonnes;
- three-axled rigid vehicles – 26 tonnes;
- rigid vehicles with four or more axles – 32 tonnes;
- articulated vehicle with three axles – 26 tonnes;
- articulated vehicles:
  - with four axles – 38 tonnes;
  - with five axles – 40 tonnes;
  - with six axles – 44 tonnes;
- lorry and trailer (ie, drawbar) combinations:
  - with four axles – 38 tonnes;
  - with five axles – 40 tonnes;
  - with six axles – 44 tonnes;
- maximum weight on drive axle – 11.5 tonnes;
- maximum weight on tandem-axle bogie – 20 tonnes;
- maximum weight on tri-axle bogie – 24 tonnes.

Note: the above maximum weights depend on the relevant plated weights of individual vehicles. Simply because a vehicle has a specific number of axles does not automatically mean that it can operate at the maximum weight shown above – the 'Ministry' plate must be examined to determine the actual maximum weights permitted by law for that particular vehicle.

GOODS VEHICLE DIMENSIONS

Maximum length

- rigid vehicles – 12 metres;
- articulated vehicles – 16.5 metres;
- drawbar trailers with four or more wheels and drawn by a vehicle over 3,500 kilograms pmw (permissible maximum weight) – 12 metres;
- all other drawbar trailers – 7 metres;
- semi-trailers (used in 16.5-metre articulated combinations kingpin-to-rear end max – 12 metres and kingpin-to-front max – 2.04 metres;
- composite trailer – 14.04 metres;
- drawbar combinations – 18.75 metres.

Maximum width

- goods vehicles and trailers – 2.55 metres;
- trailer drawn by vehicle up to 3.5 tonnes – 2.3 metres;
- refrigerated vehicles and trailers – 2.6 metres.

Maximum height

There is no legal maximum height limit for goods vehicles in Britain, but vehicles must be able to pass under bridges. The minimum height of motorway bridges and most other unmarked bridges is 5 metres (16 feet 6 inches).

3.3

Drivers' hours, working time and pay

For reasons of public safety and particularly safety on our roads, the law requires drivers of goods vehicles to conform to strict rules on:

- the time they spend driving between breaks, in a day, a week and a fortnight;
- minimum breaks to be taken during the driving day; and
- minimum daily and weekly rest periods.

However, these rules do not apply where the vehicle is used for purely private purposes or exempted as specified in www.dft.gov.uk. Breach of the rules is a serious matter that will lead to prosecution and severe penalty, both financial and by suspension or revocation of the offender's driving licence, as well as jeopardizing the employer's 'O' licence.

WHICH RULES APPLY?

LGV drivers (and their employers) must ensure they clearly understand the rules that apply to them, depending on the vehicle being driven or the transport work they are engaged in. Three sets of rules apply:

- the EU rules;
- the AETR rules for international journeys outside the EU; and
- the British domestic rules.

THE EU RULES

The current EU rules in Regulation 56/2006/EC have been in existence since 11 April 2007, with certain other provisions concerning tachographs taking effect from 1 May 2006.

Vehicles covered

EU rules take precedence over national rules and these must be considered first by determining whether the vehicle or the transport operation is exempt (see the DfT website for details at: www.transportoffice.gov.uk (follow the links for Vehicle Drivers/drivers' hours and tachographs/new drivers' hours rules). If an exemption applies then the British domestic rules apply. If no exemption is shown, the EU rules described below must be followed.

To reiterate two key points: a vehicle not exceeding 3.5 tonnes gross weight is exempt from the EU rules; and if the vehicle is in the EU exemption list or is used for a purpose shown in the list (eg, vehicles used by the public utilities and local authorities, etc), it is exempt. In either case, the vehicle comes within the British domestic rules. Conversely, where vehicles are over 3.5 tonnes gross vehicle weight, including the weight of any trailer, and are not exempt or are not used for an exempt purpose, the EU hours law applies in full.

Off-road vehicles

The EU law applies to 'off-roader' vehicles (4x4s) used for the carriage of goods and which, when towing trailers, have a combined gross weight of the towing vehicle and the trailer of over 3.5 tonnes.

Definitions
Driver

The rules apply to the 'driver' of the vehicle, who is anybody who drives, even for a short period, or who is carried on the vehicle ready to drive if necessary.

Driving

Driving is time spent behind the wheel driving the vehicle. It does not include activities such as checking the vehicle or load, which is 'other work'. Where daily driving involves 'on-site', as well as 'on-road' driving, all the driving counts towards the maximum daily driving limit.

Driving time

Driving time is the accumulation of time spent driving:

- before a break is taken or a daily rest period is started; or
- between two daily rest periods; or
- between a daily rest period and a weekly rest period.

A day

A day is any period of 24 hours starting from when a driver commences work after a daily or weekly rest period (ie, when the tachograph is set in motion).

Note: if a vehicle to which the EU regulations apply is driven on any day (no matter how short the time spent driving or how short the journey on the road – even for just 5 or 10 minutes down the road, for example) then the legal requirements apply to the driver for the whole of that day (ie, 24-hour period) and the week in which that day falls.

Fixed week

A 'week' in the rules is a fixed week from 00.00 hours Monday to 24.00 hours on the following Sunday.

Note: all references in the rules to weeks and weekly limits must be considered against this fixed week. Reference to 'fortnight' means two consecutive fixed weeks.

Working time

Time spent by a driver doing work other than driving must be recorded on the tachograph chart and counted along with driving in the 24-hour day. For example, a driver could drive for the normal daily maximum of nine hours, taking his 45-minute break period where appropriate and his 11-hour daily rest, leaving a further three and a quarter hours in which he could work for his employer.

Drivers who travel from home to collect their vehicle from a place other than their employer's premises must record that time on the tachograph chart as working time. Where tipping vehicles are driven on off-road sites, if the driver intends driving either that vehicle or another vehicle under the regulations on the public highway, the time spent driving off-road must be counted as working time and recorded on the tachograph chart accordingly.

Employers' responsibilities

Employers must ensure that their drivers understand fully how the law applies to them and how to comply with its detailed provisions. They have specific responsibilities under the EU rules:

- to organize drivers' work so the rules on driving times, breaks and rest periods are not broken;
- to make regular checks of tachograph charts to ensure the law is complied with;
- to take appropriate steps to prevent any repetition of offences where they find drivers have breached the law.

Driving limits

Drivers are restricted in the amount of time they can spend driving:

- before taking a break;
- between any two daily rest periods (or a daily and a weekly rest period);
- in a week; and
- in a fortnight.

The driving period begins when the driver sets his tachograph in motion and begins driving. The maximum limits are as follows:

- maximum driving before a break – four and a half hours;
- maximum daily driving normally – nine hours;
- extended driving on two days in week only – 10 hours;
- maximum weekly driving – six daily driving shifts;*
- maximum fortnightly driving (two consecutive weeks) – 90 hours.

Note: where a driver spends the maximum amount of time driving in one week (ie, 4 × 9 hours plus 2 × 10 hours = 56 hours), during the next following fixed week he may drive only for a maximum of 34 hours.

Break periods

Drivers must take a break or a number of breaks if in a day the total of their driving amounts to four and a half hours or more. If they do not drive for four and a half hours, there is no legal requirement for them to take a break during that day. Break periods must not be counted as part of a daily rest period and during breaks, the driver must not do any 'other work'. However, 'other work' does not include:

- waiting time;
- time spent riding as a passenger in a vehicle; or
- time spent on a ferry or train.

The requirement for taking a break is that immediately the four and a half hour driving limit is reached, a break of 45 minutes must be taken, unless a daily or weekly rest period starts at that time. This break may be replaced by a number of other breaks of *at least* 15 minutes each spread over the driving period, or taken during and immediately after this period, so as to equal at least 45 minutes and taken in such a way that the four and a half hour maximum driving limit is not exceeded. Any break taken in excess of the required 45 minutes after driving for four and a half hours cannot be counted as part of the break period legally required in respect of the next four and a half hour driving period.

Rest periods

Rest periods are defined as uninterrupted periods of at least one hour during which the driver 'may freely dispose of his time'. Daily rest periods, and particularly rest periods that are compensating for previously reduced rest periods, should not be confused with, or combined with, statutory break periods required to be taken during the driving day as described above.

Time spent by drivers on weekend training courses (eg, Hazchem [hazardous chemicals] courses and suchlike), even where there is no direct payment of wages by the employer, breaches the requirements under EU rules for drivers to have a period of weekly rest during which they may freely dispose of their time.

Daily rest

Once each day drivers are required to take either a normal, a reduced or a split daily rest period during which time they must be free to dispose of their time as they wish. These daily rests are to be taken once in each 24 hours starting when the driver activates the tachograph following a daily or weekly rest period.

Where the daily rest is taken in two or three separate periods (see below), the calculation must commence at the end of a rest period of not less than eight hours. Thus in each 24-hour period one or other of the following daily rest periods must be taken:

- normal daily rest – 11 hours; or alternatively
- reduced rest (max three times weekly) – nine hours – the reduced time must be compensated by an equal amount of additional rest taken with other rest periods before the end of the next following fixed week;
- split rest – where the daily rest period is not reduced (as above), the rest may be split and taken in two separate periods during the 24 hours, provided:
  - the first continuous period is of at least three hours' duration;
  - the second period is of at least nine hours' duration;
  - the total daily rest period is increased to 12 hours.

Split daily rest

When a daily rest period is split into two separate periods, the eight-hour period must be in the last portion of the rest.

Multi-manned vehicles

Where a two-man crew operates a vehicle, the daily rest period requirement is that each man must have had a minimum of nine hours' rest in each period of 30 hours. Daily rest, however, cannot be taken on a moving vehicle (see opposite).

A multi-manned vehicle can be driven for a maximum of 20 hours within the

21-hour period left after deducting nine-hours' rest from the 30-hour spreadover mentioned above – each crew member driving for a maximum of 10 hours.

Note: the law applies to both crew members from the commencement of the journey (or their day's work if that started prior to the start of the journey).

Daily rest on vehicles

Daily rest periods may be taken on a vehicle provided it has a bunk so the driver (but not necessarily a mate or attendant) can lie down, and it is stationary for the whole of the rest period. A driver on a double-manned vehicle cannot be taking part of his *daily rest period* on the bunk while his co-driver continues to drive the vehicle. He could, however, be taking a break at this time while the vehicle is moving or he could merely spend his time lying on the bunk with his tachograph chart recording other work.

Daily rest on ferries/trains

Daily rest periods that are taken when a vehicle is to be carried for part of its journey on a ferry crossing or by rail may be interrupted *twice only* provided that:

- part of the rest is taken on land before or after the ferry crossing/rail journey;
- the interruption is 'as short as possible' and in any event not more than one hour before embarkation or after disembarkation (not both) and includes dealing with Customs formalities;
- during both parts of the rest (ie, in the terminal and on board the ferry/train) the driver has access to a bunk or couchette.

Weekly rest

Once each fixed week (and after six driving shifts) a daily rest period must be combined with a weekly rest period to provide a weekly rest period totalling 45 hours. A weekly rest period that begins in one fixed week and continues into the following week may be attached to either of these weeks, but not both. In two consecutive fixed weeks the driver must take two weekly rest periods, one of which must total 45 hours.

While the normal weekly rest period is 45 hours as described above, this may be reduced to 24 hours.

Reduced weekly rest periods must be compensated (ie, made up) by an equivalent amount of rest period time taken:

- en bloc;
- added to another rest period of at least eight hours' duration; and
- before the end of the third week following the week in which the reduced weekly rest period was taken.

Compensated rest periods

When reduced daily and/or weekly rest periods are taken, the compensated time must be attached to another rest period of at least eight hours' duration, and granted, at the request of the driver, at the vehicle parking place or at the driver's base. Compensation in this respect *does not* mean compensation by means of payment; it means the provision of an equivalent amount of rest time taken on a later occasion but within the specified limits; that is:

- by the end of the next week for compensated daily rest; and
- by the end of the third following week in the case of compensated weekly rest period; and
- in either case added to other rest periods.

Emergencies

Drivers are permitted to exceed the EU rules when an emergency arises, but only by as much as is necessary to reach a suitable stopping place and provided road safety is not jeopardized. An emergency is defined as an event where action is necessary to ensure the safety of persons, the vehicle, or its load. The driver must note the nature of and reasons for exceeding the rules on his tachograph chart.

Prohibition on certain payments

The EU rules prohibit any payment to wage-earning drivers of bonuses or wage supplements related to distances travelled and/or the amount of goods carried unless they do not endanger road safety.

Enforcement and penalties

The hours rules are applied to protect road users from the dangers of over-worked and tired drivers being in control of heavy vehicles. For this reason, the police and VOSA enforce them vigorously. Convicted offenders are dealt with severely by the courts to emphasize the importance of these road safety measures; they can expect to be fined heavily while the most serious offenders may end up in prison. Those who hold LGV driving entitlements may lose these, and possibly their jobs.

Enforcement officers can detain drivers found on the road to be in breach of the drivers' hours rules and where a UK driver has not taken sufficient break or rest periods he will be prohibited from continuing his journey. Where break periods have been infringed, the delay at the roadside will last until a full 45-minute break period has been taken. Where breaches of the daily or weekly rest period requirements are found, the driver and his vehicle will be escorted by the police to a suitable parking area (eg, a service area or truck stop) where he will have to remain until he has taken a full 11-hour daily rest or 24-hour weekly rest. A relief driver may be sent to take over the vehicle and continue its journey, but this driver will be subjected to scrutiny to ensure he has sufficient driving time available within legal limits.

In Europe, breaches of the rules may result in heavy on-the-spot fines, which must be paid immediately, otherwise the vehicle may be impounded and the driver held until it is paid.

AETR RULES

Drivers on international journeys beyond the European Union are required to observe the AETR rules (an internationally recognized agreement), which are fully harmonized with the EU rules.

BRITISH DOMESTIC DRIVERS' HOURS RULES

The British domestic rules comprise only limits on daily driving (maximum 10 hours in 24 hours) and daily duty (maximum 11 hours in any 24 hours – but no limit on non-driving days). Drivers who are exempt from the EU rules, either because their vehicle does not exceed 3.5 tonnes permissible maximum weight, or they are otherwise exempt, must comply with the British domestic rules as set out below. However, it is important to note that drivers of light goods vehicles not exceeding 3.5 tonnes gross weight must still conform to the British domestic limits on maximum daily driving and maximum daily duty despite the fact that no records of driving or working times have to be kept. Also, if a trailer is attached to a vehicle not exceeding 3.5 tonnes permissible maximum weight (which itself is exempt from the EU rules on account of its weight), making the combined weight more than 3.5 tonnes, then the EU rules must be followed as described above, unless it is exempt for other reasons.

Exemptions and concessions

The British domestic rules apply to drivers of all goods vehicles exempt from the EU regulations, but with the following further exceptions, which are totally exempt from all hours rules control:

- armed forces;
- police and fire brigade services;
- driving off the public road system;
- driving for purely private purposes (ie, not in connection with any trade or business).

Additionally, the British domestic rules do not apply to a driver who on any day does not drive a relevant vehicle; or to a driver who on each day of the week does not drive a vehicle within these rules for more than four hours.

Note: this exemption does not apply to a driver whose activities fall within the EU rules.

Definitions

For the purposes of the British domestic rules:

- Driving means time spent behind the wheel actually driving a goods vehicle. Driving on off-road sites and premises such as quarries, civil engineering and building sites and on agricultural and forestry land is counted as duty time, not driving time.
- Driving time is the maximum amount of time spent driving on roads to which the public has access.
- Duty time is the time a driver spends working for his employer and includes any work undertaken including the driving of private motor cars, for example, which is not driving time for the purposes of the regulations. The daily duty limit does not apply on any day when a driver does not drive a goods vehicle.

Emergencies

The daily driving and duty limits specified above may be suspended when an emergency situation arises. This is defined as an event requiring immediate action to avoid:

- danger to life or health of one or more individuals or animals;
- serious interruption in the maintenance of essential public services for the supply of gas, water, electricity, drainage, or of telecommunications and postal services;
- serious interruption in the use of roads, railways, ports or airports; or
- damage to property.

The driver must enter details of the emergency on his record sheet when the statutory limits are exceeded.

Light vehicle driving

Drivers of light goods vehicles not exceeding 3.5 tonnes permissible maximum weight must observe the daily limits on driving (10 hours) and duty (11 hours). However, only the 10-hour daily driving limit applies when such vehicles are used:

- by doctors, dentists, nurses, midwives or vets;
- for any service of inspection, cleaning, maintenance, repair, installation or fitting;

- by a commercial traveller and carrying only goods used for soliciting orders;
- by an employee of the AA, the RAC or the RSAC;
- for the business of cinematography or of radio or television broadcasting.

MIXED EU AND BRITISH DRIVING

When a goods vehicle driver, on the same day or within the same week, drives within scope of both the EU and the British domestic hours' rules, he may choose to conform solely to the EU rules throughout the whole of the driving/working period *or* follow the more liberal British domestic rules where appropriate. If he decides on the latter and thereby combines both British and EU rules, he must beware of the following points:

- Time spent driving under the EU rules cannot count as an off-duty period for the British rules.
- Time spent driving or on duty under the British rules cannot count as a break or rest period under the EU rules.
- Driving under the EU rules counts towards the driving and duty limits for the British rules.
- Where any EU rules' driving is done in a week, he must observe the EU daily and weekly rest period requirements for the whole of that week.

DOMESTIC RECORD KEEPING

Where a goods vehicle is outside the scope of the EU rules as described previously, then the British domestic driving hours rules apply and the driver is required to keep written records of his driving and working activities using the 'logbook' system.

Exemptions from record keeping

Written records do not have to be kept in the following cases:

- by drivers of vehicles that are exempt from 'O' licensing, except that the exemption does not apply to drivers of Crown vehicles that would have needed an 'O' licence if the vehicle had not been Crown property;
- by drivers of goods vehicles on any day when they drive for four hours or less and within 50 kilometres of the vehicle's base (*Note: this exemption is applicable only in the case of domestic operations – it does not apply to tachograph use.*);
- by drivers voluntarily using an EU tachograph for record-keeping purposes (ie, which has been calibrated and sealed at a DfT-approved tachograph centre).

Record books

Record books must be a standard A6 format (105 millimetres × 148 millimetres) or larger and comprise:

- a front sheet;
- a set of instructions for the use of the book;
- a number of individual weekly record sheets with facilities for completing these in duplicate (ie, with carbon paper or carbonless copy paper); and
- a duplicate sheet, which can be detached for return to the employer when completed.

There is no legal requirement for the numbering of record books or for their issue against an entry in a register of record book issues. The following entries must be made in the weekly record sheets:

- driver's name;
- period covered by sheet week commencing... week ending...;
- registration number of vehicle(s);
- place where vehicle(s) based;
- time of going on duty;
- time of going off duty;
- time spent driving;
- time spent on duty;
- signature of driver;
- certification by employer (ie, signature and position held).

Issue and return of record books

Drivers must be issued with record books when they are required to drive vehicles to which the British domestic driving hours regulations apply and where records must be kept. Before issuing the book, the employer must complete the front cover to show the firm's name, address and telephone number, preferably with a rubber stamp if one is available. When a record book is issued to the driver, he should complete the front cover with:

- his surname;
- first name(s);
- date of birth;
- home address; and
- the date when the book was first used.

When the book is completed, he should also enter the date of the last entry (ie, date of last use). Books issued by an employer to an employee-driver must be returned to that employer when complete (subject to the requirement for the driver to retain it for two weeks after use), or when the employee leaves that employment.

The driver must not take with him a record book issued by one employer when he joins a new employer. When returning a record book to his employer under these circumstances any unused weekly sheets and all duplicates must be included (ie, left in situ).

Two employers or change of employer

Where a driver has two employers who employ him to drive goods vehicles to which the British domestic hours rules apply, the first employer must issue the record book as described above and completed weekly record sheets and completed record books must be returned to this employer. The second employer must write or stamp his firm's name and address on the front cover of the record book with a statement that the holder is also a driver in his employment. Space is provided for this purpose.

When a driver does part-time driving work for another employer he must disclose to each employer, if requested, details of his working and driving times with the other employer. Similarly, when a driver changes to a new employer the former employer must give the new employer details of the driver's previous driving and working times if requested.

Record book entries

The driver must make entries on the weekly sheet for each day on which a record is required (instructions on the correct use of the book are printed inside the cover). He must take care to ensure that an exact duplicate of the entry is made simultaneously (ie, two separately written repeat entries are *not* acceptable even if no carbon paper is available). When completing a daily sheet he must enter all the required details under each of the headings. If he changes vehicles during the day he must enter the registration number for each vehicle. He must then sign the sheet before returning it to his employer. Completion of the record is straightforward, the driver having to enter only:

- the vehicle registration number (and the number for any subsequent vehicle driven);
- the time of coming on duty;
- the time at which he went off duty at the end of the day; and
- his signature.

He may enter any remarks concerning his entries, or point out corrections that should be made, in the appropriate box at the foot of the record sheet. The employer may also use this space if required for making comments regarding the record. This space may also be used for recording the name of a second driver who accompanies the vehicle.

Corrections to entries

Entries in the record book must be in ink or made by a ballpoint pen and there must be no erasures, corrections or additions. Mistakes may only be corrected by writing an explanation or by showing the correct information in the remarks space. Weekly sheets must not be mutilated or destroyed.

Return and signing of record sheets

When he has completed the weekly sheet and signed it, the driver must detach the duplicate copy from the book and hand it to his employer within seven days of the date of the last entry on the sheet. Within a further seven days the employer must examine and sign the duplicate sheet. If in either case it is not reasonably practicable to do so within this time, these actions must be carried out as soon as possible.

Retention and production of record books

The driver should carry his record book with him at all times when working and must produce it for inspection at the request of an authorized examiner. The book should be shown to the employer at the end of every week or as soon as possible after the week so the employer can examine and countersign the entries.

Following completion of the book the driver must keep it with him for a further two weeks to have it available for inspection by the enforcement authorities if required. After this time he should return the book to his employer. Completed record books must be retained by the employer, and also be available for inspection by the enforcement authorities if required, for not less than 12 months (counting from the date of the last entry).

Record books for Germany

Germany requires foreign drivers of goods vehicles between 2.8 and 3.5 tonnes gross weight entering the country to use AETR-type log books. Failure to do so could result in delays and penalties.

Checking of records

Police and examiners of the VOSA can demand to see a driver's domestic record book, which he should carry with him at all times when on duty under the regulations. A police officer may seize a record book if he considers it provides evidence of an offence.

WORKING TIME

The Road Transport Directive came into force from March 2005 and applies to road haulage and logistics drivers who are subject to the EU drivers' hours rules.

Self-employment

The Road Haulage Directive mentioned above will not apply to self-employed road hauliers (ie, owner-driver lorry operators) until 23 March 2009. However, not all existing self-employed persons are genuinely self-employed in terms that meet legal requirements of HM Revenue & Customs and the Department for Work and Pensions (DWP) with regard to payment of National Insurance contributions. To satisfy both the IR and the DWP a self-employed person must meet a series of 'tests' under which they:

- decide, broadly, how and when specified work is to be carried out, the actual hours they work and when they take breaks and holidays and are not subject to disciplinary provisions of the employer;
- provide their own tools and equipment and are free to send another person (or sub-contractor) in their place to carry out work where necessary;
- have no entitlement to payment for public or annual holidays or sickness; are not included in the employer's pension scheme, and have no rights to claim redundancy payments, unfair dismissal or any entitlement to unemployment benefit if their services are no longer required;
- take financial risk with the aim of making a profit, are responsible for paying their own income tax and National Insurance contributions and charge for their services by submitting an invoice;
- are free to work for other employers as required if they so wish (a self-employed person who works for only one employer is likely to be considered to be an employee of that employer).

Working week

The working week is 48 hours work (with a maximum of 60 hours over a 4-month (17-week) reference period, which may be extended by agreement to 6 months. Total working time is calculated excluding breaks during the working day and waiting time (ie periods of availability). It should be noted that there is *no* opt-out from the working time limits under this Directive as there is with the main Working Time Directive.

Breaks

Breaks taken during the working period must amount to a minimum 30 minutes if working takes place for between 6 and 9 hours, or 45 minutes if working over 9 hours.

Night work

This is defined as a 4-hour period between midnight and 4.00am. Night working is limited to 10 hours in any 24-hour period, although an agreed derogation will allow this to be extended to 12 hours.

Note: This night work definition should not be confused with the night work definition contained in the main Working Time Directive.

Holidays

Holidays, including those under a British amendment to the Horizontal Amending Directive (HAD), will comprise from 2009 a minimum of 5.6 weeks (including bank holidays) paid at the average rate of earnings for the previous 12 weeks. Average earnings in this case should include overtime payments.

Other employers

Mobile workers must inform their employer in writing of any time they spend working for any other employer (even if it does not come within scope of the RTD). Such time worked will count towards the weekly working limit of 48 hours.

Record keeping

Employers must keep detailed records of employee working times and provide copies of such records to their employees when requested to do so. There is no officially prescribed system for record keeping or special format for individual records, but whatever system is used the records must be kept for two years and be made available to VOSA enforcement officers on request.

Health assessments

Employers must provide free health assessments for night workers. Employers have a duty to determine exactly who is a night worker for this purpose and provide the health assessment accordingly. The assessment should include a questionnaire devised and monitored by a qualified health professional and where necessary be backed up by a medical examination.

THE NATIONAL MINIMUM WAGE

The National Minimum Wage rules require that workers (other than self-employed persons) aged 22 years or over must be paid at least £5.52 per hour, and workers aged from 18 to 21 years at least £4.60 per hour (rates from 1 October 2007). The Minimum Wage applies to most workers in the United Kingdom including agency drivers.

DRIVER OVERNIGHT ALLOWANCES

The amount paid to drivers for overnight subsistence varies considerably from area to area – the national general figure is currently £28.62 applicable for nights-out where no receipt is provided.

3.4

Tachograph fitment and use

There are currently two types of tachograph in use in goods vehicles (where fitment is a statutory requirement); the old-type analogue tachograph and the new-type digital instrument fitted to new (non-exempt) goods vehicles over 3.5 tonnes gross weight from 1 May 2006. LGV drivers need to be familiar with the operation of both types, since they may be required to drive goods vehicles with either type of instrument installed. Failure by a driver to comply with the relevant requirements in either case is an offence for which they may be heavily fined on conviction. This section of the *Handbook* describes the legal requirements relating to both types of instrument (see this page and p 93).

ANALOGUE TACHOGRAPHS

The analogue-type tachograph is a cable or electronically driven speedometer with an electric clock and a chart recording mechanism that is fitted into the vehicle dashboard. It indicates time, speed and distance and permanently records this information on a circular chart along with driving and working activities. Charts show:

- speeds (and the highest speed) at which the vehicle was driven;
- total distance travelled and distances between individual stops;
- times when the vehicle was being driven and the total amount of driving time;
- times when the vehicle was standing and whether the driver was indicating other work, break or rest period during this time.

RECORDINGS

Recordings are made on circular charts, each covering 24 hours, by special styli that press through a wax recording layer on the chart, revealing the black carbonated layer between the top surface and the backing paper. The charts are accurately premarked with time, distance and speed reference radials and when the styli have marked the chart with the appropriate recordings these can be easily identified and interpreted against the printed reference marks:

● Movement of the vehicle creates a broad running line on the time radial, indicating when the vehicle started running and when it stopped. After the vehicle has stopped, the time-group stylus continues to mark the chart but with an easily distinguishable thin line.

● The speed trace gives an accurate recording of the speeds attained at all times throughout the journey, continuing to record on the speed baseline when the vehicle is stationary to provide an unbroken trace except when the instrument is opened.

● The stylus moving up and down over a short stroke makes the distance recording, each movement representing 5 kilometres travelled; thus, every 5 kilometres the stylus reverses direction, forming a 'V' for every 10 kilometres of distance travelled. To calculate the total distance covered the Vs are counted and multiplied by 10 and any 'tail ends' are added in, the total being expressed in kilometres.

When a second chart is located in the rear position of a two-man tachograph, only a time recording of the second man's activities (ie, other work, break or rest) is shown. Traces showing driving, vehicle speed or distance cannot be recorded on this chart.

Precautions against interference with the readings are incorporated – a security mark is made on the chart every time the instrument is opened so it can be easily established at what time the instrument was opened. Interference with the recording mechanism to give false readings, particularly of speed, can easily be seen.

VEHICLES REQUIRING TACHOGRAPHS

The law requires the fitment and use of tachographs in most goods vehicles over 3.5 tonnes gross weight with certain EU exemptions (see exemptions on the DfT website at www.roads.dft.gov.uk/roadsafety/tachograph/gv262). Unless a vehicle is used solely for private purposes, or is specifically exempted as shown by the exemption list, the law applies.

There is no exemption for short-distance operations, infrequent-use vehicles or occasional driving: once a relevant vehicle is on the public highway (ie, any road to which the public has access – and that includes public car parks and so-called private dock roads) – the law applies in full.

Where the law applies, a tachograph instrument must be fitted and whoever drives the vehicle must produce a tachograph record and comply fully with the EU drivers' hours law on the day on which the driving takes place, and the week in which that day falls.

DRIVER RESPONSIBILITIES

Responsibility for the legal use of tachographs rests with the driver, who must fully understand what the law requires, and how to comply with it. Drivers must ensure that the tachograph in their vehicle works correctly throughout the whole of their working shift so a proper recording is made for a full 24 hours. They must also ensure they have sufficient quantities of the right type of charts.

Not knowing what the law requires or how to comply with it are not acceptable excuses in defence of a prosecution for tachograph offences. The courts take the view that it is the driver's duty to know these things. Drivers must:

- Keep a proper record, ie, a continuous and 'time right' record (ie, recordings must be in the correct 12-hour section of the chart – daytime or night-time hours).
- Make manual recordings on the chart if the tachograph fails while working, or when no tachograph-fitted vehicle is available – these must be legible and must not dirty the chart.
- Produce for inspection on request by an authorized inspecting officer:
  - a current chart for that day;
  - charts relating to the current week; and
  - a chart for the last day of the previous week in which he drove.
- Return completed charts to their employer no later than 21 days after use.
- Allow any authorized inspecting officer to inspect the charts they have with them and the tachograph calibration plaque, which is usually fixed inside the body of the instrument. This means allowing the officer into the vehicle cab where necessary.
- When they take their vehicle (or just the tractive unit) home at the end of their working shift, record this time on the tachograph chart and count it as part of their daily maximum driving time and their day's work – it is not part of the rest period.

TWO-CREW OPERATION (MULTI-MANNING)

Where a vehicle is multi-manned a two-man tachograph must be fitted and both drivers must use it simultaneously to produce records as follows. The person driving must have his chart located in the uppermost (ie, number 1) position in the instrument and use the number '1' activity mode switch to record his activities and vehicle speed and distance on the chart as appropriate.

The person riding passenger must have his chart in the rearmost (ie, number 2) position *from the start of the journey* and use the number '2' activity mode switch to record his other work activities, or break or rest periods. Only time group recordings are made on this chart; driving, speed and distance traces are not produced.

TACHOGRAPH BREAKDOWN

If the tachograph breaks down, or the seals are broken for whatever reason, including authorized breakage to carry out repairs, or unauthorized interference, it must be repaired at an approved centre as soon as 'circumstances permit', but in the meantime the driver must continue to make records manually on the chart of his working, driving, breaks and rest times. There is *no* requirement to record speed or distance.

When a vehicle returns to base with a defective tachograph, it should not leave again until the instrument has been repaired and recalibrated (if necessary) and the seals replaced. If it cannot return to base within one week from the day of the tachograph breakdown, it must be repaired and recalibrated at an approved centre *en route* within that time.

Defence

There is a defence in the regulations against using a vehicle with a defective tachograph allowing continued use provided steps have been taken to have it restored to a legal condition as soon as circumstances permit and provided the driver continues to record his driving, working and break period times manually on a tachograph chart. It is also a defence to show that at the time the tachograph was examined by an enforcement officer, the vehicle was on its way to an approved tachograph centre to have repairs carried out. But this defence will fail if the driver did not manually record his activities in the meantime.

TIME CHANGES

Tachograph clocks must be set and recordings made in accordance with the official time in the country of registration of the vehicle. British drivers travelling in Europe should not change the clock to show local European time.

DIRTY OR DAMAGED CHARTS

If a chart becomes dirty or damaged in use, it must be replaced and the old chart should be securely attached to the new chart that is used to replace it.

COMPLETION OF THE CHART CENTRE FIELD

Before starting work with a vehicle the driver must enter on the centre field of his chart for that day the following details:

- his surname and first name (not initials);
- the date and place where use of the chart begins;
- vehicle registration number;
- the distance recorder (odometer) reading at the start of the day.

At the end of a working day, he should then record the following information on the chart:

- the place and date where the chart is completed;
- the closing odometer reading;
- by subtraction, the total distance driven – in kilometres.

MAKING RECORDINGS

When the centre field has been completed, the chart should be inserted in the tachograph, ensuring that it is the right way up and that recording will commence on the correct part of the 24-hour chart (day or night). The instrument face should be securely closed. The activity mode switch (number 1) should be turned as necessary throughout the work period to indicate driving, other work, break or rest periods. Failure to do this is an offence.

Other work and overtime recordings

Drivers must record *all* periods of work on their tachograph charts including work for the employer after the daily driving shift has been completed (eg, in a yard, warehouse, workshop or office), either by the instrument if this is convenient or manually.

Overnight recordings

At the end of his shift the driver can leave the chart in the tachograph overnight to record the daily rest or remove it and record the rest period manually. Generally, enforcement officers prefer an automatic recording of daily rest, but this is not always practicable where the vehicle may be:

- used by other drivers on night-shift work;
- driven for road testing or other purposes by workshop staff; or
- moved around the premises by others when the driver is taking his statutory rest period.

When the driver is scheduled to start work later on the following day, there will be an overlap recording if he leaves the chart in the tachograph overnight, which is illegal.

Vehicle changes
If the driver changes to another vehicle during the working day he must take the existing chart with him and record:

- details of the time of change;
- the registration number of the further vehicle(s); and
- distance recordings in the appropriate spaces on the chart.

That same chart is used in the next vehicle to record the driver's continuing driving, working and break periods. This procedure is repeated no matter how many different vehicles (except those not driven on the public highway) are driven during the day so the one chart shows (where possible) the driver's entire daily activity – but see also below.

Mixed tachographs
There is more than one make of tachograph, each using different charts, which are not interchangeable – although some 'universal charts' are available. The driver who switches from one make of instrument to another during the working day must make fresh entries on a second or even third chart. At the end of the day, all the charts used should be attached together to present a comprehensive (and legal) record for the whole day.

MANUAL RECORDS
Drivers are responsible for ensuring that the tachograph is kept running while they are in charge of the vehicle. If it fails or stops making proper records, the chart should be removed and they should continue to record their activities manually on the chart. Similarly, they must make manual recordings of work done or time spent away from the vehicle (eg, when working in the yard or warehouse). Manual recordings must be made legibly, the chart must not be dirtied or damaged and existing recordings made by the tachograph must not be defaced.

RECORDS FOR PART-TIME DRIVERS

The rules on the use of tachographs described above apply equally to part-time or occasional drivers, such as yard and warehouse staff, and even if the driving on the road is for a very short distance or period of time – a five-minute drive without a tachograph chart in use would be sufficient to break the law and risk prosecution.

Vehicle fitters and other workshop staff who drive vehicles on the road for testing or repair are exempt from the need to keep tachograph records but this *does not* apply when using vehicles for other purposes (eg, collecting spare parts, taking replacement vehicles out to on-road breakdowns, taking vehicles to and from goods vehicle test stations etc).

RETENTION, RETURN AND CHECKING OF TACHOGRAPH CHARTS

Drivers must retain and be able to produce, on request by authorized examiners (including the police), completed tachograph charts for the current day and for the previous 28 days, plus their driver 'smart card' if they have one – charts are not required for non-driving or rest days. After this period charts must be returned to the employer no later than 42 days after use and the employer must check them to ensure that the law has not been broken.

More than one employer

Where a driver has more than one employer in a week, as may be the case with an agency driver, he must return the tachograph charts to the employer who first employed him in that week.

OFFICIAL INSPECTION OF CHARTS

An authorized inspecting officer may require a driver to show him any tachograph chart on which recordings have been made. The examiner may enter a vehicle to inspect a chart or a tachograph instrument and the calibration plaques. Where a chart is suspected of showing a false entry an examiner may 'seize' the chart (but not for other reasons) and retain it for a maximum of six months, after which time, if no charges for offences have been made, the chart should have been returned. It is an offence to fail to produce records for inspection as required or to obstruct an enforcement officer in his request to inspect records or tachograph installations in vehicles.

OFFENCES

Some specific tachograph-related offences have already been mentioned above, but there are other overriding and very serious offences, in particular:

- using, or causing or permitting the use of, a vehicle without a fully calibrated tachograph installed;
- drivers failing to keep tachograph records (or manual records if the instrument is defective); and
- making false recordings.

Further, it is an offence for the driver to fail to return used charts to his employer within 21 days after use, or notify his first employer or any other employer for whom he drives vehicles to which the regulations apply.

Penalties

On summary conviction for tachograph offences a fine of up to £2,500 may be imposed and both the driver's LGV driving entitlement and the employer's 'O' licence may be jeopardized. More serious offences of making false entries on a tachograph chart and forgery can result in fines of up to £5,000 per offence and/or imprisonment for up to two years. Tachograph falsification is a 'recordable' offence leaving the convicted offender with a criminal record. Drivers convicted for using wires to interfere with their tachograph will be disqualified from holding an LGV driving licence for a period of one year.

DIGITAL TACHOGRAPHS

A new generation of digital tachographs for goods vehicles was introduced from 1 May 2006 under EU Regulation 561/2006/EC, which amended the previous tachograph regulations. From that date all new goods vehicles exceeding 3.5 tonnes gross weight (except those specifically exempt under the regulations) have had to be fitted with a digital tachograph instrument into which the driver inserts his own personalized micro-chip 'smart card' to record his working times.

The driver card is crucial to the whole system. It is personal to the individual and carries identification information and other essential data about him. It has the capacity to store and print out relevant data on driving and working times, breaks and rest periods covering at least 28 days, and comprises the legal record in place of the current tachograph chart. The card itself is tamper-proof, and strict regulatory systems are established by national governments to prevent fraudulent issue, use and transfer of cards within their territories.

A tachograph smart card (officially called a 'tachograph card') is a plastic card similar in size to a photo-card driving licence or credit card, with a microchip embedded into it. There are four such cards for use with digital tachographs as follows:

- driver cards – which the driver inserts at the commencement of his journey to record driving and working activities;
- company cards – for use by vehicle operators to protect and download the data;
- workshop cards – available only to approved tachograph calibration centres;
- control cards – for use only by VOSA examiners and the police for carrying out enforcement activities.

Before commencing a journey the driver should insert his driver card into the 1st (driver) or 2nd (co-driver) slot on the front of the Vehicle Unit. The time setting and all manual entries made on the print-out must be in UTC (Universal Time Co-ordinated), which is the same as Greenwich Mean Time (GMT), and must remain so both in the UK and throughout Europe. The 'centre field' details, formerly entered by the driver on the tachograph chart, will be recorded automatically by the digital instrument (the driver's name, vehicle registration number, start and finish odometer readings and name of place code).

In the same way that drivers and co-drivers currently record their different activities – driving, other work, breaks and rest – by changing the mode switch and by swapping the position of charts in the tachograph head, with digital tachographs the mode switch will have to be turned and digital smart cards will need to be swapped between driver and co-driver slots in the instrument when multi-manning a vehicle.

Details of time spent working away from the vehicle that are normally written on the rear of the analogue tachograph chart need to be entered manually into the digital tachograph. The digital instrument also records details of any faults, interference, errors and over-speeding that occur.

DOWNLOADING AND STORING DATA

All this data will be stored for at least 28 days on the driver's personal smart card and for at least a year in the Vehicle Unit. This data must be regularly downloaded by the vehicle operator to the office computer to ensure that the legal records are not lost – this means complying with the law by downloading driver cards every 28 days (otherwise the data will be overwritten) and the Vehicle Unit at least once every 56 days. Small hand-held downloading devices are available for this purpose, similar to memory sticks. These computerized records along with any print-outs from digital tachographs must be kept available for inspection for at least one year.

PRODUCTION OF RECORDS

Enforcement officers of VOSA have the right to examine computerized and printed records as well as examining any analogue tachograph charts. For this purpose, it is a legal requirement that the driver is able to produce:

- his driver smart card if he has one (even if not driving a digital tachograph-equipped vehicle at the time);
- any analogue tachograph records for the current day and any records made in the previous 28 days when driving analogue tachograph-equipped vehicles.

At the request of an enforcement officer the driver must also be able to produce a print-out from his digital tachograph which will show his driving up to that time.

3.5

Driver licensing and testing

THE LAW ABOUT LICENCES

Any person wishing to drive a motor vehicle on a public road must hold a driving licence, obtainable from the Driver and Vehicle Licensing Agency (DVLA), showing a valid entitlement for the type of vehicle being driven. This may be a full entitlement for the vehicle, where the relevant driving tests (theory and practical) have been passed, or a provisional entitlement for a learner driver who has not yet passed the test for that category of vehicle.

Driving without a licence
It is a serious offence to drive a vehicle without a current and valid driving licence, or to encourage (cause) another person to do so. These offences carry heavy fines and offenders may be disqualified. Driving by an unlicensed or incorrectly licensed person invalidates the vehicle insurance.

Steering and pushing a vehicle
Where a person sits in and steers a vehicle being towed (whether broken down or even with vital parts missing) he is 'driving' for licensing purposes and must hold a current and valid driving entitlement covering that vehicle. Conversely, a person pushing a vehicle from the outside with both feet on the ground is not legally 'driving' or 'using' the vehicle.

Eligibility for a driving licence
Any person may apply for a driving licence provided they meet the minimum standards of age, health and eyesight specified to ensure that those who drive motor vehicles on public roads are in a fit state of health and are safe to drive. (Medical standards for drivers are described on pages 102–08.) New drivers

are issued with a provisional licence until the appropriate driving test has been passed when application can be made for a full entitlement for that category of vehicle – see list of categories below.

Photocard licences

Credit card-sized plastic photocard licences showing a passport-type photo-graph of the holder are issued to new drivers in the United Kingdom and to existing licence holders who apply for replacements for lost or damaged licences and to those who need to change their name or address or who have qualified for additional entitlements by passing further driving tests. Existing licences will not be recalled for change and will remain valid until their expiry or revocation.

Licence counterpart

Photocard licences are accompanied by a green paper 'counterpart' showing the categories of vehicle the holder is qualified to drive and any endorsements, penalty points and periods of disqualification. This should be carried with the photocard licence.

Minimum age for driving motor vehicles

The law specifies minimum ages for drivers of goods vehicles as follows:

- small goods vehicles not exceeding 3.5 tonnes gross weight – 17 years;
- medium-size goods vehicles exceeding 3.5 tonnes but not exceeding 7.5 tonnes gross weight – 18 years;
- heavy goods vehicles over 7.5 tonnes gross weight – 21 years.

Young drivers

The minimum age for driving large goods vehicles is reduced to 17 years for members of the armed forces, and 18 years for learner LGV drivers of over-7.5-tonne vehicles undergoing registered training by their employer or by a registered training establishment – see pages 127–28 on the Young LGV Driver Scheme.

VEHICLE LICENCE CATEGORIES

Goods vehicles are classified under EU categories as shown in Table 3.5.

Validity of licences in the categories

Full driving entitlements in licence categories B, B+E, C1 and C1+E are valid from the date of issue until the applicant's 70th birthday (unless previously restricted or revoked due to a medical condition), after which each new licence will be valid for three years only.

Table 3.5   *Goods vehicle categories*

Category	Vehicle type
Cars and light vans	
B1	Motor tricycles and three/four-wheeled cars and vans not exceeding 550 kg unladen and capable of exceeding 50 kph. Additional categories covered: K, P.
B	Motor vehicles not exceeding 3.5 tonnes gross weight (gross vehicle weight) and with not more than eight seats (excluding the driver's seat) including drawing a trailer not exceeding 750 kg gross weight where the combined weight does not exceed 3.5 tonnes and the weight of the trailer does not exceed the unladen weight of the towing vehicle. Additional categories covered: F, K, P.
B+E	Motor vehicles in category B drawing a trailer but where the combination does not fall within category B.
Medium goods vehicles	
C1	Medium goods vehicles over 3.5 tonnes but not over 7.5 tonnes gross weight (including drawing a trailer of not more than 750 kg gross weight).
C1+E	Medium goods vehicles over 3.5 tonnes but not over 7.5 tonnes gross weight and drawing a trailer over 750 kg but not exceeding the unladen weight of the towing vehicle and the combination not exceeding 12 tonnes. Additional category covered: B+E.
Large goods vehicles	
C	Large goods vehicles over 3.5 tonnes gross weight (but excluding vehicles in categories D, F, G and H) including those drawing a trailer not exceeding 750 kg.
C+E	Large goods vehicles in category C drawing a trailer over 750 kg gross weight. Some C+E licences, where the holder was previously qualified to drive vehicles in old HGV class 2 or 3, show a restriction limiting driving to drawbar combinations only. Additional category covered: B+E.

VOCATIONAL LICENSING

Vocational licensing is the scheme for licensing drivers of goods vehicles over 3.5 tonnes gross weight. It is called 'vocational' licensing because it relates specifically to the driver's job – it is the indication of a professional driver. For obvious reasons of road safety, drivers of these vehicles are required to meet higher standards of driving competence and stricter medical and eyesight standards than ordinary driving licence holders. Hence the more extensive LGV driving tests to be passed and the stringent medical examination required.

The requirement to hold an LGV driving licence

Any person who wishes to drive a goods vehicle over 3.5 tonnes maximum gross weight, whether for private purposes or in connection with their own or their employer's business (unless they are otherwise exempt – see below), must hold a driving entitlement covering medium goods vehicles in category C1 and/or large goods vehicles in category C. If such vehicles are to tow a trailer weighing more than 750 kilograms maximum authorized weight, additional driving entitlements covering categories C1+E and/or C+E must be shown on the licence.

Note: a list of exemptions from LGV driver licensing is to be found on the DVLA website at www.dvla.gov.uk/drivers and on Form D100 – see also below.

Application for an LGV entitlement

Any person who meets the legal requirements of age, health and conduct as described below may apply for an LGV entitlement. Initially, the application will be for a provisional entitlement, which will be upgraded to a full entitlement on passing the relevant LGV theory, hazard perception and practical driving tests.

Medical examination

Strict medical standards that apply to vocational licensing require LGV drivers to pass a thorough examination conducted by a doctor and meet stringent eyesight requirements. The medical examination is needed initially to obtain a provisional LGV driving entitlement and then for subsequent licence renewals after passing the age of 45. These medical and eyesight standards are described on pages 102–08.

Good conduct

Both provisional licence holders and qualified LGV drivers must be of good conduct, determined initially by their declaration on the licence application form of any past convictions for offences relating to:

- goods vehicle drivers' hours and records (including tachographs);
- the roadworthiness of goods vehicles; and/or
- overloading of such vehicles.

Any subsequent conviction for such offences may be taken into account by the Traffic Commissioner when determining whether they are still of good conduct.

Validity of LGV driving entitlements

LGV driving entitlements are normally valid for five years or until the holder reaches the age of 45, whichever is the longer. After the age of 45, five-year entitlements are granted subject to medical fitness, but may be granted for lesser periods where the holder suffers from a relevant or prospective relevant disability. From the age of 65 years, vocational entitlements are granted only on an annual basis.

Responsibility for driver licensing

It is the individual's own legal responsibility to ensure that they hold a current and valid driving licence covering the category of vehicle being driven. Heavy penalties are imposed on offenders for driving:

- without a current licence;
- without a licence covering the correct category of vehicle being driven; or
- while disqualified from driving.

It is also the responsibility of the employer who requires any person to drive his vehicle/s for business purposes to ensure that such persons, irrespective of their function, status or seniority (and including agency drivers), are correctly licensed to drive company vehicles. The fact that a driver may be disqualified, or has allowed his licence to lapse, without the employer's knowledge is no defence for the employer against prosecution for causing or permitting an unlicensed person to drive a vehicle.

PRODUCTION OF DRIVING LICENCES

Police and enforcement officers of the Vehicle and Operator Services Agency (VOSA) can request a driver – and the person accompanying a provisional licence holder – to produce their driving licence showing their entitlements to drive. If they are unable to do so at the time, they may produce it later, in person, within certain time intervals. Firstly, if the request was by a police officer, the licence must be produced at a police station of their own choosing (eg, near to their home or workplace) within seven days. The officer will issue the driver with a form containing their details notifying them to produce documents (eg driving licence, vehicle insurance and annual test certificate where appropriate). Secondly, if the request was by an enforcement officer or the Traffic Commissioner, the driving licence must be produced within 10 days at the Traffic Area Office.

If a licence cannot be produced (for a good reason) within the 7 or 10 days mentioned above, it can be produced as soon as reasonably practicable thereafter. Failure to produce a licence either immediately on request, or later as described above (unless the licence holder can show that it was produced as soon as was reasonably practicable), is an offence for which the driver may be arrested and brought before a court and face a heavy fine.

Information to be given on request

A police officer can ask a driver, for purposes of identification, to state his date of birth – driving licences carry a coded number that indicates the holder's surname and their date of birth. The name and address of the vehicle owner can also be requested.

When required by a VOSA examiner to produce his licence, an LGV entitlement holder may be required to give his date of birth and to sign the examiner's record sheet to verify the fact of the licence examination. This should not be refused.

Production of licences by fixed penalty offenders

Drivers apprehended for *endorsable* fixed penalty (yellow ticket) offences (see page 146) must produce their driving licence to the police officer at that time, or later (within seven days, as previously described) to a police station, and surrender the licence, for which they will be given a receipt. Failure to produce a licence in these circumstances means that the fixed penalty procedure will not be followed and a summons for the alleged offence will be issued requiring the offender to attend court.

Production of licences to court

Drivers summoned to appear in court for driving and road traffic offences must produce their driving licence to the court at least on the day before the hearing.

ISSUE OF DRIVING LICENCES AND INFORMATION

All driving licences are issued by the DVLA at Swansea. Information on driver licensing can be obtained from the Customer Enquiries (Drivers) Unit, DVLA, Swansea SA6 7JL, Tel: 0870 240 0009, Fax: 01792 783071 or by accessing the DVLA website at: www.dvla.gov.uk/drivers. See also DVLA Form D100

(*What you need to know about driving licences*), available free from many Post Offices.

MEDICAL REQUIREMENTS FOR ALL LICENCE HOLDERS

Strict medical standards are required for driving motor vehicles. Applicants for all driving licences must declare information about their health, particularly when they have or have had:

- an epileptic event (seizure or fit);
- sudden attacks of disabling giddiness, fainting or blackouts;
- severe mental handicap;
- a pacemaker, defibrillator or anti-ventricular tachycardia device fitted;
- diabetes controlled by insulin;
- angina (heart pain) while driving;
- a major or minor stroke;
- Parkinson's disease;
- any other chronic neurological condition;
- a serious problem with memory;
- serious episodes of confusion;
- any type of brain surgery, brain tumour or severe head injury involving hospital in-patient treatment;
- any severe psychiatric illness or mental disorder;
- continuing or permanent difficulty in the use of arms or legs that affects the ability to control a vehicle safely;
- been dependent on or misused alcohol, illicit drugs or chemical substances in the previous three years (excluding drink-driving offences);
- any visual disability that affects both eyes (short/long sight and colour blindness do not have to be declared).

Applicants for LGV entitlements (unless submitting a medical report – Form D4 – see below) are required to state whether they have:

- sight in only one eye;
- any visual problems affecting either eye;
- angina;
- any heart condition or have had a heart operation.

Where a licence applicant has previously declared a medical condition they must state what the condition is, whether it has worsened since it was previously declared and whether any special controls have been fitted to their vehicle since the last licence was issued.

MEDICAL REQUIREMENTS FOR VOCATIONAL ENTITLEMENTS

Applicants for LGV vocational entitlements must meet much stricter medical standards to ensure that they are safe to drive large goods vehicles and are not suffering from any disease or disability (especially cardiovascular disease, diabetes mellitus, epilepsy, neurosurgical disorders, excessive sleepiness, nervous or mental disorders, vision problems, or the excessive use of prescribed medicines or illicit drugs, for example) that would prevent them from driving safely.

These medical standards have to be met on first licence application, and on subsequent renewals, by undergoing a medical examination by their doctor, who completes the medical certificate portion of Form D4. This must be done not more than four months before the date when the LGV driving needs to commence.

A further examination and completed medical certificate is required for each five-yearly licence renewal after reaching 45. After 65 a medical examination is required for each annual licence renewal. Further medical examinations may be called for at any time if there is any doubt as to a driver's fitness to drive.

Driving following medical disqualification

Where an application for a full driving licence is made following the revocation of a licence, or its renewal has been refused on medical grounds, the applicant may need to take a driving test (or an 'on-road assessment') to see if he is fit to regain his licence. A provisional licence may be granted to authorize driving on the road, but its use is restricted to driving only during the period preceding and while taking the test; its authority ceases immediately upon conclusion of the test or assessment.

Medicals for new category C1 drivers

Since 1 January 1997 new drivers of vehicles over 3.5 tonnes gross weight (covered by driving licence category C1) have required the same medical examination as that for heavy goods vehicle drivers and must follow the same regime as described above for subsequent medical examinations.

Medical examination fees

Doctors charge candidates a fee for these medicals – they are not available on the National Health Service in the United Kingdom. The current BMA recommended fee is £58.50; although where an employer pays and an invoice is required, the cost may be around £100. The medical fee for licence renewal can be claimed as an allowable expense for income tax purposes.

Diabetes

Normally, insulin-dependent diabetes sufferers are barred from holding an LGV entitlement but if they held an old-type HGV driving licence, and the Traffic Commissioner was aware of their condition prior to 1 January 1991, an entitlement may be granted. Since 5 April 2001, new rules have allowed individual assessment of diabetic drivers wishing to drive C1 and C1+E vehicles.

Epilepsy

A person is prevented from holding an LGV entitlement only if they have a 'liability to epileptic seizures'. Applicants must satisfy the DVLA that:

- they have not suffered an epileptic seizure during the 10 years prior to the date when the entitlement is to take effect;
- no epilepsy treatment has been administered during the 10 years prior to the starting date for the entitlement; and
- a consultant nominated by the DVLA has examined their medical history and is satisfied that there is no continuing liability to seizures.

Coronary health problems

Drivers with suspected coronary health problems may retain their LGV driving entitlements while medical enquiries are made. They no longer have to submit to coronary angiography. Electrocardiograph (ECG) tests will be undertaken no earlier than three months after a coronary event, and provided the driver displays no signs of angina or other significant symptoms, he may keep his driving entitlement while investigations are made, but subject to the approval of his own doctor.

Drivers who have suffered, or are suffering from, the following heart-related conditions or have experienced or are experiencing the following procedures, must notify the DVLA:

- heart attack (myocardial infarction, coronary thrombosis);
- coronary angioplasty;
- heart valve disease/surgery;
- coronary artery by-pass surgery;
- angina (heart pain);
- heart operation (other than a heart transplant).

The DVLA's Drivers Medical Group gives the following advice to heart sufferers:

- Following a heart attack or heart operation driving should not restart for at least one month following the attack or operation and then only if recovery has been uncomplicated and the patient's own doctor has given his/her approval.

- A driver suffering from angina may continue to drive (whether receiving treatment or not) unless attacks occur while driving, in which case he must notify the DVLA immediately (see below) and *stop driving.*
- A driver who suffers sudden attacks of disabling giddiness, fainting, falling, loss of awareness or confusion must notify the DVLA immediately (see below) and *stop driving.*

Any driver who has doubts about their ability to continue to drive safely is advised to discuss the matter with their own doctor, who has access to medical advice from the DVLA.

Alcohol problems
A person with repeated convictions for drink-driving offences may be required to satisfy the DVLA (with certification from their own doctor) that they do not have an 'alcohol problem' before their licence is restored.

Other medical conditions
Other factors that may cause failure of the driver's medical examination include:

- sudden attacks of vertigo ('dizziness');
- heart disease that causes disabling weakness or pain;
- a history of coronary thrombosis;
- the use of hypertension drugs for blood pressure treatment;
- serious arrhythmias;
- severe mental disorder;
- severe behavioural problems;
- alcohol dependency;
- inability to refrain from drinking and driving;
- drug abuse and dependency;
- psychotropic medicines taken in quantities likely to impair fitness to drive safely.

A licence will be refused to a driver who is liable to sudden attacks of disabling giddiness or fainting unless these can be controlled. Those who have had a cardiac pacemaker fitted are advised to discontinue LGV driving, although driving vehicles below the 7.5-tonne LGV threshold is permitted if a person who has disabling attacks that are controlled by a pacemaker has made arrangements for regular review from a cardiologist and will not be likely to endanger the public.

Notification of new or worsening medical conditions
Once a licence has been granted (whether ordinary or vocational), the holder must notify the Drivers Medical Group, DVLA at Swansea SA99 1TU of the

onset, *or worsening*, of any medical condition likely to cause danger when driving – *failure to do so is an offence*. Examples of what must be reported are:

- giddiness;
- fainting;
- blackouts;
- epilepsy;
- diabetes;
- strokes;
- multiple sclerosis;
- Parkinson's disease;
- heart disease;
- angina;
- 'coronaries';
- high blood pressure;
- arthritis;
- disorders of vision;
- mental illness;
- alcoholism;
- drug-taking; and
- the loss or loss of use of any limb.

Generally, the person's own doctor will advise them to report their condition to the DVLA themselves, or he/she may advise the DVLA. Either way the driving licence will have to be surrendered until the condition clears. There is no requirement to notify the DVLA of temporary illnesses or disabilities such as sprained or broken limbs where a full recovery is expected within three months. Enquiries about medical conditions can be raised with the Drivers Medical Group at the DVLA. Telephone the Customer Enquiries (Drivers) Unit on 0870 240 0009.

EYESIGHT REQUIREMENT

The statutory eyesight requirement mentioned above for ordinary (car and light goods vehicle) licence holders is for the driver to be able to read, in good daylight, a standard motor vehicle number plate from 20.5 metres (67 feet).* A 120-degree-wide field of view is also required. It is an offence to drive with impaired eyesight and the police can require a driver to take an eyesight test on the roadside. If glasses or contact lenses are needed to meet these vision standards they must be worn at all times while driving. It is an offence to drive with impaired eyesight.

Eyesight standards for vocational licence holders

Tougher, eyesight standards are required for over-3.5-tonne LGV drivers. Specifically, category C, C1, C+E and C1+E drivers must have eyesight that is at least:

- 6/9 on the Snellen scale in the better eye;* and
- 6/12 on the Snellen scale in the other eye;* and
- 3/60 in each eye without glasses or contact lenses.

Note: these standards may be met with glasses or contact lenses if worn.

To achieve these standards means being able to read the top line of an optician's chart (Snellen chart) with each eye from a distance of *at least* 3 metres without the aid of glasses or contact lenses. Wearers of spectacles or contact lenses must have vision of at least 6/9 in the better eye and at least 6/12 in the weaker eye, which means being able to read the sixth line of an optician's chart at 6 metres. Additionally, all drivers must meet existing eyesight standards, which include having a field of vision of at least 120° (horizontal) and 20° (vertical) in each eye with no double vision.

MEDICAL APPEALS AND INFORMATION

The final decision on any medical matter concerning driving licences rests with the Drivers Medical Group of the DVLA. However, there is the opportunity for appeal, within six months, in England and Wales to a magistrate's court, and within 21 days in Scotland to a sheriff's court. In other cases the refused driver may be given the opportunity to present further medical evidence for the medical adviser to consider.

DRUGS AND DRIVING

Official sources say that:
- drugs are a major cause of one in five fatal road accidents;
- driving after smoking cannabis could be a greater danger than drink-driving;
- as many as 3 million people could be driving under the influence of this drug; and
- drivers who use tranquillizers are involved in some 1,600 road accidents every year – 110 of them fatal.

Illegal drugs

Among the illegal drugs that may be detected and that can adversely affect driving are:

- cannabis – produces slow reaction times;
- cocaine – may increase reaction times, but severely affect accuracy and judgement; has potential to cause hallucination;
- amphetamines – may increase reaction times in the short term, but severely affect accuracy and judgement;
- Ecstasy – may increase reaction times, but severely affect accuracy and judgement;
- heroin – produces reduced reaction times and causes drowsiness and sleep.

Prescribed drugs

Prescribed tranquillizers, sedatives and anti-depressants, as well as diabetes and epilepsy drugs, may have an adverse effect on a driver's judgement and reactions and therefore increase the risk of an accident. These include a number of anti-stress and anxiety prescription drugs including:

- valium;
- librium; and
- ativan.

The sedative effect of these drugs is substantially compounded by the addition of alcohol, even when taken in relatively small quantities, resulting in a potentially significant loss of coordination. Similarly, sleeping tablets (eg, diazepam, temazepam, nitrazepam and zopiclone) may also have a continuing sedative effect on a driver the following morning.

Furthermore, a whole range of other proprietary medicines such as painkillers, antihistamines, cold and flu remedies, eye drops, cough medicines and common painkillers taken in sufficient quantities may have similar effects. If a driver feels drowsy, dizzy, confused, or suffers other side-effects that could affect his reaction times or judgement, *he should not drive.*

LEARNER DRIVERS

Learner drivers must hold a provisional driving entitlement to cover them while learning to drive, which they must do under tuition. This is shown on the 'counterpart' of the driving licence. A full category C LGV entitlement can be used in place of a provisional entitlement for learning to drive category C+E drawbar combinations and articulated vehicles. However, full entitlements in categories B and C1 *cannot* be used as a provisional entitlement for learning to drive category C or C+E vehicles – for which a separate provisional entitlement is required.

SUPERVISION OF LEARNER DRIVERS

Learner drivers must be accompanied, when driving on public roads, by the holder of a full driving entitlement covering the category of vehicle being driven and must not drive a vehicle drawing a trailer, except articulated vehicles.

Qualifications for car/light goods supervising drivers

Qualified drivers who supervise learner drivers in category B and C1 light vehicles (but not those in category C and C+E) must be at least 21 years old and must have held a full driving entitlement for at least three years (excluding any periods of disqualification). Contravention of these requirements could lead to a heavy fine, plus two driving licence penalty points and possibly licence disqualification for the supervising driver on conviction.

DISPLAY OF 'L' PLATES

An approved 'L' plate (ie, red letter 'L' on a white background) must be displayed on the front and rear of a vehicle being driven by a learner driver (in Wales the vehicle may alternatively display a 'D' plate).

LEARNER DRIVERS ON MOTORWAYS

Learner drivers of category B and C1 vehicles are not allowed to drive on motorways, but learner C and C+E drivers who hold full B and C1 entitlements may do so while under tuition.

DRIVING ON A TEST PASS CERTIFICATE

Provisional C or C+E licence holders who pass the LGV driving test receive a test pass certificate, which is valid for two years during which time they may continue to drive, although the DVLA's advice is to convert this to a full entitlement as soon as possible – for which there is no additional fee. Failure to apply for a full licence within two years of passing the test will mean the test having to be passed again to obtain a full licence.

COMPULSORY RE-TESTS FOR OFFENDING NEW DRIVERS

Newly qualified drivers who tot up six or more penalty points on their licence within two years will revert to learner status (ie, with the need for 'L' plates and to be accompanied by a qualified driver) and have to re-pass the theory, hazard perception and practical driving tests before regaining a full licence.

APPLICATION FOR DRIVING LICENCES

Application for a driving licence must be made to the DVLA, Swansea on Form D2, obtainable from main Post Offices, direct from Swansea, online at www.direct.gov.uk/drivers or from local Vehicle Registration Offices – see telephone directory for address. The completed and signed application, along with any previous licence, the relevant fee, a test pass certificate (if appropriate) and a medical report form D4 (also if appropriate – see below), must be sent to the DVLA, Swansea using one of the following postal codes:

- SA99 1AD for first provisional licences;
- SA99 1BJ for first full car licences;
- SA99 1AB for licence renewal, duplicate and exchange licences;
- SA99 1BR for all vocational entitlement applications.

Questions on the driving licence application form require personal details of the applicant and the type of licence required. Applicants, other than those submitting a medical report Form D4, are asked to declare information about their health as described on pages 102–08.

The form requires vocational entitlement applicants to give details of any convictions they have incurred relating to drivers' hours or records, road-worthiness or the overloading of vehicles. Applicants are warned that drivers giving false information for the purposes of obtaining a driving licence may be prosecuted.

Licence fees

The current fees for driving licences are shown in the Appendix and on the DVLA website at: www.dvla.gov.uk/drivers.

Waiting for the licence

It is illegal to drive any vehicle until a licence has been received and it comes into effect. For this reason it is important to make an application in good time for any intended driving (eg, to start driving lessons). Application for an LGV driving entitlement should be made not more than three months before the date from which it is required to run.

THE DVLA'S DECISION

The decision whether or not an applicant will be granted an LGV driving entitlement rests with the DVLA, which takes into account any motoring, drivers' hours and records, roadworthiness or vehicle loading offences against the applicant in the four years before and any drink- or drugs-driving offence during the 11 years before the application. The applicant must declare such convictions on the application form (D2), but the DVLA can check to ensure that such convictions are declared.

Powers of the Traffic Commissioners

Although LGV entitlements are issued by the DVLA, Traffic Commissioners (TCs) have statutory powers to consider the fitness of persons applying for or holding such entitlements. They can require applicants or licence holders to provide information about their conduct and to appear before them to answer in person if necessary. They can refuse the grant of an entitlement, and suspend or disqualify a person from holding such an entitlement.

CERTIFICATES OF ENTITLEMENT

UK drivers moving to live abroad who have mislaid their driving licence may obtain a temporary 'Certificate of Entitlement' (a 'cover note'), valid for one month, either from the DVLA at Swansea (free of charge) or from local Vehicle Registration Offices (VROs) subject to proof of their identity. This document proves entitlement to drive, enabling such persons to obtain an equivalent driving entitlement in their new country of residence.

THE LGV THEORY AND HAZARD PERCEPTION TEST

Driving test candidates must pass a 100-question computerized touch-screen theory test and a video-clip hazard perception test *before* taking the practical driving test. This is a tough test requiring a detailed knowledge of the *Highway Code* and of the principles and safety aspects of driving as well as testing the candidate's recognition of and reaction to road hazards. Candidates must hold a provisional licence covering the category of vehicles to which the test relates.

APPLICATION FOR THE COMBINED THEORY TEST

Application for a combined theory test may be made either by completing an application form, obtainable from a local DSA driving test centre, by telephone (0870 010 1372), or via the internet (www.dsa.gov.uk or www.driving-tests.co.uk). The test fee of £32.50 is payable with the application by cheque or postal order or by credit/debit card when booking by telephone or via the internet.

REQUIREMENTS FOR THE TEST

Candidates must take their driving licence (with provisional entitlement) to the test centre – making sure that it is signed – and must also be able to produce other evidence of identity without which they will not be allowed to sit the test. Generally, any official document with the candidate's photograph and signature will suffice (eg, a passport or works security card). As the DSA clearly states: No photo, No licence, No test – and the test fee will be forfeited. Failure to arrive at the appointed time for the theory test will result in rejection and loss of the fee.

DURATION OF THE TEST AND TEST QUESTIONS

Theory test candidates have two hours and 30 minutes in which to answer the 100 test questions and complete the 20-clip hazard perception test. At least 85 correct answers are needed by LGV drivers to pass the multiple-choice test. Normally, candidates will receive their results within 30 minutes of completing the test and be given feedback as to the questions that were answered incorrectly. Driver CPC candidates will also need to complete three case studies in 90 minutes.

The test comprises multiple-choice questions requiring the correct answers to be selected from a number of given alternatives whereas in the hazard perception test the candidate must correctly identify a number of road and traffic hazards. There are no trick questions and written (essay-type) answers are not required; candidates simply have to touch the computer screen to select an answer or click a computer mouse for the hazard perception test – the point scoring in this is based on identification of the hazard and speed of response.

Topics covered

The questions cover a wide range of goods vehicle subjects such as the following:

- goods vehicle weights and dimensions;
- secure load stowage and safe loading;
- the polluting effects of excessive exhaust smoke;
- legal markings on vehicles;
- vehicle braking systems – types of brake and how they work;
- maintenance and inspection of vehicle brakes;

- correct use of heavy vehicle braking systems;
- the risks and adverse effects of tailgating;
- the effects of freezing weather conditions on vehicle braking systems;
- how power steering systems work;
- the law on speed limiters;
- drivers' hours rules and rest period requirements;
- legal requirements on record keeping;
- the law on tachograph fitment and use of tachographs;
- the effects of tiredness on drivers;
- driver responsibility for the security of his vehicle and load;
- stability of high and long vehicles;
- the carriage and use of safety equipment;
- how to reduce the risk of road accidents;
- dealing with injuries;
- what to do if an accident involves hazardous materials;
- how to deal with casualties;
- reporting accidents;
- carrying out safety checks, particularly on brakes, steering and tyres to ensure the vehicle is in a safe and legal condition;
- understanding the legal requirements about vehicles being kept safe and roadworthy;
- the effects of windy weather, particularly cross-winds, on high-sided vehicles;
- the use of air deflectors to reduce wind resistance and improve fuel consumption;
- the adverse effects of heavy rain causing excessive spray, which affects other road users and reduces the grip of tyres on wet roads.

All these topics are covered in this handbook and in the *Highway Code* (2007 edition, from bookshops and newsagents) or in the DSA publication *The Official Theory Test for Drivers of Large Vehicles* (The Stationery Office).

TEST FAILURE

Candidates who fail either the multiple-choice theory test or the hazard perception test will fail the whole test. A different set of questions will be used for any second or subsequent attempts at the test.

THE LGV DRIVING TEST

The purpose of the LGV driving test is to ensure that drivers are competent to drive large goods vehicles on the roads in safety. The test is more comprehensive and more complex than the car and light vehicle driving test and, consequently, demands greater skill and knowledge from the driver. Effectively, it ensures standards of professionalism among drivers of the heaviest vehicles on our roads.

PROOF OF IDENTITY

Candidates for LGV driving tests must produce satisfactory photographic evidence of identity on arrival (eg, an existing driving licence, a passport or an employer identity card bearing the holder's name, signature and photograph). Without this identification the test will not be conducted and the fee will be forfeited. This measure is necessary to combat a rising incidence of people with false identities taking multiple LGV driving tests on behalf of others.

APPLICATION FOR THE TEST

Applications for the LGV practical driving test are made on Form DLG 26 obtainable from local DSA offices (see local telephone directory or contact the DSA direct at: www.dsa.gov.uk or by telephone on 0300 200 1122) and should be made in good time. This is important if an LGV driving entitlement is required – subject to passing the test – from a particular date.

Candidates must produce a theory/hazard perception test pass certificate before being permitted to take the practical LGV driving test as well as their driving licence showing a full entitlement for category B driving and a provisional entitlement for driving goods vehicles in category C1 or C.

New drivers wishing to progress to an LGV category C+E entitlement to drive the heaviest vehicles must do so via the lower licensing categories as follows:

- first obtaining a category B entitlement;
- then with provisional entitlement qualifying to drive category C1 (ie, 3.5 to 7.5 tonnes) or category C (ie, over 7.5 tonnes) vehicles;
- followed by a C1+E test to drive vehicles in category C1 towing trailers above 750 kilograms with a combination weight exceeding 12 tonnes gross weight;
- finally passing a category C test before qualifying in the top category C+E.

Test fees

LGV driving tests currently cost £89 on weekdays and £107 at other times (eg, weekday evenings and Saturdays). Higher test fees of £78 on weekdays and £96 on Saturdays are payable where an extended re-test is ordered following obligatory disqualification of a driving licence. Test fees are forfeited unless at least 10 clear days' notice of cancellation of a previously booked test is given. See Appendix II for a full list of test fees.

VEHICLES FOR THE LGV DRIVING TEST

The candidate has to provide the vehicle (or arrange for the loan of a suitable vehicle) on which he wishes to be tested and it must:

- be unladen and of the category (ie, a 'minimum test vehicle') for which an LGV driving entitlement is required – see below;
- display 'L' plates front and rear;*
- be in a thoroughly roadworthy condition;
- have seating in the cab for the examiner;
- have sufficient fuel for a test lasting up to two hours.

Note: learner drivers in Wales may display a 'D' plate instead of the usual 'L' plate.

Minimum test vehicles (MTVs) for the LGV driving test (effective from September 2003) are as follows:

The vehicle and its equipment

Category C

Category C vehicles must meet the following criteria:

- be at least 12,000 kilograms maximum authorized weight (mam);
- be at least 8 metres long;
- be at least 2.40 metres wide;
- be capable of at least 80 kph;
- be fitted with anti-lock brakes;
- have a gearbox with at least eight forward gear ratios;
- have a calibrated tachograph;
- have a closed box body at least as wide and as high as the cab; and
- have a minimum total weight of 10,000 kilograms.

Category C+E

Articulated vehicles or a combination of a category C test vehicle and a trailer of at least 7.5 metres in length must:

- both have a mam of at least 20,000 kilograms;
- be at least 14 metres long;
- be at least 2.40 metres wide;
- be capable of at least 80 kph;
- be fitted with anti-lock brakes;
- be equipped with at least eight forward gear ratios;
- have a calibrated tachograph;
- have a closed box body at least as wide and as high as the cab; and
- both have a minimum total weight of 15,000 kilograms.

Sub-category C1:
A sub-category C1 vehicle must:

- be at least 4,000 kilograms mam;
- be at least 5 metres long;
- be capable of at least 80 kph;
- be fitted with anti-lock brakes;
- be equipped with a calibrated tachograph;
- have a closed box body that is at least as wide and as high as the cab.

Sub-category C1+E
A combination of a C1 test vehicle and a trailer must:

- be at least 1,250 kilograms mam,
- be at least 8 metres long;
- be capable of at least 80 kph;
- have a closed box body trailer at least as wide and as high as the cab;*
- have a minimum total trailer weight of at least 800 kilograms.

Note: the closed box body may be slightly less wide than the cab provided the view to the rear is only possible by use of the external rear-view mirrors of the motor vehicle.

Deferred implementation

Minimum test vehicles for categories C, C+E, C1, C1+E that do not conform with the minimum criteria described above, but that were in use on or before 11 October 2000, may still be used until October 2010. The requirements relating to the load to be carried by test vehicles (as shown above) may also be deferred until October 2010.

KNOWLEDGE REQUIRED FOR THE TEST

Driving test candidates must be:

- fully conversant with the contents of the *Highway Code*;
- able to read in good daylight (with the aid of spectacles, if worn) a motor vehicle's registration number in accordance with the vision requirements (see pages 106–07);
- competent to drive without danger to and with due consideration for other road users, including being able to:
  - start the engine of the vehicle;
  - move away straight ahead or at an angle;

- overtake, meet or cross the path of other vehicles and take an appropriate course;
- turn right-hand and left-hand corners correctly;
- stop the vehicle in an emergency and in a normal situation, and in the latter case bring it to rest at an appropriate part of the road;
- reverse the vehicle and while doing so enter a limited opening either to the left or to the right;
- cause the vehicle to face the opposite direction by the use of forward and reverse gears;
- carry out a reverse parking manoeuvre that involves stopping the vehicle next to and parallel with a parked vehicle, then reversing to position and park the vehicle in front of or behind the other vehicle, level with and reasonably close to the kerb;
- indicate their intended actions at appropriate times by giving appropriate signals in a clear and unmistakable manner (in the case of a left-hand drive vehicle or a disabled driver for whom it is impracticable or undesirable to give hand signals there is no requirement to provide any signals other than mechanical ones);
- act correctly and promptly on all signals given by traffic signs and traffic controllers and take appropriate action on signs given by other road users.

Test failure
Candidates who fail the test will be given an oral explanation of the reasons for their failure.

DURATION OF THE DRIVING TEST

The practical driving test lasts approximately 90 minutes, so it is important for candidates to have sufficient legal driving hours left on that day/week to be able to complete the test within legal limits. It is also important that the vehicle has sufficient fuel for the test and to get it back to base afterwards. Running out of fuel on the test may be embarrassing, but it will also result in test failure and loss of the test fee.

INSURANCE FOR TEST VEHICLES

Test candidates are responsible for ensuring that the vehicle supplied for the test is correctly insured and will be required to sign a declaration to this effect on arrival at the test station.

PREPARING FOR THE LGV DRIVING TEST

Candidates preparing for the LGV driving test should acquire a thorough prior knowledge and understanding of all the topics covered in the DSA's publication *Driving Goods Vehicles – the Official DSA Syllabus* (available from The Stationery Office and most bookshops). The *Highway Code* should also be carefully studied.

Driving skills and behaviour for LGV drivers

Driving test candidates must demonstrate the following key skills:

- Preparation and technical check of the vehicle for road safety purposes. They are capable of preparing to drive safely by:
  - adjusting the seat as necessary to obtain a correct seated position;
  - adjusting rear-view mirrors, seat belts and head restraints if available;
  - making random checks on the condition of the tyres, steering, brakes, lights, reflectors, direction indicators and audible warning device;
  - checking the power-assisted braking and steering systems; the condition of the wheels, wheel-nuts, mudguards, windscreen, windows and wipers, fluids (eg, engine oil, coolant, washer fluid); checking and using the instrument panel including the tachograph;
  - checking the air pressure, air tanks and the suspension;
  - checking the safety of the vehicle loading: body, sheets, cargo doors, loading mechanism (if available), cabin locking (if available), way of loading, securing load;
  - checking the coupling mechanism and the brake and electrical connections (categories C+E, C1+E only);
  - reading a road map, route planning, including the use of electronic navigation systems (optional).
- Special manoeuvres to be tested with a bearing on road safety:
  - coupling and uncoupling, or uncoupling and recoupling a trailer – must involve the towing vehicle being parked alongside the trailer (ie, not in one line) (categories C+E, C1+E only);
  - reversing along a curve;
  - parking safely for loading/unloading at a loading ramp/platform or similar installation.
- Behaviour in traffic. Applicants must perform all the following actions in normal traffic situations, in complete safety and taking all necessary precautions:
  - driving away: after parking, after a stop in traffic, when exiting a driveway;
  - driving on straight roads: passing oncoming vehicles, including in confined spaces;

- driving round bends;
- crossroads: approaching and crossing of intersections and junctions;
- changing direction: left and right turns; changing lanes;
- approach/exit of motorways or similar (if available): joining from the acceleration lane; leaving on the deceleration lane;
- overtaking/passing: overtaking other traffic (if possible); driving along-side obstacles, eg, parked cars; being overtaken by other traffic (if appropriate);
- special road features (if available): roundabouts; railway level crossings; tram/bus stops; pedestrian crossings; driving up-/downhill on long slopes;
- taking the necessary precautions when alighting from the vehicle.

MARKING OF THE SKILLS AND BEHAVIOUR TESTS

The examiner will be looking for the ease with which the applicant handles the vehicle controls and his capacity to drive in complete safety in traffic. Importantly, the examiner must be made to feel safe throughout the test. He will also pay special attention as to whether the applicant shows defensive and social driving behaviour, in particular ensuring the safety of all road users, especially those who are the weakest and most exposed, by showing due respect for others. Overall, drivers are expected to make progress in an economical and environmentally friendly manner.

During the test, the examiner will check to ensure that the candidate makes proper use of safety belts, rear-view mirrors, head restraints; driving seat; lights and other equipment; clutch, gearbox, accelerator, braking systems (including third braking system, if available) and the steering. He will also check the driver's control of the vehicle under different circumstances and at different speeds; his steadiness on the road (ie, meaning no fast acceleration, smooth driving and no hard braking); the weight and dimensions and characteristics of the vehicle; the weight and type of load.

Additionally, drivers must show that they are capable of detecting any major technical faults in their vehicles, especially those posing a safety hazard, and know how to have them remedied in an appropriate fashion.

ON PASSING THE TEST

On completion of the test, a successful candidate will be given a Pass Certificate, which means that they no longer need to be accompanied by a qualified driver or display 'L' plates. They will also be given a copy of the examiner's report (Form DLV25) that will show any minor faults recorded during the test –

this is to help further improve the individual's driving skills. The Pass Certificate and full ordinary licence together authorize the holder to drive LGVs of the category shown on the Pass Certificate and will enable the applicant to have an LGV driving entitlement of the appropriate category added to his driving licence.

ON FAILING THE TEST

A candidate who fails the test will be given a Statement of Failure Guidance Notes. Matters requiring special attention will be marked accordingly and the examiner will allow a few minutes to explain the driving errors shown on the statement. Anybody who has difficulty in understanding the driving errors shown on the Guidance Notes or feels that the test was unfairly conducted can write to the Supervising Examiner (Driving Tests) at the DVLA.

According to an experienced LGV driving instructor, there are only two ways to fail the LGV driving test. Firstly, by not being good enough to pass in the first place (ie, having entered for the test too soon). More practice is needed and more miles behind the wheel to gain the experience and confidence required. Secondly, by being basically good enough to pass the test, but by making a specific mistake serious enough to warrant the failure.

Application for a re-test

Candidates who fail the practical driving test on category C or C+E vehicles may apply to take a re-test after three clear working days. Failed category C1 and C1+E drivers must wait 10 clear working days before being allowed a re-test.

HELPFUL ADVICE

A little bit of extra advice is always useful so the following information from an experienced LGV driving instructor is given for this purpose. On the day of the test candidates should:

- leave plenty of time to get to the test station;
- check over the vehicle thoroughly (not forgetting to take some spare light bulbs);
- take their provisional driving licence and test appointment card with them;
- ensure their vehicle is suitable for the test and is unladen;
- clean the vehicle well both inside and outside;
- clean the vehicle windows and wing mirrors;
- have no loose articles in the cab likely to move about during the test.

The driving examiner may refuse to travel in the vehicle and consequently refuse to conduct the test if it is too dirty or if there is an excessive amount of equipment around the floor area and passenger seat. If he says the vehicle is unsuitable for test on these grounds, the test fee will be lost.

When arriving for the test, candidates should:

- have checked the vehicle thoroughly and have enough fuel for the duration of the test;
- check and clean stop-lights and indicators (the test could be terminated and test fee forfeited if the brake lights are faulty – but time may be allowed for a minor repair);
- ensure that 'L' plates are correctly displayed on the front and rear of the vehicle;
- ensure there is ample time for the test to be completed without exceeding legally permitted hours of work.

Tests are arranged to a strict timetable so candidates must be at the test centre not later than the time shown on the appointment card. On arrival at the centre the vehicle should be parked in the area provided and the candidate should report to Reception. There is usually a room or an area where candidates can wait until the driving examiner arrives. He will ask for his test sheet to be signed before commencing the test.

The reversing exercise

The first part of the driving test is the reversing exercise. This takes place on a special manoeuvring area within the test centre. The examiner will give clear directions as to how the manoeuvring area should be approached and where to position the vehicle prior to the actual manoeuvre taking place. Great care must be taken when carrying out this exercise, as there is very little margin for error. The driver who tends to over-steer or under-steer or fails to position the vehicle correctly or tends to reverse too fast or erratically, will undoubtedly bring pressure upon himself. The vehicle must be positioned correctly, and correct use made of the accelerator, clutch and steering. A slow but constant speed should be maintained, particularly with articulated vehicles. Ideally the driver should be able to position the vehicle correctly and complete the exercise without having to stop or without having to take a shunt. If unable to do this, a driver should not be taking the test, as he is clearly not ready.

The braking exercise

The second part of the test is the controlled stop or braking exercise. Here the candidate will be directed to another part of the manoeuvring area where this exercise can be carried out safely. He will be directed to the start line/position where he has to park the vehicle in order to allow the driving examiner to climb aboard. Only when he is settled in and has secured all his paperwork will he give clear instructions as to how the exercise is to be carried out. The vehicle will need to be accelerated vigorously in order to attain a speed of 20/25 mph (32/40 kph) within the prescribed distance of 200 feet (60 metres). When the front of the vehicle is in line with the finishing line the foot brake must be applied firmly, but without locking the wheels, and keeping it depressed until the vehicle has come to an abrupt stop. Locking the wheels, stalling the engine or, in the case of articulated vehicles, jack-knifing the trailer, are to be avoided at all costs. The candidate should practise this manoeuvre as often as possible on a suitable site before attempting the test.

Vehicle and trailer driving

If the test vehicle is an articulated combination the examiner will ask questions about the safe procedures for coupling and uncoupling the tractive unit and semi-trailer.

Driving on the road

When all the off-road manoeuvres and exercises have been completed, the on-the-road driving will begin, following the directions and route given by the examiner. It is important to concentrate on the job in hand, ignoring the examiner's presence. Normally examiners make themselves as inconspicuous as possible, thus allowing the candidate to concentrate and demonstrate his skills and abilities. Particular attention will be paid to control of the vehicle throughout the test and to the courtesy and consideration shown to other road users. It is essential to drive the vehicle safely and progressively while adhering to all the rules of the road. The driving must be adjusted to suit the different road conditions and also the different weather conditions. During the test the examiner will require various road exercises and procedures, such as gear changing, stopping and moving off and hill starts, to be carried out. Confidence when negotiating right and left turns, roundabouts and traffic lights and other traffic obstacles is essential.

Stopping procedure

One of the first exercises will be to stop the vehicle at the side of the road and then to move away again safely. When telling the driver to pull up at a convenient place on the left, the examiner will expect the driver to:

- observe and assess the situation ahead and select a safe parking position for the vehicle;
- observe the situation behind in the rear-view mirrors and act accordingly in relation to what can be seen;

- give the correct signal clearly and in good time;
- slow the vehicle down gradually in a safe and convenient manner, not stopping abruptly or extending the slowing down process over an excessive distance;
- bring the vehicle to rest close to and parallel to the kerb in a safe, legal and convenient position.

Once the vehicle is stopped, the hand brake should be applied, the gear lever put into neutral and the direction indicator signal cancelled. It is not necessary to stop the engine. The examiner will normally acknowledge the stop and then ask the driver to move off.

Moving off
The examiner will expect the candidate to:

- look in both mirrors and react sensibly to what is seen;
- select the correct gear for moving off according to the gradient;
- give the correct signal in good time;
- physically look all round, checking the blind spots;
- move off only when it is safe to do so and under no circumstances if evasive action would have to be taken by other road users.

Moving off uphill and on the level
Moving off on an uphill gradient demands smooth coordination in use of the accelerator, clutch and hand brake and is very important in getting an LGV moving. The use of excessive engine revolutions or clutch slipping must be avoided except on the steeper gradients, and under no circumstances should the vehicle be allowed to roll backwards.

Moving off downhill
If asked to move off on a down gradient the driver should:

- use mirrors;
- select the correct gear – this may be one gear higher than normal;
- apply the foot brake;
- release the hand brake, holding the vehicle firmly on the foot brake;
- signal;
- look all round;
- release the foot brake allowing the vehicle to roll forward and at the same time bring the clutch into play taking up the drive;
- move only when it is safe to do so.

Moving off at an angle

In order to move off at an angle, the examiner will first select a convenient place on the left to stop, just before reaching a parked vehicle. When pulling up behind a parked vehicle, be mindful of the need to move off again and leave sufficient room to do so. The precise procedure to follow when moving off will be determined by the gradient. When moving off on the flat or uphill the hand brake should be used as normal. When moving off on a down gradient the foot brake should be used. Naturally the examiner will expect all normal precautions to be taken, such as looking round, signalling as required and maintaining a smoothness in the use of the controls.

Extra care is needed to avoid getting too close to the parked vehicle, allowing plenty of room for the cut-in from your vehicle, and particularly the trailer in the case of an articulated vehicle. Extra care must also be taken so as not to inconvenience other road users, as during the move out from the nearside to the offside when passing the parked vehicle.

Gear changing

In normal driving with most large goods vehicles, it would be unusual for a driver to use first gear when moving off. However, in order to demonstrate the ability to engage any of the low gears when necessary, the examiner will require the candidate to perform a gear changing exercise – usually early on in the test. He will select a suitable road where this part of the test can be conducted with a minimum of inconvenience to other traffic and will give very clear instructions as to what he requires.

This will be a demonstration of gear changing from first gear, through the gearbox until the examiner feels that sufficient ability has been shown. He will then request a series of down-changes until the lowest gear is engaged. It will not be necessary in this exercise to demonstrate the use of any auxiliary transmission systems, ie, splitter box or two-speed axles (a splitter box should not be confused with a range change). The foot brake may be used as necessary to slow the vehicle down before any downward gear change.

Arm signals

Arm signals are not included as a separate part of the test. However, they will be expected to be demonstrated when required, eg, at pedestrian crossings and as confirmation signals. Only those arm signals illustrated in the *Highway Code* should be used.

Note: signals to other drivers by means of flashing the headlights should not be used except to indicate only the presence of your vehicle on the road.

PRIMARY FAILURE POINTS

Experience has shown that the most common driving test failings are:

- not acting correctly at road junctions;
- not making proper use of gears;
- not making proper use of mirrors.

Each stage of the driving test has its own individual failure points as described below and the examiner will be watching these very carefully.

Approach

When approaching any type of road junction including crossroads and round-abouts, driving examiners will be observing that:

- the mirrors are used properly and that candidates act sensibly in relation to what they see in them;
- signals are used (if required) and that they are given correctly, clearly and in good time;
- the vehicle is (if necessary) manoeuvred safely into the correct position.

Once in position, driving examiners will judge your ability to regulate the speed of the vehicle and will assess the use of the brakes and gears as the final stage of the approach is completed. (It is this part of the approach that proves the most difficult, and where a large number of candidates have problems.)

Negotiation

Negotiating road junctions involves a particular sequence of events, which in the main will include:

- Proper observation before emerging or turning, including the use of the nearside mirror when about to turn left. Particular attention should be paid to the nearside mirror when about to negotiate a roundabout, and care should be taken to ensure that the cut-in of a large LGV does not endanger other road users.
- Emerging or turning safely with due regard for approaching traffic, not forgetting that an LGV is generally slower moving and larger than most other vehicles and this must be taken into account.
- Correct positioning of the vehicle throughout the negotiation. Depending upon the size of the vehicle, examiners will allow some degree of tolerance in positioning, but care must be taken not to endanger or inconvenience any other road users.
- Proper use of mirrors and all-round observation.

- Securing the correct road position for the vehicle when the negotiation/turn has been completed. Changing gear on the turn is accepted, provided that it is done when the steering wheel is held firmly on course. Do not change gear and turn the wheel at the same time, and avoid crossing hands on the wheel.

Departure
The ingredients of a good departure from any road junction will include:

- following a straight preplanned course;
- sound acceleration in accordance with road and traffic conditions;
- proper use of the gears, each gear to be fully used before changing into the next higher gear;
- constant use of mirrors throughout the departure;
- keeping a watchful eye all round including on the speedometer and rev counter.

OTHER MAJOR FAILURE POINTS
If you fail the test you can expect to have one or more of the following comments shown on the document the examiner gives you:

- *Exercise proper care in the use of speed:* this means that you drove too fast, either by breaking the legal speed limit or, more often than not, by driving through low-speed situations much too fast.
- *Make normal progress to suit varying road and traffic conditions:* this implies that you drove too slowly throughout the whole of the test, but this is not always the case. It can include situations such as stopping unnecessarily at road junctions or roundabouts, failing to recognize and take advantage of a safe gap in traffic in order to emerge, or failing to take advantage of the opportunity to accelerate away from a hazard (as described above).
- *Make proper use of gears* (other than at road junctions): this usually means you have changed up a gear too early when the vehicle has not reached the correct speed for the next higher gear; or changed up a gear too late, where the vehicle's speed and road conditions are right for the next higher gear but you did not change up; or selected the wrong gears (eg, by changing gear from 2nd to 3rd but missing 3rd and accidentally selecting another gear – not to be confused with block changing).
- *Make proper use of mirrors* (other than at road junctions): this is of the utmost importance and must be done often throughout the whole test. There is a right way and a wrong way to use mirrors and the examiner will observe if you are using them correctly (eg, using the right mirror at the right time).

When you are about to drive round a right bend you should check the offside mirror as you do so as this will afford a far better view of the road behind than the nearside mirror would. Likewise, when you are about to drive round a left-hand bend you should use the nearside mirror as this will not only afford a better view of the road behind but will also allow you to see where the end of your vehicle is in relation to the kerb. This is particularly important in the case of articulated vehicles. Obviously mirrors should be used before any change of direction no matter how slight and before signalling, moving off or stopping. When negotiating a left turn at a road junction, you must look in the nearside mirror to check the back wheels of your vehicle in relation to the kerb, to ensure all is well behind and that there are no cyclists or pedestrians. When you are about to overtake a parked vehicle, you should look in the offside mirror first to ensure it is safe to move out (do not forget the signal if necessary) and then check the nearside mirror when you have passed the parked vehicle before returning to the nearside.

TEST ROUTES

LGV driving test routes are carefully selected to include a large variety of driving conditions. You must be able to adjust your driving to suit the different conditions that you will encounter under test conditions. You will be given the opportunity to demonstrate your driving skills at high speeds one moment, then you will have to change your style of driving altogether the next moment as you are directed through a congested town centre. A test route is designed to test the ability of the driver and should never be underestimated.

QUESTIONS AND ANSWERS DURING THE TEST

The oral part of the old-style driving test is largely replaced by the theory test, but this does not preclude the examiner asking questions during the test to test the candidate's knowledge, especially about vehicle safety matters.

THE YOUNG LGV DRIVER SCHEME

To encourage an inflow of new driver entrants to the road haulage industry, Skills for Logistics (formerly the Road Haulage and Distribution Training Council (RHDTC)) has devised the Young LGV Driver Scheme (YDS). The scheme is managed by SFL on behalf of the Department for Transport (DfT), run in conjunction with the Road Haulage Association (RHA), the Freight

Transport Association (FTA) and the transport trades unions and supported and operated by a number of approved training organizations.

AIM OF THE SCHEME

The scheme is aimed at young persons from the age of 18 years who wish to take up LGV driving as a career in its own right or as part of wider ambitions to progress in the road transport industry. Its specific purpose is to enable a young person to obtain a full category C licence and subsequently a C+E LGV driving entitlement from the age of 18 years rather than having to wait until reaching the normal 21-year minimum age limit.

This scheme is to be replaced at the time of the introduction of the new Driver CPC scheme as described on page 7.

FURTHER DETAILS

Further information on the Young LGV Driver Scheme can be obtained from the SFL help desk: Tel: 01908 313360, or direct from: Skills for Logistics, 14 Warren Yard, Warren Farm Office Village, Stratford Road, Milton Keynes MK12 5NW, or by accessing the website: www.skillsforlogistics.org

3.6

Road traffic law

Road traffic law in the United Kingdom is complex and contained in numerous Road Traffic Acts and many associated regulations. However, for drivers, the key starting point lies in the *Highway Code* (2007 edition) – readily available from bookshops and newsagents. It sets out in plain language most of what the learner LGV driver, as well as other road users, need to know, particularly for answering the theory test questions on traffic rules, for passing the driving test itself and for driving safely on the road after passing the test. Whether you are a newcomer, or a qualified and experienced driver, there is always something to be learned from the *Highway Code* so it is useful to carry a copy at all times.

STOPPING, LOADING/UNLOADING AND PARKING

When you are leaving a vehicle on a road, the engine must be stopped (except when the engine is used to drive auxiliary equipment). In any case, this is good practice for reasons of fuel conservation and in helping to reduce unnecessary traffic noise and exhaust pollution, which blight urban environments.

Restrictions on stopping and parking

A vehicle must not be left where it is likely to cause obstruction or danger to other road users. Lorry trailers and articulated semi-trailers must not be left on a road or in a lay-by when detached from the towing vehicle. Vehicles must not stop or park on clearways to load or unload.

Loading and unloading restrictions

In some areas yellow lines painted on the kerb at right angles to it indicate loading and unloading restrictions. A single yellow line at intervals indicates restrictions during certain hours, for example, peak hours (eg, no loading or unloading Mon–Sat 8.30 am–6.30 pm). Double yellow lines at intervals indicate a complete ban on loading and unloading. Single, double or broken yellow lines painted on the road parallel to the kerb apply to waiting and parking at various times, but do not indicate a ban on loading or unloading.

Parking meter zones

Loading and unloading in parking meter zones during the working day (the times are indicated on signs) is not allowed unless a gap between meter areas or a vacant meter space can be found. A goods vehicle using a meter space for loading or unloading can stop for up to 20 minutes without having to pay the meter fee (this does not apply when parking for any purpose other than loading or unloading the vehicle).

Parking on verges

It is an offence to drive a motor vehicle on to common land or other land that does not form part of a road, or on any footpath or bridleway, beyond a distance of 15 yards (13.5 metres), except where legal permission exists, but then only for parking or to meet an emergency such as saving life or extinguishing fire.

It is an offence to park a vehicle over 7.5 tonnes gross weight on the verge of a road, on any land between two carriageways or on a footway whether the vehicle is totally parked on those areas or only partially so except with the permission of a police officer in uniform, in an emergency, or for loading and unloading, providing this could not have been done properly otherwise.

Overnight parking in lay-bys

Sleeping overnight in sleeper cabs while parked in lay-bys (which are part of the highway) is usually considered illegal on the grounds that the vehicle is causing an obstruction – it is not illegal under the drivers' hours law. Drivers can expect to be moved on by the police. A similar offence is committed when detached drawbars and semi-trailers are left in lay-bys.

London lorry control

Certain vehicles over 18 tonnes gross weight are prohibited from travelling on many routes through Greater London at certain times unless the operator holds an exemption permit issued under the ALG (Association of London Government) Transport and Environment Scheme. This must be carried on the vehicle, which must also display exemption plates at the front and rear in a conspicuous position. The routes on which the ban applies and the times of its operation are well signposted. It is an offence to break these rules.

London 'Red Route' Scheme

The 'Red Route' scheme in London is designed to prevent traffic congestion on certain primary routes. Each section of the route is identified by single or dual red road markings painted parallel to the kerb edging and accompanied by a red route sign. Failure to comply with the Red Route restrictions can lead to severe penalties.

London congestion charging scheme

The London congestion charging scheme is designed to reduce traffic congestion and allow for more reliable delivery times in the capital. The daily charge of £8 applies to all vehicles (except those exempt) entering the zone on weekdays between 7 am and 6.30 pm.

The charging zone covers any route that crosses the River Thames by Lambeth, Westminster, Waterloo, Blackfriars, Southwark or London bridges. Excluded from the charging area are Euston Road, Tower Bridge, Elephant and Castle, Vauxhall Bridge, Victoria and Park Lane. Cameras, located at 85 per cent of the boundary intersections and at random points within the zone, record vehicle registration numbers and cross-check computer records or charges paid.

Vehicles running on gas or electricity are exempt after paying a £10 registration fee. All other commercial vehicles are included in the scheme, unless they are emergency service vehicles or are vehicles on municipal duty, not competing with private firms.

Drivers who regularly enter the charging zone may preregister and pay a fee, otherwise payment of the £8 daily fee may be made by credit card or by carnets purchased from newsagents and convenience stores and from ticket terminals in car parks, hospitals and other local amenities. Any driver who has not paid prior to entry into the charging zone may pay later that day – up to midnight. Failure to pay the daily charge will result in evaders incurring a £120 penalty, issued to the vehicle owner (not necessarily the driver), but this is halved to £60 if paid within two weeks.

'BUS-ONLY' LANES

Vehicles, except for pedal cycles (and taxis if signed to this effect), are prohibited from using the bus lanes, marked by a single solid white line, when the signs indicate that the restrictions are in operation.

LEVEL CROSSINGS

Most railway level crossings have automatic half-barrier crossing gates with advance warning by red flashing lights and ringing bells that a train is approaching. Once these warnings start, the barrier comes down immediately, and drivers should not zigzag around the barriers. When the train has passed, the barriers will rise unless another train is following, in which case the warnings will continue.

Drivers of abnormal load-carrying vehicles that are large or slow (ie, with loads that are more than 2.9 metres (9 feet 6 inches) wide or more than 16.8 metres (55 feet) long or weighing more than 38 tonnes gross or incapable of a speed of more than 5 mph (8 kph) wishing to cross must, before attempting to cross, obtain permission from the signal operator via the special telephone provided at the crossing. If this is not answered or there is no ringing tone, the police should be contacted. Failure to follow these requirements is an offence that can result in penalty points being endorsed on the driver's licence, or he may be disqualified from driving. If a vehicle becomes stuck on the crossing the driver should advise the signal operator immediately by using the telephone.

WEIGHT-RESTRICTED ROADS AND BRIDGES

Where signs indicate that a particular section of road or a bridge is restricted to vehicles not exceeding a specified weight limit or axle weight limit, unless otherwise expressly stated the weight limit relates to the actual weight of the vehicle or to an individual axle of the vehicle, not the relevant plated weights.

Signs, particularly to protect weak bridges, restrict vehicles according to their maximum authorized gross weight (ie, their plated weight) – indicated as 'mgw'. The signs apply even if the vehicle, if it has a plated weight greater than the limit shown, is unladen at the time and therefore well below the maximum weight limit for the bridge (unless the sign permits 'empty vehicles').

SPEED LIMITS

Speed kills! It is a major contributor to the many accidents on our roads in which some 3,500 people are killed annually and a further 45,000 are seriously injured. Statutory speed limits are set to ensure road safety. For this reason, it cannot be stressed too highly that you should observe all relevant speed limits when driving. Speeding can result in heavy fines and loss of driving licence – and if somebody is killed through speeding the offending driver could be sent to prison. There are three levels of speed limit as follows and it is the lowest limit that should always be observed:

1. permanent speed limits applying to vehicles using particular roads;
2. permanent speed limits applying to particular classes of vehicle (including limits imposed by the mandatory fitment of speed limiter devices on certain goods vehicles);

3.   temporary speed limits introduced for special reasons such as in potentially hazardous situations.

Speed limits on restricted roads

On roads where street lights are positioned at intervals of not more than 200 yards (about 180 metres) (ie, 'restricted' roads), a speed limit of 30 mph (48 kph) applies to all vehicles unless alternative lower speeds are indicated by signs or unless the vehicle itself is subject to a lower limit due to its construction or its use.

Speed limits on other roads

Maximum speed limits on roads outside built-up areas are 60 mph (96 kph) on single-carriageway roads and 70 mph (112 kph) on dual carriageways and motorways, except where specified temporary or permanent lower limits are in force. In certain high-accident risk areas (eg, housing estates) 20mph (32kph) speed limit zones are applied in conjunction with road humps. Other so-called 'traffic calming' measures are used to improve road safety, including road-narrowing chicanes.

Speed limits at roadworks

Mandatory speed limits may be encountered at roadworks sections on motor-ways (and other roads). These are indicated by circular white signs with black letters indicating the maximum permissible speed and with a red border – see the *Highway Code* for illustration. Failure to obey these mandatory speed limits can result in prosecution and, on conviction, the endorsement of penalty points on the offender's driving licence.

Advisory speed limits on motorways

Advisory speed limits on motorways should be observed. These are shown by illuminated signs that indicate hazardous situations and road works ahead and by temporary speed limits signs at road works. Warning lights positioned at intervals on motorways indicate temporary maximum speed limits, which should be observed until a sign appears indicating an end to the speed restric-tion.

Speed limits on vehicles

All vehicles are restricted to certain maximum speeds according to their construction, weight or use, but when travelling on roads that themselves are subject to speed restrictions it is the lowest permitted speed (ie, of the vehicle or of the section of road) that must always be observed.

Light goods vehicles

Light goods vehicles for the purposes of speed limits are vehicles up to and including 7.5 tonnes maximum weight. Speed limits for rigid vehicles in this category are 50 mph (80 kph) on single-carriageway roads, 60 mph (96 kph) on dual-carriageway roads and 70 mph (112 kph) on motorways.

The maximum speed for rigid vehicles up to 7.5 tonnes maximum laden weight drawing trailers and articulated vehicles up to 7.5 tonnes maximum laden weight on single-carriageway roads is 50 mph (80 kph) and on dual carriageways and motorways the limit is 60 mph (96 kph).

Large goods vehicles

There is no distinction in terms of maximum speed between rigid and articulated large goods vehicles and those with drawbar trailers. Large goods vehicles are those over 7.5 tonnes maximum laden weight (mlw), which, under other regulations, are required to display rear reflective markers, so making them readily identifiable to the police for speed limit enforcement purposes. Speed limits for all vehicles in this category are 40 mph (64 kph) on single-carriageway roads, 50 mph (80 kph) on dual-carriageway roads and 60 mph (96 kph) on motorways.

Most over-7.5-tonne gross weight goods vehicles are required by UK law to be fitted with speed limiters set to restrict their top speed to 60 mph (96 kph), while EU rules restrict certain other heavy vehicles over 12 tonnes gross weight to a maximum speed of 56 mph (approximately 90 kph).

Note: in all cases mentioned above, it must be stressed that these maximum speed limits may be attained only where no lower limit is in force.

Abnormal loads vehicles

Vehicles used for carrying abnormal indivisible loads are restricted to the following maximum speeds:

Table 3.6a   Speed limits for abnormal load vehicles

Vehicle category	Motorways mph (kph)	Dual carriageways mph (kph)	Single carriageways mph (kph)
Category 1	60 (96)	50 (80)	40 (64)
Category 2	40 (64)	35 (56)	30 (48)
Category 3	30 (48)	25 (40)	20 (32)

Emergency service vehicles

Fire, police and ambulance emergency service vehicles are exempt from statutory speed limits if, by observing the speed limit, they would be hampered in carrying out their duties.

Table 3.6b *Vehicle speed limits*

	Motorways mph (kph)	Dual carriageways mph (kph)	Other roads mph (kph)
Car-derived vans			
solo	70 (112)	70 (112)	60 (96)
towing caravan/trailer	60 (96)	60 (96)	50 (80)
Not exceeding 7.5 tonnes mlw			
solo	70 (112)	60 (96)	50 (80)
articulated	60 (96)	60* (96)	50 (80)
drawbar	60 (96)	60* (96)	50 (80)
Over 7.5 tonnes mlw			
solo	60 (96)	50 (80)	40 (64)
articulated	60 (96)	50 (80)	40 (64)
drawbar	60 (96)	50 (80)	40 (64)

Notes: mlw means maximum laden weight (ie maximum gross weight for a vehicle as specified in construction and use regulations).
* In Northern Ireland the speed limit for vehicles in these two categories is 50 mph (80 kph) only.

Speed-enforcement cameras

Speed-enforcement cameras are authorized under the Road Traffic Acts, which allow the use of photographic evidence in cases of alleged speeding and traffic light jumping. Most speed cameras, of which there are now very many, are of the digital type linked directly to a central control from which fixed penalty notices are sent out immediately to speeding drivers.

MOTORWAY DRIVING

Driving on motorways requires special care and attention, due to vehicles travelling at higher speeds and in close proximity. It is important to know and observe the motorway regulations.

Stopping on a motorway

Drivers should not stop on a motorway except for reasons of:
- mechanical defect;
- lack of fuel, water or oil;
- an accident;
- the illness of a person in the vehicle;
- other emergency situations (including giving assistance to other persons);
- a person from the vehicle having to remove objects from the carriageway.

Use of the hard shoulder

It is illegal to drive on the hard shoulder or the central reservation of a motorway, or to reverse or make a 'U-turn'. Where it is necessary to use the hard shoulder for emergency reasons such as those listed above, the vehicle must remain there only for so long as is necessary to deal with the situation.

Use of lanes

The following vehicles must not use the outer or offside lane of three- and four-lane motorways:

- goods vehicles with a maximum laden weight over 7.5 tonnes;
- vehicles with more than eight passenger seats excluding the driver and with a maximum laden weight over 7.5 tonnes;
- vehicles drawing trailers;
- motor tractors and locomotives.

Temporary speed limits

Where carriageway repairs take place on motorways or where contraflow traffic systems are used an *advisory* lower speed limit may be imposed. This is considered by the police to be a maximum speed, and they may prosecute drivers found speeding in these sections. However, it is more common for a mandatory speed limit to be imposed. Drivers found to be speeding in these sections will be prosecuted. A *mandatory* maximum speed sign is circular with black figures on a white background with a red border – see illustration in the *Highway Code*.

Learner drivers on motorways

Learner drivers are not normally allowed to drive on motorways, but holders of provisional LGV driving entitlements covering vehicles in categories C1, C1+E, D1 and/or D1+E may drive these vehicles on motorways provided they are accompanied by a qualified driver holding a full vocational entitlement for the category of vehicle being driven.

Motorway lights and signs

Hazard warning lights on rural motorways

Rural motorways have amber lights, at not more than 2-mile (approx 3-kilometre) intervals and usually located in the central reservation, which flash and indicate either a maximum speed limit or, by means of red flashing lights, that one or more lanes ahead are closed. The speed limit indicated applies to *all* lanes of the motorway and should not be exceeded. When these lights flash, drivers must slow down until the danger that the lights are indicating, and a non-flashing light or 'All clear' sign, has been passed.

Lights on urban motorways

Urban motorways have overhead warning lights placed at 1,000-yard (approx 1,600-kilometre) intervals. Amber lights flash when there is danger ahead and indicate a maximum speed limit or an arrow advising drivers to change to another lane. If red lights flash above any or all of the lanes, vehicles in those lanes must stop at the signal. It is as much of an offence to fail to stop at these red lights as it is to ignore automatic traffic signals.

Local radio station frequency signs

Some local radio stations have their broadcasting frequencies shown on motorway signs indicating that they provide local-area traffic news 24 hours a day, seven days a week.

RDS radios

Many modern vehicle radios have RDS or RDS-EON functions that enable the set to be tuned to automatically receive traffic announcements issued by local radio stations. Generally, with the function switched on, the announcement interrupts normal radio programme reception, or temporarily pauses cassette tape or CD playback for the duration of the announcement.

Emergency telephones on motorways

Emergency telephones are located at 1-mile (approx 1.6-kilometre) intervals on the hard shoulder each side of motorways – there is no need (and it is both dangerous and illegal) to cross the carriageways to reach an emergency telephone. Arrows on the back of posts on the hard shoulder indicate the direction to the nearest telephone. The use of the telephone is free, and it connects directly to the police, who should be given full details of the emergency, the name of the person calling and details of the vehicle involved. After making the call the driver should return to his vehicle immediately to await help – a police patrol may arrive within minutes. A woman driver travelling alone is advised to tell the police of this fact.

DRIVING IN FOG

Fog presents a major driving hazard on occasions and results in numerous accidents, some with fatal consequences. For this reason it is important to drive with great care and to observe the sensible advice given in the *Highway Code* (rules 234–36) as follows:

- Use your headlights (ie, switch them on when visibility is reduced to 100 metres – 328 feet).
- Keep a safe distance behind the vehicle in front, remembering that the other vehicle's rear lights can give you a false sense of security.
- Be able to pull up within the distance you can see clearly, especially on motorways and dual carriageways, where vehicles are travelling much faster.
- Use your windscreen wipers and demisters to give you clear vision ahead.
- Watch out for other drivers who are not using their headlights.
- Do not accelerate to get away from a vehicle that is being driven too closely behind you.
- Check your mirrors before you slow down and use your brakes so that your brake lights warn drivers behind that you are slowing down.
- Stop in the correct position at a road junction with limited visibility and listen for traffic until you are sure it is safe to cross, then do so positively without hesitating in a position that leaves you directly in the path of approaching vehicles.

The *Highway Code* also states that you *must not* use front or rear fog lights unless visibility is seriously reduced as they dazzle other road users and can obscure your brake lights. You must switch these lights off when visibility improves.

VEHICLE EXCISE DUTY (VED)

All mechanically propelled vehicles, whether used for business or private purposes, which are driven or parked on public roads in Great Britain must display a current and valid excise licence unless they are being driven, by previous appointment, to a place for their annual test.

It is an offence to use or keep an unlicensed vehicle (or trade licensed only vehicle) on a road, even for a short period of time.

Exceptions

Exceptions apply to certain official vehicles such as those belonging to fire brigades and ambulance services, those operated by the Crown, those used for snow clearance and certain other public utility vehicles. An exemption also applies when vehicles used solely for forestry, agriculture or horticultural purposes travel on public roads for not more than 1.5 kilometres per journey between land occupied by the same firm or person who is the registered owner of the vehicle. An 'exempt' disc is provided for display on the vehicle windscreen.

Duty rates

Goods vehicle excise duty is based on a set of 7 bands (A – G) relating to the vehicle gross weight and the number of axles, with concessionary rates for vehicles covered by a reduced pollution certificate (RPC). Duty for light goods vehicles (those not over 3,500kg gross weight) is based on a single rate with a reduction for those with a Euro-IV emission engine. Car duty is based on the vehicle's CO_2 emissions.

Documents for licensing

When licensing a vehicle, the following documents must be provided:

1. the registration document (form V5) for the vehicle;
2. a current certificate of insurance (or a temporary cover note, but not the policy);
3. a current MoT or goods vehicle test certificate (where applicable);
4. a completed application form
   (a) form VE55 for first registration
   (b) form V11 renewal reminder (or V85/1 for certain vehicles);
5. the type approval certificate (for first registration only);
6. a reduced pollution certificate (where relevant);
7. the appropriate amount of duty.

On first registration of the vehicle a registration number will be allocated. This must be made into plates to be displayed on the front and rear of the vehicle. A circular windscreen disc is also provided to indicate that duty has been paid (the colouring of these discs is varied to provide ready indication that duty for the current period has been paid). This disc must be displayed on the vehicle windscreen on the nearside, where it can be easily seen. Failure to display the disc (even if the duty has been paid) is an offence.

When a vehicle is off the road (ie not licensed) a Statutory Off Road Notice (SORN) declaration is required, otherwise the vehicle keeper/owner will be prosecuted.

MOTOR VEHICLE INSURANCE

Compulsory cover

Motor vehicles using the public highway must be covered against third party claims. Basic motor vehicle insurance covers the insured against claims by injured parties for personal injury (ie death or bodily injury) and medical expenses. This, together with mandatory cover for passengers – except those in the employ of the vehicle owner/operator – and for damage to roadside property, is the minimum legal requirement (sometimes referred to as 'Road Traffic Act cover'). Beyond this, an insurance policy may cover other third-party risks including damage to other property or loss of the vehicle by fire or theft, or it may entail fully comprehensive cover to provide full protection against third-party claims and compensation for damage to the vehicle.

The insured person or organization must have in their possession a current and valid certificate of insurance (the policy is not acceptable proof of cover) showing the cover provided, and it must give particulars of any conditions subject to which the policy is issued. It should indicate:

- the vehicles covered, by registration number or by specification;
- the persons authorized to drive the vehicle;
- the dates between which the cover is effective;
- permitted use of the vehicle.

3.7

Road traffic offences and penalties

Drivers may incur penalties following conviction by a court for offences committed on the road with a motor vehicle. These range from fixed penalty notices to driving licence penalty points endorsement or, in the case of more serious offences, driving licence disqualification from a few weeks or months extending to a number of years – for example, in the case of drink-driving related offences. LGV drivers who are convicted of offences risk their LGV driving entitlements being suspended or revoked or, in really serious circumstances, being disqualified from holding a vocational entitlement altogether. Besides the above penalties, convicted drivers can expect to pay fines (heavy at times, plus court costs) and may also face imprisonment for certain very serious offences.

FINES

Maximum fines vary according to a standard scale between £200 at level 1 to £5,000 at level 5.

OFFENCES INCURRING LEVEL 5 FINES

Offences such as dangerous driving, failing to stop after an accident or failure to report an accident and drink-driving offences, carry the current maximum fine of £5,000, as do certain vehicle construction and use offences (eg, overloading, insecure loads, using a vehicle in a dangerous condition etc) and using a vehicle without insurance.

NEW-DRIVER PENALTIES

Newly qualified drivers are required to undergo a two-year probationary period after first passing their driving test, during which time they are liable to have their driving licence revoked if more than six penalty points are endorsed on their licence. They must also retake the driving test before their licence will be restored to them.

THE PENALTY POINTS SYSTEM

The penalty points system grades road traffic offences according to their seriousness with a number or range of between 2 and 10 penalty points, which are endorsed on the offender's driving licence. Once a maximum of 12 penalty points has been accumulated (ie, totted-up, in common parlance) on a licence within a three-year period counting from the date of the first offence to the date of the current offence (not from the date of the relevant convictions), disqualification of the licence for at least six months will follow automatically.

The endorsement of penalty points on a driving licence will also arise where the driver is convicted for offences where disqualification is discretionary and the court has decided that immediate disqualification is not appropriate (for example, if acceptable 'exceptional' reasons are put forward – see also below). In this case, the offender's driving licence will be endorsed instead with four penalty points. The courts remain free to disqualify an offender immediately on conviction if the circumstances justify this.

When a driver is convicted of more than one offence at the same court hearing, only the points relating to the most serious of the offences will normally be endorsed on the licence.

Periods of disqualification

Once 12 points have been endorsed on the driving licence and a period of disqualification has been imposed (six months for the first totting-up of points), the driver's 'slate' will be wiped clean and those points will not be counted again. Twelve more points would have to be accumulated before a further disqualification would follow.

However, to discourage drivers from repeatedly committing road traffic offences the courts will impose progressively longer periods of disqualification on each successive occasion. For example, a minimum 12-month disqualification will be imposed for a second totting-up within three years and 24 months' disqualification for a third totting-up within three years.

Driving licence endorsement codes and penalty points

A convicted offender's driving licence will be endorsed with both a code (from which employers can assess the offences that drivers have committed) and the number of penalty points imposed.

DISQUALIFICATION OFFENCES

Road traffic offences carrying obligatory disqualification are as follows:

- causing death by dangerous driving and manslaughter;
- dangerous driving within three years of a similar conviction;
- driving or attempting to drive while unfit through drink or drugs;
- driving or attempting to drive with excess alcohol in breath, blood or urine;
- failure to provide a breath, blood or urine specimen;
- motor racing on the highway.

Driving while disqualified is a serious offence carrying a fine of up to £5,000, or six months' imprisonment, or both.

Special reasons for non-disqualification

The courts have discretion, when there are 'special reasons', not to impose a disqualification but four penalty points will be added to the driver's licence. The mitigating circumstance must attempt to make the offence appear less serious and no account will be taken of hardship other than 'exceptional' hardship.

DANGEROUS DRIVING

A person is driving dangerously if the way he drives 'falls far short of what would be expected of a competent and careful driver, and it would be obvious to a competent and careful driver that driving in that way would be dangerous', or if he is driving a vehicle in a dangerous mechanical condition or one that is loaded dangerously.

Other dangerous actions

It is an offence for any person to cause danger to road users unlawfully by placing objects on a road, interfering with motor vehicles, or directly or indirectly interfering with traffic equipment (eg, road signs etc).

REMOVAL OF PENALTY POINTS AND DISQUALIFICATIONS

Penalty points endorsed on driving licences can be removed by applying to the DVLA Swansea on form D1 and paying the appropriate fee.

Waiting period for removal of penalty points

The waiting period before making an application for removal of penalty points endorsed on a driving licence is four years from the date of the offence, except in the case of endorsements for reckless/dangerous driving convictions, when the four years is taken from the date of conviction. Endorsements for alcohol-related offences must remain on a licence for 11 years.

Waiting period for removal of a disqualification

Application may be made to the DVLA at Swansea by disqualified drivers for reinstatement of their licence after varying periods of time depending on the duration of the disqualifying period as follows:

- less than two years – no prior application time;
- less than four years – after two years has elapsed;
- between four years and 10 years – after half the time has elapsed;
- in other cases – after five years has elapsed.

Licences returned after disqualification will show no penalty points but previous disqualifications (within four years) will remain on the licence and if a previous alcohol/drugs-driving offence disqualification has been incurred, this will remain on the licence for 11 years.

Court order to retake the driving test

Disqualified drivers may be required by the courts to retake the driving test before restoring a driving licence. These 'extended' re-tests (involving at least one hour's driving) must be taken before the driving licence is restored following disqualification for the most serious of driving offences, namely, dangerous driving and causing death by dangerous driving.

THE TRAFFIC COMMISSIONERS' ROLE IN DRIVER LICENSING

The TCs fulfil a disciplinary role under the driver licensing scheme with regard to the conduct of LGV and PCV vocational entitlement holders, but only at the request of the DVLA. They have powers to call drivers to public inquiry (PI) to give information and answer questions as to their conduct. Their duty is to report back to the DVLA if they consider that an LGV/PCV entitlement should be revoked or the holder disqualified from holding an entitlement – the DVLA must follow the TC's recommendation in these matters.

Failure to attend a public inquiry when requested to do so (unless a reasonable excuse is given) means that the DVLA will automatically refuse a new vocational entitlement or suspend or revoke an existing entitlement.

REMOVAL OF AN LGV DRIVING LICENCE DISQUALIFICATION

Drivers disqualified from holding an LGV/PCV entitlement, as described above, may apply to have the disqualification removed after:

- two years if it was for less than four years;
- after half the period if the disqualification was for more than four years but less than 10 years;
- five years in any other case, including disqualification for an indefinite period.

If an application for the removal of a disqualification fails, another application cannot be made for three months.

THE FIXED PENALTY SYSTEM

Drivers who commit road traffic offences may find themselves receiving a fixed penalty notice issued by a traffic warden or a police constable. These notices, which are either handed to the driver personally or are affixed to the vehicle windscreen if the driver is not present, require the vehicle driver or owner to pay the fixed penalty or to elect to have the case dealt with in court.

Types of fixed penalty

There are two types of fixed penalty notice: (1) non-endorsable offences (mainly dealt with by traffic wardens), and (2) driving licence endorsable offences, which only the police can deal with since traffic wardens have no general authority to ask drivers to produce their driving licences (they may do so only in prescribed instances concerned with parking, obstruction, traffic signs and excise licence offences). Additionally, two London-area parking offences are included in the fixed penalty system (see overleaf).

Fixed penalty for non-endorsable offences

For non-endorsable offences either a white notice (penalty £30, £40 or £60) is handed to the driver personally if he is present or it is fixed to the vehicle windscreen. Since no driving licence penalty points are involved for such offences, there is no requirement to examine the licence. Traffic wardens have authority to issue fixed penalty tickets for the following non-endorsable offences:

- leaving a vehicle parked at night without lights or reflectors;
- waiting, loading, unloading or parking in prohibited areas;
- unauthorized parking in controlled parking zone areas;

- contravention of the Vehicle Excise and Registration Act 1994 by not displaying a current licence disc;
- making 'U' turns in unauthorized places;
- lighting offences with moving vehicles;
- driving the wrong way in a one-way street;
- overstaying on parking meters, returning to parking places before the expiry of the statutory period, or feeding meters to obtain longer parking facilities than those permitted in a meter zone;
- parking on pavements or verges by commercial vehicles over 3,050 kilograms unladen weight.

Fixed penalty for endorsable offences

The extended fixed penalty system covers driving licence endorsable offences, which can be dealt with only by the police (ie, not by traffic wardens) – this includes some 250 driving and vehicle use offences. For endorsable offences, a yellow notice with a different level of penalty applies as described below.

For driving licence endorsable offences the police issue a yellow notice for which a penalty of £200 is payable. These tickets are only issued after the police officer has examined the offender's driving licence and has established that the addition of penalty points appropriate to the current offence, when added to any points already on the licence, will not result in automatic disqualification under the 12-point totting-up procedure (see page 142). If this is the case, the ticket will be issued and the driving licence will be confiscated (an official receipt, covering the holder for non-possession or production of his licence, will be given – valid for two months), being returned to the holder with the appropriate penalty points added when the fixed penalty has been paid.

If the offender does not have his driving licence with him at the time, the penalty notice will not be issued on the spot but will be issued later at the police station when the driving licence is produced there within seven days – subject again to the number of penalty points already on the licence.

Where the addition of further points in respect of the current offence would take the total of penalty points on the licence to 12 or more, thus leading to automatic disqualification, the ticket will not be issued and the offence will be dealt with by the offender being summoned to appear in court in the normal manner.

London-area parking offences

The fixed penalty system includes two specific London-area parking offences, namely parking on a marked 'Red Route', for which the penalty is currently £120, and parking in other prohibited places, for which the penalty is also £120. Parking in less congested areas may incur an £80 penalty charge. Offending vehicles may be removed which will entail much higher charges.

Payment or attending court

Fixed penalty notices must be paid in accordance with the instructions on the notice and within the specified time limit of 28 days. Alternatively, offenders can elect to have the charge dealt with by a court so they have the opportunity to defend themselves against the charge or, even if they accept that they are guilty of the offence, of putting forward mitigating circumstances, which may lessen any penalty that may be imposed.

The address of the fixed penalty office to which the penalty payment should be sent is given in the notice together with instructions for making an application for a court hearing if this course of action is chosen.

Failure to pay penalties

With both the white and the yellow ticket systems, failure to pay the statutory penalty within the requisite period of 28 days will result in the offender being automatically considered guilty and the penalties being increased by 50 per cent (ie, to £60, £80 and £90 respectively). These increased amounts become fines and continued non-payment will result in the offender being arrested and taken before a court in the district where the offence was committed. This could be many miles from where the offender lives and may necessitate him being held in custody, possibly overnight, and then being transported under arrest to the court.

3.8

Driving on drink and drugs

Driving any vehicle while under the influence of drink or drugs is illegal and is both highly dangerous and morally indefensible. With large goods vehicles the situation is much worse, first because the driver is supposed to be professional, but more importantly because of the greater risk of a heavily loaded vehicle being in the hands of a driver whose judgement and reaction times are impaired.

BREATH TESTING

It is an offence to drive or attempt to drive when the level of alcohol in the breath exceeds 35 micrograms per 100 millilitres of breath. This is measured by an on-the-spot breath test, when the driver is stopped, and later substantiated by an approved breath-testing machine at a police station.

The breath/alcohol limit mentioned above is equal to the alternative measures of blood/alcohol, where the limit is 80 milligrams of alcohol in 100 millilitres of blood, or urine/alcohol, where the limit is 107 milligrams of alcohol in 100 millilitres of urine.

Police powers to conduct breath tests

The police may require suspected drink-drivers to take a breath test and will arrest a person in charge of a vehicle, or who is driving or attempting to drive on a road or other public place, if he is unfit to drive through drink or drugs. They may also arrest a person who fails (or refuses) to take a breath test but who is believed to have been drinking. A driver who has been arrested following a breath test and is required to provide a specimen of blood or urine may be detained at a police station till he is fit to drive, but not if there is no likelihood of him driving or attempting to drive while still unfit.

The police *do not* have powers to carry out breath tests at random but they *do have* powers to enter premises to require a breath test from a person suspected of driving while impaired through drink or drugs, or who has been driving, or been in charge of a vehicle that has been involved in an accident in which another person has been injured.

Alternative blood/urine tests

If the suspected drink-driver cannot produce a breath sample for health reasons, or if a breath test shows a reading of not more than 50 micrograms of alcohol per 100 millilitres of breath, he may be offered an alternative test to produce a sample of either blood or urine, for laboratory analysis. This can only be carried out at a police station or a hospital and the decision as to which is chosen rests with the police, unless a doctor present decides that for medical reasons a blood test cannot or should not be taken.

Failing or refusing the breath, blood or urine test

Drink-driving offenders who fail or refuse the breath, blood or urine tests will be prosecuted, resulting in a fine or imprisonment and automatic long-term disqualification from driving or driving licence endorsement on conviction (endorsements for such offences remain on a driving licence for 11 years – see p 144).

DRINK-DRIVING PENALTIES

Conviction of a driver for a first drink-driving offence will result in a minimum one-year period of driving licence disqualification. Longer periods of disqualification will be imposed by the courts for a second or subsequent offence of driving or attempting to drive under the influence of drink or drugs. If the previous such conviction took place within 10 years of the current offence the disqualification must be for at least three years.

'High-risk' offenders

Drivers convicted twice for drink-driving offences may have their driving licence revoked altogether. Offenders who are disqualified twice within a 10-year period for any drink-driving offences and those found to have an exceptionally high level of alcohol in the body (ie, more than two and a half times over the limit) or those who twice refuse to provide a specimen will be classified as high-risk offenders (HROs) by the Driver and Vehicle Licensing Agency. These HROs will be required to show that they no longer have an 'alcohol problem' by means of a medical examination (including blood analysis of liver enzymes) by a DVLA-approved doctor before their licence will be restored to them. These drivers are charged a higher than normal fee (ie, £85) for the renewal of driving licences following disqualification.

DRINK-DRIVING COURSES

Certain (but not all) drink-driving offenders may have the period of their driving licence disqualification for drink-driving offences reduced if they agree to undertake an approved rehabilitation course and satisfactorily complete the course. This applies only where the court orders the individual (who must be over 17 years of age) to be disqualified for at least 12 months following conviction for:

- causing death by careless driving when under the influence of drink or drugs;
- driving or being in charge of a motor vehicle when under the influence of drink or drugs;
- driving or being in charge of a motor vehicle with excess alcohol in the body; or
- failing to provide a specimen (of breath, blood or urine) as required.

Before ordering the offender to attend the training course, the court has a duty to ensure that a place on an approved course is available. Further, the court must explain to the offender 'in ordinary language' the effect of the order (ie, to reduce the disqualification period), the amount of the fees and that these must be paid in advance, and it must seek the offender's agreement that the order should be made – in other words, it is a completely voluntary scheme and there is no question of compulsion.

Given these provisos, the court can order the period of disqualification imposed on the offender to be reduced by not less than three months and not more than one-quarter of the unreduced period (for example, with a 12-month disqualification, the reduction will be three months, leaving a nine-month disqualification period to be served). The latest date for completion of one of these rehabilitation courses is two months prior to the last day of the reduced disqualification period (so, in the nine-month example given above, the course would have to be completed by the last day of the seventh month).

On completion of the course the offender is given a certificate, which must be returned to the clerk of the supervising court (named in the order) in order to secure the reduction. Failure to complete the course or to produce the certificate on time will result in the loss of this facility.

The courses

A number of approved courses have been established requiring attendance for between 16 and 30 hours, made up of a number of separate sessions, during which the offender learns about the effects of alcohol on the body and on driving performance and behaviour, about drink-driving offences and the alternatives to drinking and driving. Relevant advice will also be given.

DRUG TESTING OF LGV DRIVERS

Random drug testing of LGV drivers is becoming an increasing practice in the United Kingdom, especially among road tanker fleet operators.

Drugs and driving

Official sources say that drugs are a major cause of one in five fatal road accidents and that as many as 3 million people could be driving under the influence of cannabis. Drivers who use tranquillizers are involved in some 1,600 road accidents every year – 110 of them fatal. See Chapter 3.5 for further information on drug use and abuse.

Warning
Drivers feeling drowsy, dizzy, confused, or with other side-effects from drink or drugs that could affect their reaction times or judgement *SHOULD NOT DRIVE.*

3.9

Enforcement authority powers and prohibitions

LGV drivers will be familiar with the front-line enforcement of traffic regulations by police and, in towns, by traffic wardens. However, they are also likely to encounter other enforcement officials, principally:

- examiners from the Vehicle and Operator Services Agency (VOSA), who examine goods vehicles, tachographs and drivers' records;
- officers of HM Revenue & Customs who have extensive powers regarding illegal use of rebated heavy oil (ie, red diesel) and smuggling of alcohol, cigarettes and drugs;
- trading standards officers who represent local authority interests with regard to overweight vehicles;
- local authority environmental health officials concerned with hygiene standards of food-carrying vehicles;
- livestock inspectors from DEFRA who enforce regulations on the welfare of animals during transit;
- health and safety inspectors enforcing provisions of the Health and Safety at Work Act; and
- immigration officers at ports who track down illegal immigrants.

POLICE CONSTABLES

The police have wide-ranging powers with regard to crime prevention and investigation, for maintaining public order and for protection of the public. They also have specific powers regarding goods vehicle operations: for example, a police constable *in uniform* can stop a moving vehicle on a road ('constable' includes any rank of uniformed police officer). They can test any vehicle or trailer on a road to check that legal requirements regarding brakes, silencer, steering, tyres, lights and reflectors, smoke and fumes are complied with. They may drive the vehicle for this purpose.

POLICE, EXAMINERS AND CERTIFYING OFFICERS

Authorized examiners may test and inspect vehicles and examine vehicle records as follows:

- They can test any vehicle or trailer on a road to check that legal requirements regarding brakes, silencer, steering, tyres, lights and reflectors, smoke and fumes are complied with, and may drive the vehicle for this purpose.
- They may at any time enter and inspect any goods vehicle and inspect goods vehicle records, and at any reasonable time enter premises on which they believe such a vehicle or records are kept.
- They can ask the driver of a stationary goods vehicle to take it to a place for inspection up to 5 miles away.
- They may request a driver to take his vehicle to a weighbridge to be weighed.
- When a goods vehicle has been weighed and found to be overweight and its use on a road would be a risk to public safety, they can prohibit its use (with Form TE160) until the weight is reduced to within the legal limit.
- If they find that a goods vehicle is unfit or likely to become unfit for service they can prohibit it being driven on the road either immediately or from a later date and time by a Form PG9 prohibition notice.
- Where a prohibition notice has been placed on a vehicle for various reasons, they can remove it (with Form PG10) when they consider the vehicle is fit for use. Clearance of prohibitions requires the vehicle to be subjected to a full roadworthiness test by VOSA at a Goods Vehicle Testing Station – and payment of the full test fee.
- They can ask the driver of a vehicle fitted with a tachograph to produce his tachograph charts and they can examine the official calibration plaque in the instrument.

TRAFFIC WARDENS

Besides issuing fixed penalty tickets, traffic wardens may also act as parking attendants, carry out traffic control duties, act as school crossing patrols, inquire into the identity of drivers and act in connection with the custody of vehicles at car pounds.

They may demand to know the names and addresses of drivers believed to have committed parking, obstruction, traffic sign and excise licence offences and to see the driving licence of anybody who is suspected of such offences. If the licence cannot be produced at that time the warden may require its production at a police station within seven days.

Since December 2002, certain traffic wardens can stop moving vehicles for the purposes of testing their condition, and escort vehicles carrying abnormal loads.

TRADING STANDARDS OFFICERS

Trading standards officers employed by local authorities can ask a driver to produce the official conveyance note for ballast loads (eg, sand, gravel, shingle, ashes, clinker, chippings, including coated material, hardcore and aggregates) and take the vehicle to a weighbridge. Goods may have to be unloaded if it is overweight.

CHECKS ON VEHICLES

In addition to carrying out annual vehicle tests at goods vehicle testing stations, VOSA operates roadside checks on goods vehicles, usually in main-road lay-bys and occasionally during the night and at weekends. A uniformed police officer directs vehicles required for examination into the lay-by where they are inspected, mainly for visible wear and defects of the brakes, steering gear, silencers, tyres, lights and reflectors and for the emission of black smoke when the engine is revved up.

INSPECTION NOTICES AND PROHIBITIONS

Vehicle inspection notice – Form PGDN35

Following an inspection of a vehicle that is found to have no serious road safety defects, Form PGDN35 (inspection notice) is issued to indicate either that one or more minor defects were found, which for safety reasons should be rectified at an early date (it is not actually a prohibition), or the vehicle has no apparent defects – subject to a disclaimer – to save further inspection later on that journey or that day.

Direction notice

Form GV3 is authorization for VOSA examiners to direct a vehicle to proceed to a specified place to be inspected (normally not more than 5 miles away).

Prohibition notices

The driver of any vehicle found to have serious defects is given a Form PG9 on which these are listed. This form is the examiner's authority to stop the use of the vehicle on the road for carrying goods. Depending on how serious the defects are, the prohibition will take effect either immediately, in which case the vehicle, if loaded, has to remain where it is until it is repaired or has been unloaded and taken away for repair, for which the examiner will give authority by issuing Form PG9B, or it may be delayed for 12 to 24 hours or more depending on the seriousness of the fault. In this case the vehicle may continue to operate until the limit of the period of exemption of the prohibition by which time, if it is not repaired and cleared, it must be taken off the road.

If defects recorded as requiring immediate attention are repaired quickly on the roadside (either by the driver or by a mechanic or repair garage staff who come out to the vehicle) the examiner may issue a variation to the PG9 notice with Form PG9A, which allows the vehicle to be removed and used until the new time specified on the variation notice.

A copy of the PG9 is given to the driver and this must be carried on the vehicle until the prohibition is removed. Further copies are sent to the operator and to the Traffic Commissioner.

C&U (construction and use) offences

If defects are found at a roadside check that make the vehicle unsafe to be on the road (usually brakes, steering or suspension defects) or if they are such that an offence under the construction and use regulations is committed (particularly in respect of lights, reflectors, smoke emission or the horn), the VOSA examiners will consider prosecution of the driver and/or the operator.

Effects of prohibitions

Under no circumstances must a vehicle be used to carry goods while it is the subject of a PG9 prohibition notice. However, despite the prohibition a vehicle may be driven unladen to a goods vehicle test station, by previous appointment only, to have it inspected. It may also be driven on the road for test purposes, provided it is unladen, within 3 miles of where it has been repaired.

Clearance of prohibitions

An operator having a vehicle placed under an immediate or a delayed prohibition notice has to get the defects repaired and then submit the vehicle to his local Goods Vehicle Testing Station either for a full roadworthiness examination in the case of serious defects (with payment of the relevant fees) or, in the case of minor defects, a 'partial clearance' or 'mini' test. A clearance certificate PG10 is issued if the examiner is satisfied with the repair; if not, he will issue a Form PG9C 'Refusal to Remove a Prohibition' or Form PG9A if some of the defects are cleared and others are not. If he finds further defects another Form PG9 may be issued.

Part 4

Heavy vehicles and the law

4.1

Construction and use of vehicles

Heavy goods vehicle operations in the United Kingdom and in Europe are controlled by a mass of complicated technical regulations, most of them imposed for reasons of public safety, but others are concerned with environmental issues, such as the control of noise and exhaust emissions. In these changing times, the professional LGV driver increasingly needs to know a great deal more than just how to drive his truck, like understanding many of these technical provisions.

For starters, manufacturers are required by law to build goods vehicles and trailers to comply with the dimensions and technical specifications laid down in the construction and use (C&U) and authorized weight regulations. However, once vehicles are built and put into service, it is the operator and the driver, as legal 'users' of a vehicle, who must ensure they comply with the law. Both can be prosecuted if the legal requirements or safety standards of the C&U regulations are not met. Fines of up to £2,500 may be imposed on conviction for such offences and driving licences can be endorsed with three penalty points.

BRAKES

Good brakes are essential and all goods vehicles must meet specified efficiencies for the service brake (ie, the foot brake), for the secondary brake, and for the parking brake or hand brake, which must be an independent system preventing at least two wheels from turning when the vehicle is not being driven. The specified braking efficiencies are:

- service brake – 50 per cent;
- secondary brake – 25 per cent;

- parking brake – must be capable of holding the vehicle on a gradient of at least 1 in 6.25 without the assistance of stored energy (ie, 16 per cent).

Braking systems and their means of operation on all vehicles and trailers must be maintained in good and efficient working order and be properly adjusted.

TYRES

Tyres are an important safety item on which the life of the driver and other road users may depend. All heavy truck and trailer tyres must have *at least* 1 millimetre of tread depth (on cars and light goods vehicles up to 3.5 tonnes gross weight the minimum is 1.6 millimetres) across three-quarters of their breadth and in a continuous band around the entire circumference, and the base of the original grooves must be clearly visible over the remaining one-quarter of the breadth of the tyre.

Tyres must be inflated to the manufacturer's recommended pressures. They must not have breaks in the fabric or deep cuts (reaching the body cords) more than 25 millimetres long (or longer than 10 per cent of its section width) and there must be no lumps, bulges or tears caused by separation or partial fracture of the structure. No part of the ply or cord structure must be exposed. It is an offence for a vehicle to be on the road with tyres that are unsuitable or are of different types on opposite wheels.

WINDSCREEN WIPERS AND WASHERS

Vehicles must have efficient windscreen wipers and washers for cleaning the windscreen. The wipers must be in good and efficient working order and be adjusted properly.

MIRRORS

Goods vehicles must have at least two mirrors, one externally on the offside and the other either in the driver's cab or externally on the near side, which show traffic to the rear or on both sides rearwards. Vehicles over 12 tonnes gross weight must be fitted with additional mirrors providing close proximity and wide-angle vision.

Under recent EU directives heavy goods vehicles must now have a close-proximity kerb mirror and a mirror giving a view across the front of the vehicle.

HORN

Goods vehicles must be fitted with a horn with a continuous and uniform sound. Gongs, bells, sirens, musical and two-tone horns are not permitted. Horns must not be sounded while the vehicle is stationary (except in an emergency involving another vehicle) or in built-up areas between 11.30 pm and 7 am.

REVERSING ALARMS

Reversing alarms may be fitted to goods vehicles over 2 tonnes gross weight (but not to vehicles below this weight) but they must not operate in built-up areas after 11.30 pm and before 7 am.

SPEEDOMETER

Light goods vehicles must have a working speedometer, but most over-3.5-tonne gross weight goods vehicles need a tachograph (see Chapter 3.4).

SEAT BELTS

All goods vehicles must have seat belts for the driver and one front-seat passenger. They will fail their annual test if belts are not fitted, or if they are permanently obstructed or not in good condition. Drivers and passengers must wear the seat belts provided – it is illegal not to do so.

SILENCER

Vehicles must have an adequate silencer.

SAFETY GLASS

Vehicle windscreens and windows in front of and on either side of the driver's seat must be of safety glass (ie, toughened or laminated).

WINGS

Goods vehicles and trailers (with certain exceptions) must have wings to catch mud and water thrown up by the wheels unless the bodywork provides adequate protection.

REAR UNDER-RUN BUMPERS AND SIDEGUARDS

Most rigid vehicles over 3.5 tonnes gross weight and trailers and semi-trailers over 1,020 kilograms unladen weight must have sideguards and rear under-run bumpers although some specialized vehicles and trailers are exempt. These must be free from obvious defect and comply with the legal fitting dimensions.

ANTI-SPRAY EQUIPMENT

Certain vehicles and trailers (with exemptions applying to some specialized vehicles) must have one or the other following types of effective anti-spray device: a straight valance across the top of the wheel and a vertical flap hanging behind the wheel made from approved spray-suppressant material; or a semi-circular valance following the curvature of the wheel with either air/water separator material round the edge or a flap of spray-suppressant material hanging from the rear edge.

NOISE

It is an offence to allow a vehicle or trailer to cause excessive noise due to a defect, lack of repair or faulty adjustment of components or of the load. Vehicles must not be used on the road if they cause excessive noise that the driver could have reasonably avoided (tipper and skip-loader drivers please note!).

SMOKE

Vehicles must not emit avoidable smoke, visible vapour or oily substances that may cause damage to property or injury or danger to any person.

EXCESS FUEL DEVICES

Excess fuel (ie, cold-start) devices must not be used while the vehicle is moving. Their use when the engine is warm slightly increases power, but causes black smoke, which is illegal.

SPEED LIMITERS

Most UK registered goods vehicles over 3.5 tonnes gross weight must have speed limiters restricting their top speed to 60 mph (96 kph), while separate EU legislation requires goods vehicles over 12 tonnes gross weight to have their speed limiters set to a maximum speed of 90 kph (56 mph). They must be in good working order, but it is a defence if a vehicle was being driven to a place for a speed limiter to be repaired.

TOWING

Goods vehicles may tow only one trailer (but see below) except when a rigid vehicle tows a broken-down vehicle on a towing ambulance – although legally counted as towing two trailers, this is allowed. A rigid vehicle may tow a broken-down *unladen* articulated vehicle, when it counts as one trailer only, but if the articulated vehicle is loaded it counts as two trailers and cannot legally be towed by a normal goods vehicle – only by a vehicle classed as a locomotive.

A rigid goods vehicle can tow two trailers instead of only one, when one of the trailers is a towing dolly and the other is a semi-trailer – legally known as a composite trailer and counted as a single trailer.

Two vehicles joined by a tow rope or chain must not be more than 4.5 metres apart – there is no limit when a solid tow bar is used. If the distance between the two vehicles is more than 1.5 metres the rope, chain or bar must be made clearly visible from both sides.

TELEVISIONS IN VEHICLES

It is illegal for a vehicle to have a television that the driver can view directly or by reflection, except where it displays only information about the state of the vehicle or its equipment, its location and the road on which it is travelling, to assist when reversing and to help the driver find his destination (eg, sat/nav equipment).

OPENING OF DOORS

It is an offence to cause injury or danger to other road users by opening vehicle doors carelessly. Particular care should be taken when opening rear van doors to ensure that no danger is caused to pedestrians or other road users, and if they are left open for on-street loading/unloading they should be secured so as not to swing or blow into pedestrians or cyclists.

EURO EXHAUST EMISSIONS

Post-1991 diesel vehicles over 3.5 tonnes gross weight must comply with exhaust emission limits on the amount of nitrous oxide (NOx), carbon monoxide (CO) and unburned hydrocarbons (HC) discharged into the atmosphere. EU standards apply as follows: Euro-1 from 1 July 1992, Euro-2 from 1 October 1996, Euro-3 from 1 October 2001, Euro-4 from 1 October 2005 and Euro-5 from 1 October 2008. Users must maintain vehicle engines and emission control equipment (ie the catalytic converter) in good working order.

4.2

Goods vehicle lighting and marking

It is common these days to see heavy trucks festooned with an array of spot and fog lights mounted either on the cab roof or below the front grill, or both. While there is freedom for truck drivers or operators to fit these additional lights it is important that the law is complied with as to how they are positioned and used. It is illegal:

- to show a red light to the front;
- to show a white light to the rear except when reversing (and apart from a shielded white light illuminating the rear number plate);
- for front headlights, spot lights and fog lights, and rear fog lights to cause dazzle to other road users;
- to use front fog lights mounted in pairs (but *not* above 1,200 millimetres from the ground), *without* the headlamps being lit, except in seriously reduced visibility.

Vehicles used on a public road after lighting-up time must display the following obligatory lights, other lights and reflectors:

- two white main-beam headlamps (capable of being dipped);
- two white front position lamps (ie, side lamps);
- two red rear position lamps (ie, rear lamps);
- two red rear stop lamps;
- two red reflex reflectors at the rear;
- one or two red rear fog lamps on post-1 April 1980 vehicles;
- direction indicators on either side showing to the front and rear and capable of giving hazard warning on post-1 April 1986 vehicles;

- rear number plate light (shielded);
- certain vehicles/trailers require side and end-outline marker lamps, side-facing reflectors and rear reflective markings.

Lighting-up time is from sunset to sunrise for sidelights and from half an hour after sunset until half an hour before sunrise (ie, defined as the 'hours of darkness') for dipped-beam headlamps.

All lights and reflectors must be kept clean and in good working order at all times and maintained so vehicles can be used legally on the road during the hours of darkness.

NIGHT PARKING OF GOODS VEHICLES

Goods vehicles over 1,525 kilograms unladen weight (ulw), trailers and vehicles with projecting loads must show side- and rear lights at all times when parked during lighting up time. Light goods vehicles (ie, up to 1,525 kilograms ulw) do not need to show lights at night when parked on restricted roads (ie, a 30mph (48kph) or lower, speed limit area), if they are either in a recognized parking place (outlined by lamps or traffic signs) or on the nearside, close to and parallel to the kerb, facing the direction of travel and with no part of the vehicle within 10 metres of a road junction (ie, on either side of the road).

Parking in lay-bys separated from the main carriageway only by a broken white line, after lighting-up time without sidelights and other obligatory lights as appropriate being lit is an offence, and the driver will be prosecuted if caught. This does not apply where the lay-by is segregated from the highway.

On any road where these conditions are not met, front and rear position lights must be shown. Vehicles parked overnight should be on the nearside unless they are in a one-way street or a parking place and they must not cause obstruction.

HEADLAMPS

Vehicles must have two headlamps showing white or yellow lights to the front – both lamps must be the same colour. They must have dipping equipment and be adjusted so they do not cause dazzle. Headlamps must be used on unlit roads* at night, but switched off when the vehicle is stationary, except at traffic stops.

*Note: roads with no street lamps or street lamps more than 200 yards (180 metres) apart.

Lights in poor visibility

Sidelights and headlights must be used in poor daytime visibility conditions such as fog, smoke, heavy rain, spray or snow. If matching fog or fog and spot lights are fitted in pairs these may be used instead of headlights, but sidelights and other marker lights must be on. The rear fog light must also be used in such conditions, but it must be switched off when visibility improves (see also below).

SIDE MARKER LAMPS

Red and white side marker lights must be fitted to certain long vehicles and trailers.

END-OUTLINE MARKER LAMPS

Two white lights at the front and two red lights at the rear are required on vehicles 2.1 metres or more wide.

FOG AND SPOT LAMPS

Fog and spot lamps if fitted should be mounted and used in pairs. They must show either white or yellow lights, be adjusted so as not to dazzle other road users and used *only* in reduced visibility (ie, less than 100 metres). If fitted and used singly, the headlamps must also be used. They must be no more than 1,200 millimetres from the ground and 400 millimetres in from the outer edges of the vehicle.

REVERSING LAMPS

One or two white reversing lamps may be fitted that are operated automatically when in reverse gear or by a switch in the cab so long as a warning tells the driver the lights are on. They must not dazzle other road users.

STOP LAMPS

Most goods vehicles must have two red stop lamps.

DIRECTION INDICATORS

Vehicles must have amber direction indicators at the front and rear and side repeater indicators that flash between 60 and 120 times a minute with a warning in the cab.

HAZARD WARNING

Vehicles must have direction indicators that operate as a hazard warning to other road users with a warning light to advise the driver when they are in use. These may be used when the vehicle, or another vehicle, is broken down, for an accident or other emergency or when causing a temporary obstruction while loading or unloading.

REAR FOG LAMPS

Vehicles and trailers need either one or two rear fog lamps, which are wired so they operate only when the other statutory vehicle lights are on – but not into the brake/stop light circuit – and must not cause dazzle. An indicator in the cab must show when they are on. They should be used only in poor visibility (ie, in fog, smoke, heavy rain or spray, snow, dense cloud, etc), while the vehicle is moving or during an enforced stop (eg, a motorway hold-up). The *Highway Code* recommends their use only when visibility is below 100 metres.

REAR REFLECTORS

Vehicles must have two red reflectors facing squarely to the rear.

SIDE-FACING REFLECTORS

Vehicles more than 6 metres long and trailers more than 5 metres long must have amber side-facing reflectors on each side.

SWIVELLING SPOT LAMPS

White swivelling spotlights may be used to illuminate an accident or breakdown scene provided the vehicle also has an amber rotating beacon.

BLUE FRONT-FACING LIGHTS

Blue front-facing lights may be fitted on goods vehicles, provided the light remains static. Flashing blue lights may be used only on emergency service vehicles (eg police, fire, ambulance, lifeboat or mines rescue vehicles) – not on commercial trucks or private cars.

VEHICLE MARKINGS

Number plates

Vehicles must have reflective number plates, except those over 7.5 tonnes, which need rear reflective markers. Drivers should ensure that number plates are securely fixed, especially those on semi-trailers, and are indirectly illuminated when the other lights are on. It is an offence to fail to display a rear number plate, to display a wrong number plate, or a number plate made up using an unauthorized lettering style, or for the plate not to be illuminated at night.

Height warning

Vehicles and trailers with a travelling height greater than 3 metres must have a notice in the cab showing the overall travelling height, and vehicles with high-level power-operated equipment must also have a visible warning device to alert the driver if the equipment moves while travelling.

Hazard marking

Vehicles carrying dangerous, radioactive or explosive loads whether in bulk or in packages must display appropriate dangerous goods markers and hazard symbols in accordance with ADR requirements.

Rear reflective markings

Goods vehicles (with some exceptions such as car or boat transporters) over 7.5 tonnes gross weight and trailers over 3.5 tonnes must have rear reflective markers.

4.3

Vehicle checks and defect reporting

An essential part of the process for achieving high standards of safety for goods vehicles and trailers is their regular inspection and maintenance. While it is the operator's duty to ensure that, at all times, vehicles and trailers are in a safe, fit and roadworthy condition when used on the road and that they have been tested annually at a Department for Transport (ie VOSA) Goods Vehicle Testing Station, the LGV driver also has responsibilities with regard to the mechanical condition of his vehicle.

The penalties for failing to maintain vehicles properly are high. Besides the risk of heavy fines, the operator may lose his 'O' licence since a satisfactory state of maintenance is one of the factors taken into account by the Traffic Commissioner when reviewing such licences. The driver too can be penalized for driving a defective or unsafe vehicle on the road. Additionally, it is a well-known fact that inadequately maintained vehicles tend to cause or become involved in a greater proportion of road accidents.

DAILY SAFETY CHECKS

Drivers should carry out daily safety checks of their vehicle *before* starting out on the first journey of the day. These include:

- the engine oil, water and battery levels;
- wheels and wheel-nuts (ie, looking for signs that the nuts may be loose);
- tyre condition (ie, for wear and signs of damage) and making a visual check of pressures (ie, looking for signs of partial deflation, especially on the inner tyre of twin wheel sets);
- lights, reflectors, direction indicators and vehicle markers (ie, check for

cleanliness, correct operation of all lights and for signs of damage to lenses and marker boards etc);

- windscreen wipers and washers (ie, for functionality and that washer reservoirs are full);
- the horn;
- driving mirrors (ie, for cleanliness, signs of damage and correct adjustment);
- the trailer coupling, brake hoses and electrical connections (ie, ensuring proper connections are made, that lights work and that landing legs are properly retracted);
- the vehicle/trailer body to ensure it is secure, that closures work properly and that there is no damage (especially jagged edges or projections that might injure anybody walking past);
- the load to ensure it is secure either on or within the bodywork, that all securing devices have been correctly applied and tightened, that there is no risk of the load shifting during transit and that loose loads have been fully covered or netted to stop them falling or being blown from the vehicle;
- warning instruments; and
- testing the brakes *before* driving out on to the road.

Ideally, these daily checks should be carried out against a printed checklist to ensure that nothing is missed.

DEFECT REPORTING BY DRIVERS

Besides their legal obligation to carry out daily safety checks of their vehicles and trailers, LGV drivers also have a duty, as a condition of their employer's 'O' licence, to report, in writing, any mechanical or safety defect in their vehicle. This is to ensure that safety faults on heavy vehicles are not ignored or left unrepaired, when they may cause an accident.

The vehicle operator must establish a proper system for drivers to make these reports in writing, which should clearly state the vehicle registration number, the nature of the defect, the name of the driver making the report and the date of the report. Reported defects must be rectified at the earliest opportunity and a record made showing when the repair was carried out, by what means, by whom and the date.

4.4

Legal requirements for special loads

While most LGV drivers spend their working lives working with mundane everyday products, others are involved with highly specialized loads requiring special training, especially in safety and legal responsibilities. The most obvious example is the carriage of dangerous goods, but similarly there is the carriage of abnormal and projecting loads, livestock, food, sand and ballast loads and shipping containers, all of which are strictly regulated for safety reasons.

DANGEROUS SUBSTANCES

LGV drivers involved in the carriage of dangerous goods either in bulk in road tankers or in packages have particular responsibilities to ensure that their activities are carried out with the utmost safety. They need to understand the complex legal requirements applying to this form of transport, as indeed their dangerous goods vocational training certificate, which they must hold to be able to undertake this sort of work, will testify. Euro-wide regulations cover the carriage of dangerous goods by road based on:

- their classification, packaging and labelling;
- their carriage by road in bulk loads or in small consignments or packages;
- the training and certification of dangerous goods drivers;
- the certification of Dangerous Goods Safety Advisors (DGSAs).

Carriage requirements

Drivers must not carry unauthorized passengers and must not open any package containing dangerous goods unless authorized. No matches or lighters (or anything capable of producing a flame or sparks) must be carried on vehicles. Drivers must be provided with the following 'transport documentation', in writing:

- information on the products provided by the consignor;
- the weight or volume of the load;
- the emergency action code (where appropriate) and the prescribed temperature for the goods;
- emergency information;
- any relevant additional information about the particular type of dangerous goods being carried.

It is an offence to provide false or misleading information to drivers about the particular type of dangerous goods being carried.

This documentation must be kept readily available during journeys and produced when asked for by the police or a goods vehicle examiner. When a dangerous goods-carrying trailer is detached and left parked, the transport documentation (or an authenticated copy) must be given to the owner/manager of the premises, or attached to the trailer in a readily visible position.

Documentation relating to dangerous goods no longer on a vehicle must be either removed completely, or placed in a securely closed container clearly marked to show that it does not relate to dangerous goods still on the vehicle.

Information to be displayed on containers, tanks and vehicles

Containers, tanks and vehicles used for carrying dangerous goods must display relevant information. All panels and danger signs must be kept clean and free from obstruction. It is an offence to display information when the container, tank or vehicle is not carrying dangerous goods, and to cause or permit the display of any information likely to confuse the emergency services. Signs and panels relating to dangerous goods no longer being carried must be covered or removed. It is an offence to remove panels or signs from a container, tank or vehicle carrying dangerous goods (except for updating the information) and to falsify information on any panel or sign.

Emergency action codes

Emergency action codes displayed on dangerous goods vehicles are as follows: numbers 1 to 4 indicating the equipment suitable for fire fighting and for dispersing spillages (ie, 1 = water jet, 2 = water fog, 3 = foam, 4 = dry agent). Letters indicating the appropriate precautions to take are shown in Table 4.4a.

A letter 'E' at the end of an emergency action code means that people should be evacuated from the neighbourhood.

Table 4.4a   *Emergency action cold letters and relevant precautions*

Letter	Danger of violent reaction	Protective clothing and breathing apparatus	Measures to be taken
P	Yes	Full protective clothing	Dilute
R	No	Full protective clothing	Dilute
S	Yes	Breathing apparatus	Dilute
S*	Yes	Breathing apparatus for fire	Dilute
T	No	Breathing apparatus	Dilute
T*	No	Breathing apparatus for fire	Dilute
W	Yes	Full protective clothing	Contain
X	No	Full protective clothing	Contain
Y	Yes	Breathing apparatus	Contain
Y*	Yes	Breathing apparatus for fire	Contain
Z	No	Breathing apparatus	Contain
Z*	No	Breathing apparatus for fire	Contain

*These symbols are shown as orange (or can be white) letters reversed out of a black background.

Emergency provisions

Vehicles must be equipped so the driver can take emergency measures and, where toxic gases are carried, must carry respiratory equipment to enable the crew to escape safely. In accident or emergency situations drivers must comply with the emergency information given to them. Where an incident cannot be immediately controlled, the emergency services must be notified by the quickest practical means.

Vehicles must carry portable fire extinguishers with a minimum total capacity of 12 kilograms; one must have a minimum capacity of 2 kilograms of dry powder (or other extinguishant with an equivalent test fire rating of at least 5A and 34B), suitable for fighting a fire in the engine (unless the vehicle has an automatic extinguisher system) or cab, and not likely to aggravate a fire in the load.

Vehicles must also carry at least one portable fire extinguisher with a minimum capacity of 6 kilograms of dry powder (or other extinguishant with an equivalent test fire rating of at least 2IA and 183B),* suitable for fighting a tyre or brake fire, or a fire in the load, and not likely to aggravate a fire in the engine or cab.

Note: an extinguisher is not required on a detached trailer.

* *Note: where the vehicle has a gross weight of not more than 3.5 tonnes, a 2-kilogram dry powder extinguisher (or another suitable extinguishant with a test fire rating of at least 5A and 34B) will suffice.*

It is an offence to carry an extinguisher with an overdue inspection date.

Supervision and parking of vehicles

When parked, dangerous goods vehicles must be supervised at all times by a competent person over 18 years of age. Otherwise they must be parked:

- in an isolated position in the open, but in a secure depot or factory premises;
- in a vehicle park supervised by an appropriate person who knows both the nature of the load and the whereabouts of the driver;
- in a public or private vehicle park where they are not likely to suffer damage from other vehicles;
- in a suitable open space separated from the public highway and from dwellings, and where the public does not normally pass or assemble.

None of these requirements applies when the vehicle has been damaged or has broken down on the road and the driver has left to seek assistance, provided he has taken all reasonable steps to secure it and its contents before leaving it unattended.

Driver training

Operators must ensure their drivers hold valid 'vocational training certificates' (VTCs), which they gain through training in the dangers of the dangerous goods being carried, the emergency action to be taken and their other health and safety responsibilities. VTCs are granted on successful completion of an approved course of theoretical study and practical exercises and passing an approved examination. They are valid for five years and may be extended for further five-yearly periods if in the 12 months preceding their expiry the holder has successfully completed a refresher course and passed the examination. Drivers must carry their vocational training certificates with them on all dangerous goods journeys and produce them on request by the police or a goods vehicle examiner.

CARRIAGE OF POISONOUS WASTE

Many drivers are involved with the transport and disposal of waste materials and, as such, are affected by strict regulations that make it an offence to dispose of poisonous waste in an irresponsible way. Poisonous, noxious or polluting waste must not be deposited on land where it is liable to cause an environmental hazard and anyone removing or depositing poisonous material must notify both the local authority and the river authority before doing so. Failure to comply with any of the legal requirements can result in heavy fines and the possibility of vehicles being impounded by the courts.

CONTROLLED WASTE

It is illegal for any transport operator who is not a registered carrier with the local waste authority to handle controlled waste or move it to or from any place in Great Britain. Controlled waste is any household, commercial or industrial waste. Charities, voluntary organizations and waste authorities are exempt from the rules, as are producers of controlled waste (apart from builders and demolition contractors). A Waste Transfer Note containing details of waste material being carried must show where it is from and where it is going to and the date of transfer.

OVERSIZE LOADS

Loads on normal goods vehicles (ie, within C&U regulations), which are wider or longer than the actual vehicle dimensions, may be carried provided certain special conditions regarding notification of the police and the need for attendants (ie, drivers' mates) are observed. These provisions apply where loads are more than 18.3 metres long and more than 2.9 metres wide.

ABNORMAL LOADS

C&U regulation limits on vehicle lengths, widths and weights do not apply to vehicles specially designed, constructed and used solely for the carriage of abnormal indivisible loads (known as Special Types vehicles which operate under the Special Types General Order – STGO). These are loads that cannot, without undue expense or risk of damage, be divided into two or more loads for transport by road and cannot be carried on a normal C&U vehicle. Normally, only one abnormal load is permitted, but two such loads can be carried on a single vehicle in category 1 or 2 if they are both from the same place and for the same delivery address. Special Types vehicles and their loads can be up to 2.9 metres wide (or exceptionally up to a maximum of 6.1 metres wide) and up to 27.4 metres long (where the load is carried on a combination of vehicles and trailers or on a long articulated vehicle, the 27.4 metres excludes the drawing vehicle).

The maximum weight of a Special Types vehicle must not exceed 150,000 kilograms. Three separate weight categories apply to Special Types vehicles as follows:

- category 1 – up to 50 tonnes;
- category 2 – up to 80 tonnes;
- category 3 – up to 150 tonnes.

Identification sign

Vehicles operating under the Special Types Order must display an STGO identification sign at the front with white letters on a black background.

Speed limits

Maximum permitted speeds for Special Types vehicles (subject to having suitably rated tyres) are as follows in Table 4.4b:

Table 4.4b   Maximum permitted speeds for Special Types vehicles

Vehicle category	Motorways mph (kph)	Dual carriageways mph (kph)	Other roads mph (kph)
1. Up to 46 tonnes	60 (96)	50 (80)	40 (64)
2. Up to 80 tonnes	40 (64)	35 (56)	30 (48)
3. Up to 150 tonnes	30 (48)	25 (40)	20 (32)

HIGH LOADS

While there are no legal height restrictions on vehicles or loads (except where routes are constrained by bridge heights, for example), when planning to move loads over 19ft (5.7 metres) high contact must be made with National Power to check on overhead power cables. British Telecom should also be contacted regarding its overhead lines on the route.

Most motorway bridges are at least 16ft 6in (4.95 metres) high; otherwise roadside signs on the approach to the bridge indicate the height from the road surface to the centre point. Special care is needed when attempting to pass through arched bridges where the sides may have reduced clearance and where an offset approach may be necessary (sometimes signified by road markings). Hitting a bridge is an offence and in the case of railway bridges it may involve considerable legal problems and costs resulting from infringement of railway byelaws as well as risking the lives of train travellers should the track be dislodged.

PROJECTING LOADS

A projecting load is one that projects beyond the front or rear or the side of the vehicle. Depending on the length or width of the projection, certain conditions such as the need to carry marker boards and notification of the police apply when such loads are carried.

Where a load projects more than 1 metre beyond the rear vehicle it must clearly be marked – how this should be done is not specified, but a piece of rag tied to the end is usually sufficient.

When a vehicle is carrying a load projecting more than 1 metre beyond the rear end of the vehicle an additional rear light must be carried within 1 metre of the end of the load or, if the projecting load covers the rear lights and reflectors of the vehicle, additional lights and reflectors must be fixed to the load.

When a load projects sideways more than 400 millimetres beyond the vehicle sidelights and rear lights, extra lights must be carried within 400 millimetres of the outer edges of the load at both the front and the rear.

CARRIAGE OF ANIMALS

Strict regulations exist to ensure that animals carried by road do not suffer distress or discomfort and that risk of the spread of disease is minimized. It is illegal to transport any animal in a way that causes injury or unnecessary suffering. Animals must be fed and watered before and during a journey at specified intervals according to the regulations and must be transported to their destination without delay.

CARRIAGE OF FOOD

Special regulations apply to vehicles used for the carriage of food, excluding milk and drugs. Mobile shops and food delivery vehicles and their equipment must be constructed and maintained so any food carried can be kept clean and fresh. Drivers of food vehicles should wear clean overalls and should wear a hat to prevent the meat touching their hair if they have to carry meat or bacon sides over their shoulder. They must not smoke while loading or unloading or serving the food (but they may do so in the cab of the vehicle if this is separate from the part of the vehicle in which the food is carried), and any cuts or abrasions on their hands must be covered with waterproof dressings.

If a driver or any other person concerned in the loading and unloading of food develops any infectious disease, their employer must notify the local authority health department immediately.

A local authority officer may enter and detain (but not stop while it is in motion) any food-carrying vehicle except those owned by British Rail or vehicles operated by haulage contractors.

Perishable food

Strict legislation covers the carriage of perishable food both in the United Kingdom and in Europe, mainly concerned with maintaining proper temperatures to prevent the possibility of listeria or salmonella poisoning.

SAND AND BALLAST LOADS

Sand and ballast loads must be sold in weighed quantities (normally by volume in metric measures – in multiples of 0.2 cubic metres) and carried in calibrated vehicles displaying a stamp placed on the body by the Trading Standards department of the local authority. The driver must have a signed note (ie, conveyance note) from the supplier indicating the:

- name and address of the sellers;
- name of the buyer and the address for delivery of the load;
- description of the type of ballast;
- quantity by net weight or by volume;
- details of the vehicle;
- date, time and place of loading the vehicle.

This document must be handed to the buyer before unloading begins and if he is not there it must be left at the delivery premises. Where a delivery is to be made to two or more buyers each must be given a separate document containing the details shown above. Similar requirements apply to the carriage of ready-mixed cement.

SOLID FUELS

The driver of a vehicle carrying a solid fuel load must have a document giving similar details to those mentioned above for sand and ballast loads.

CARRIAGE OF CONTAINERS

Many dangers arise from inadequate securing of ISO-type shipping containers on road vehicles. Ideally they should be carried only on vehicles fitted with proper twist locks or, failing this, should be secured by chains of sufficient strength with tensioners for adjustment.

FLY TIPPING

The tipping of rubbish (ie, waste goods and materials), demolition rubble and such materials in unauthorized places (commonly referred to as fly tipping) is illegal.

4.5

Security of vehicles and loads

The theft of goods vehicles and loads is escalating on an unprecedented scale, causing hauliers and their customers considerable disruption and substantial extra costs, not least by way of ever-increasing insurance premiums. LGV drivers may feel this is not a problem for them, but rather for their boss. However, the key to many of these thefts is where and how the driver parks his vehicle overnight or even while stopped for a daytime break. He has a duty to his employer to do everything possible to safeguard both the vehicle and its load. This is best achieved by the driver thinking carefully about what is going on around him, by following specified routes and complying with his firm's security instructions, and by being constantly vigilant about people who may be following him or observing his vehicle or about other suspicious events on the road.

OVERNIGHT PARKING

When away from base, drivers should park their vehicles in guarded security parks, particularly if loaded with high-value goods. While the number of suitable security parks is limited and they are not conveniently located, it is in everybody's interest that vehicles should not be left overnight on the roadside or on odd bits of wasteland. Keys should never be left in or on a vehicle even if supposedly secreted (eg, for another driver to pick up). Most insurers refuse to meet loss or theft claims if keys are left with a vehicle.

Most thefts occur while vehicles are parked overnight, mainly at the weekend – very few are on-road hijacking. More than half of all truck thefts are from operators' own premises, with less than 1 per cent being from supervised lorry parks. While the absence of a nationwide chain of secure lorry parks, which the industry bemoans, is a major deficiency, the message is very clear – security must begin at home.

It is well known that determined thieves will always find a way of defeating security devices on trucks and trailers, and of entering secure premises. Security for overnight lorry parking must include a strongly fenced compound with locked gates and controlled entrance and exit, floodlighting, round-the-clock manning with regular security patrols and closed-circuit TV coverage.

For many hauliers the greatest protection against lorry or load theft is for the driver to sleep in the cab. However, this has its shortcomings both in legal terms (since the driver could be considered to be still working, even when supposedly resting, if instructed to remain with the vehicle for security reasons), and in the fact that the presence of the driver is still not a guarantee that the vehicle or its load will not be stolen.

GOOD SECURITY

Good security starts with the driver – the need to employ good and honest drivers goes without saying. But the question is how to establish whether they are good and honest. Only by very careful checking of their past history and references when they are first recruited, and by careful scrutiny of their driving licence (fortunately now condensed into a single document – and for new drivers, now in photocard form with a photograph and signature of the holder), can an employer be certain.

Drivers should be trained and their attitude to security developed. They wouldn't leave their own car unlocked, windows down, radio playing etc, so why should they leave their employer's truck like that? They must learn to set the immobilizers and alarms without fail, and to lock the vehicle and remove the keys every time they leave the cab. The fact that they are likely to be gone for only a minute or two is no excuse – determined thieves only need a minute. Besides which, the small print in insurance policies invariably specifies that failure to set immobilizers and alarms will invalidate the insurance.

The same applies when delivering from the tailboard, especially in public places such as in the High Street. Drivers should seek the assistance of customer staff to stand guard before they lower the tail-lift and open the doors or raise the shutter, otherwise the vehicle should be locked every time they leave it.

A key aspect of security is the need to maintain secrecy about the loads carried, routes followed and stopping places, and so on. If criminals know that vehicles carrying valuable loads (probably overheard in a pub or roadside cafe) follow regular routes and that drivers stop at particular cafes and truckstops at regular times, it makes their job so easy. But remember, it serves no purpose for the operator to go to the trouble of planning different routes and timings if drivers always filter back to the same old cafes for their breaks, which they often do.

Truck thieves can pinpoint a place for a hijack, assess the timing and check it out a number of times before actually making a hit. The driver may not be aware that his vehicle is being watched for such purposes, but this is where observation and vigilance pays off. Strange happenings on a journey – unusual sightings, such as the same car or van parked in the same odd place on a number of occasions; the same people hanging around the depot or a delivery location – should all be reported and logged; it may help to prevent a theft or it may help the police to track down a missing vehicle and the thieves who stole it.

Drivers are the key to combating theft in many other ways:

- by keeping vehicles locked and keys secure (not left in the ignition and not hidden on the vehicle – rest assured that every possible secure place the driver can think of on the vehicle to hide keys has already been thought of by the thieves);
- by not talking about loads and routes;
- by not giving unauthorized lifts;
- by not stopping in obscure or remote places;
- by trying to park with the vehicle within sight at cafes and truck stops;
- by backing close up to a wall, another vehicle or other obstacle at night to prevent access to the rear of the vehicle;
- by checking documentation to make sure the load is what it is intended to be – for example, the right goods and number of packages;
- by checking delivery addresses – and double-checking if an address is changed by somebody at the consignee's premises;
- by checking when help is given in unloading that only the correct items and correct number of items are off-loaded – a mistake might be made, but on the other hand, it might be deliberate;
- by making sure no unauthorized persons enter the load area. Illegal immigrants are an escalating problem, putting the driver and company at risk – check the vehicle before driving off.

Part 5
Health and safety

5.1

Driver health and safety

Heavy vehicle drivers will undoubtedly know about the keen emphasis that is placed on workplace safety. They should know too that to be a professional driver they must be aware of, and fully understand, the requirements of health and safety legislation. Virtually every newspaper and magazine has a reference to such issues, from reports of accidents where health and safety inspectors are called in to investigate the causes and prosecute those who, by failing to assess risks and take steps to ensure safety, may have caused the accident, to articles about how one can become more fit or protect one's health by making lifestyle changes such as adopting exercise regimes or changing eating habits.

Truck drivers generally, and truck driving as an occupation, are not renowned for being the epitome of a healthy lifestyle, nor for being at the forefront in adopting safe working practices. According to the Health and Safety Executive (HSE), some 400 people are killed annually and a further 25,000 are forced to leave work each year and are unable to work again due to neglect of proper workplace health and safety procedures.

Furthermore, the HSE says being struck by a moving vehicle is one of the most common causes of fatal injury among workers, while AWAKE (the sleep and fatigue research organization) says more lorry drivers are killed at work than any other type of employee, predominantly from tiredness and falling asleep at the wheel.

However, things are changing; unsafe working practices are strictly taboo since we now have a considerable body of health and safety legislation, backed up by powerful enforcement procedures and stringent penalties, and drivers are being encouraged to change their lifestyles, especially their eating habits.

RISKS ON THE ROAD AND AT WORK

We live in a world where there is a constant risk of incidents and accidents, whether on the road, at work, or even at home. The following text outlines some of these on the road and at work risks, but such is the emphasis these days on such matters by the Health and Safety Executive (HSE) that even LGV drivers need to be aware of the basic need to assess what particular risks may present themselves while at work.

Employers and employees both have a statutory duty of care under the Health and Safety at Work Act to ensure the health, safety and welfare of their employees and of other persons. In undertaking this duty they should carry out risk assessments.

Risk assessment

Many accidents could be prevented by simply examining what actually goes on in your place of work or in loading, unloading and driving your vehicle. The idea is, as far as is possible, to remove and control the hazards that are apparent and take the necessary steps to make sure that the operation is safe. This can be done in a quite simple and methodical way following just five key steps:

Step 1: Look for the hazards.
Step 2: Decide who might be harmed as a result of these hazards and how they may be harmed.
Step 3: Consider what the risks are and decide whether the existing precautions are adequate or whether more should be done to prevent harm.
Step 4: Keep a note of your findings for future reference.
Step 5: Review your assessment at regular intervals and revise it if necessary.

NB: A hazard is simply something that can cause harm. Risk is the chance of anyone suffering harm from such a hazard.

Accidents that may occur on the road are obvious and well-enough known to the skilled LGV driver, but in workplaces different dangers arise. The most common and serious of these is when lorries are being manoeuvred and reversed, especially in confined spaces. Too many people are killed and injured in such incidents each year, as indeed are many people injured by falling from lorries while loading or unloading. Taking great care at all times, driving at very slow speeds, the use of reversing bleepers and the aid of a banksman are all safety measures that can prevent accidents and may save lives.

The consequences of all accidents whether on the road or in work premises, whether the injured person was to blame or not, causes great trauma to the person/s involved, to their work colleagues, to their employer and most particularly to their family and friends. But that is not the end of the story – accidents involve considerable cost, much of which may not be recoverable through insurance. We like to think we are well covered by insurance, but there are the inconvenience costs of disrupted work schedules, the hire of replacement vehicles and equipment and, worst of all, the fact that some people may never fully recover from the loss of a loved one.

HEALTH AND SAFETY ON THE ROAD

Official statistics show that some 3,500 people are killed annually on Britain's roads, another 40,000 or so are seriously injured and more than a quarter of a million people sustain slight injuries every year in road accidents in this country. It is very useful for the LGV driver to adopt a safety code as follows:

- Wear good protective clothing and especially strong (or protective) footwear at all times when working.
- Carry a few items of essential equipment (as well as spares such as light bulbs, fuses, fan belts and wiper blades, for example), which could help them:
  - in a breakdown or emergency situation;
  - if they need to assist another stranded driver;
  - at the scene of an accident; or
  - if they are caught out by adverse weather during the winter.
- Carry a basic first aid kit and a good torch – these are most important items – plus a few simple tools (eg, screwdriver, pliers, adjustable wrench).
- Carry a fire extinguisher suitable for engine and electrical fires; a warning triangle is also useful (compulsory for dangerous goods vehicles and when driving abroad).
- Carry other items like:
  - a tow rope;
  - a set of heavy-duty jump leads; and
  - an accident reporting kit (available from the Hauliers Shop).

For winter driving it is useful to have:

- de-icer spray and a good windscreen scraper;
- a shovel;
- waterproof clothing and rubber boots;
- gloves and a hat;
- a blanket;
- a thermos flask of hot tea/coffee/chocolate; and
- a bar of chocolate or other high-calorie food.

Stranded drivers have died for the want of such items, even in Great Britain!

HEALTH AND SAFETY AT WORK

The principal objectives of the Health and Safety at Work Act are:

- to maintain and improve standards of health and safety for people at work;
- to protect people other than those at work against risks to their health or safety arising from the work activities of others;

- to control the storage and use of explosives, and highly flammable or dangerous substances, and to prevent their unlawful acquisition, possession and use;
- to control the emission into the atmosphere of noxious or offensive fumes or substances from work premises.

Duties of employees

The law says that employees (which obviously includes LGV drivers) must take reasonable care for their own safety and that of other people and cooperate in ensuring that statutory duties relating to health and safety at work are complied with. In particular, it is illegal for anybody to interfere with or misuse, either intentionally or recklessly, anything provided in the interests of health, safety or welfare.

Manual handling

Regulations exist to help reduce back and other injuries caused by manually handling loads. Employees must be given training in load handling and precise information about load weights, centres of gravity and the heaviest side of unevenly loaded packages, and employers should not expect employees to manually handle loads that involve risk of injury. Where this is not possible, injury risks should be assessed and reduced to the absolute minimum, or alternative ways found for doing the job without manual handling (eg, by mechanization or by completely eliminating some activities).

Personal protective equipment (PPE)

Employees must be provided with suitable personal protective equipment (to protect them from extreme temperatures, poor visibility and adverse weather) where there are risks to their health and safety. High-visibility clothing should be worn when working in vulnerable situations such as on docksides and in transport depots and terminals. Self-employed drivers must provide their own protective and high-visibility clothing where necessary.

Lifting operations

Regulations concerned with lifting operations also apply to forklift trucks, lorry-mounted cranes and hydraulic tail-lifts and to front-end loaders on tractors. Importantly too, they also apply to tipping vehicles. Drivers should be given adequate information about the safe operation and correct methods of use of such equipment and should also be properly trained in all relevant health and safety requirements for its use.

Work-related stress

Work-related stress is a major issue, not least because of the number of working days lost annually due to employee stress-related ailments. All employers have a legal duty to ensure that their employees are not made ill by their work or do not suffer work-related stress. Transport employers particularly need to recognize that pressures of present-day traffic conditions, tight delivery schedules and the plethora of road traffic rules and regulations can cause drivers to suffer stress-related illness.

Stress is a person's natural reaction to excessive pressure – it is not a disease. However, excessive and long-term stress can lead to mental and physical ill health causing, for example, depression, nervous breakdown and even heart disease. Stress in one person can lead to stress in other people who have to cover their work.

It has been proven that the costs of stress can be high: excessive staff turn-over, increased absence through sickness, reduced work performance, increased lateness and more customer complaints. An employer who ignores signs of stress among employees or who fails to take the necessary action to reduce stress may face claims for compensation from employees who have suffered ill health from this cause. The HSE says that half a million people in Britain are thought to suffer from work-related stress, costing industry billions of pounds in lost time.

FIRST AID

Employers should provide first aid training and first aid boxes, identified as such with a white cross on a green background, and ideally containing the following materials and nothing else:

1 × guidance card;
20 × individually wrapped sterile, adhesive dressings of assorted sizes;
2 × sterile eye pads, with attachment;
6 × individually wrapped triangular bandages;
6 × safety pins;
6 × sterile, unmedicated wound dressings (approx 13 centimetres × 9 centimetres);
2 × sterile, unmedicated wound dressings (approx 28 centimetres × 17.5 centimetres).

These materials should be replenished as soon as possible after use and items that deteriorate or become outdated must be replaced. First aid boxes and kits should be examined frequently to make sure they are fully equipped.

Note: it is unwise to store non-listed medical supplies, such as painkiller tablets, or any other items in first aid boxes. This may contravene the COSHH regulations and could result in prosecution.

Travelling first aid kits

An employer does not need to make first aid provisions for employees working away from base, but where the work involves travelling for long distances in remote areas, from which access to NHS accident and emergency facilities may be difficult, or where employees are using potentially dangerous tools or machinery, small travelling first aid kits should be provided. The contents of these may need to vary according to the circumstances in which they are to be used, but kits broadly similar to those described above will suffice.

NB: suitable first aid kits for drivers can be purchased from most chemists.

First aid on the road

Over 300,000 people are injured in UK road traffic accidents annually, unfortunately some 3,500 of them dying as a result. Any help that a road user can give at the scene of an accident may just save a life, or give much-needed comfort to a traumatized casualty. The following guidelines have been established for dealing with casualties at the scene of a road accident:

- Assess the situation:
  - What has happened?
  - Is there any further danger to you or the casualty? (Remember, roadsides are particularly dangerous places to treat a casualty.)
  - How many people are injured?
  - Is anybody else able to help?
- Assess the casualty:
  - What is wrong with the casualty?
  - Is it necessary to move them, or can they be left safely in their current position? Remember, further injuries can be caused through unnecessary movement of the casualty.
- Do you need assistance?
  - Do you need assistance from the emergency services?
  - Don't forget, other first aiders/bystanders can help you.
  - When you ask for help from the emergency services they will need to know:
    - the precise location of the incident;
    - what happened;
    - the injuries involved;
    - how many people are injured.
- Make a diagnosis:
  - What happened to the casualty? Did they fall, faint or have a bump on the head?
  - Look for signs such as bleeding, swelling or unaligned limbs.
  - If the casualty is conscious, ask them where they feel pain or if they went dizzy before the accident.

- Priorities – the priorities of first aid are usually referred to as the 'ABC of first aid':
  - *Airway* – Check inside the mouth and remove any visible obstruction. Put your fingertips under the point of the casualty's chin. Lift the chin to open the airway.
  - *Breathing* – Spend at least 10 seconds looking, listening and feeling for breathing. If the casualty is breathing, put him/her in the recovery position. Continue to monitor the patient's breathing.
  - *Circulation* – Look, listen and feel for normal breathing, coughing or movement by the victim. Only if you have been trained to do so, check the carotid pulse.
- Priorities of general treatment (the three B's):
  - *Breathing* (see above).
  - *Bleeding*. Stop bleeding by raising the injured limb above the heart. Apply pressure to the wound with pad, bandage, clean handkerchief or towel.
  - *Bones*. If necessary, immobilize a broken arm in a sling. If a broken leg is suspected, keep the casualty still.
- Whilst you're waiting for the arrival of the emergency services:
  - Look for changes in the casualty's condition, monitoring the vital signs.
  - Check that your treatment is adequate and successful.
  - Cooperate with the emergency services when they arrive.

Note: acknowledgement for these guidelines: The West Yorkshire Metropolitan Ambulance Service.

VEHICLE REVERSING

According to the HSE, nearly one-quarter of all deaths involving vehicles happen while they are reversing, hence its advice as follows to those concerned:

- Identify all the risks and decide how to remove them.
- Remove the need for reversing.
- Exclude people from the area in which vehicles are permitted to reverse.
- Minimize the distance vehicles have to reverse.
- Make sure all staff are adequately trained.
- Use a properly trained banksperson or guide (an HSE booklet illustrates the signals such a person should use to ensure safety when vehicles are reversing).
- Decide how the driver is to make and keep contact with the banksperson.
- Make sure all visiting drivers are briefed.
- Make sure all vehicle manoeuvres are properly supervised.

Additionally:

- Increase the area the driver can see.
- Fit a reversing alarm.
- Use other safety devices (ie, trip, sensing and scanning devices, and barriers to prevent vehicles over-running steep edges).

SAFE TIPPING AND LIFTING

Great care is needed when operating tipping vehicles and those with lorry-mounted cranes and suchlike. There are two principal risks. Firstly, when elevated bodies (or crane jibs) come into contact with overhead power cables or are sufficiently close for arcing to occur in wet conditions. The specific danger for the driver (or anybody else near the vehicle) lies in touching the vehicle body or tipping controls while there is contact with the power cable. Drivers are safe provided they remain in the cab, where the vehicle tyres prevent completion of an electrical circuit. The electricity supply industry advises drivers to remain in their cabs and drive clear. If this is not possible they should jump from the cab, but *NOT* touch any part of the vehicle while doing so, and then remain well clear until an electricity engineer has been contacted and reports that it is safe to return to the vehicle.

Secondly, when tipping or using lorry-mounted cranes on soft or uneven ground. The driver should always ensure he is parked on level and solid ground before raising the body to tip the load or before lowering stabilizer legs.

SAFE PARKING

Many accidents occur when parking vehicles and trailers. Proper parking procedures should be established for transport depots, especially with regard to parking areas and level standing for detached semi-trailers. A common failing is dropping semi-trailers on soft or uneven ground, allowing the landing gear to sink and the trailer to lean or even topple over to the side, which causes difficulty in recoupling. Nose-diving is another common occurrence where nose-heavy semi-trailers are not supported with trestles when left detached.

Driver deaths have arisen from the bad coupling practices whereby the driver inserts the red air-hose – releasing the emergency brakes on the semi-trailer, without first checking that both the semi-trailer ratchet brake and the tractive-unit hand brake are fully applied – allowing the vehicle combination to move while the driver is still out of the cab. Other potential sources of accident are when articulated combinations are recoupled near to walls and loading bays. If brakes are not properly set the semi-trailer may shunt backwards as the tractive unit is driven under the trailer coupling plate, damaging premises and risking the life of any unseen person walking behind the trailer.

SAFETY IN DOCK PREMISES

Drivers who work in or visit dock premises and roll-on/roll-off ferry ports must wear high-visibility clothing (eg, fluorescent jackets, waistcoats, belts or sashes) at all times when out of the vehicle cab, including when on the vehicle decks of the ferry. Protective headgear (hard hats) must be worn in areas where there is likely to be a danger of falling objects from above (eg, where cranes are working). Drivers must leave their vehicle cab when parked on straddle-carrier grids or where containers are being lifted on to or off the vehicle.

5.2

The safety of vehicles and loads

GOODS VEHICLE SAFETY

Goods vehicle drivers are under constant pressure to be more safety conscious in their work, mainly due to the demands of the health and safety at work legislation described in Chapter 5.1. Regular and efficient maintenance of vehicles and trailers, as required by law (see also Chapter 4.3), is a crucial means of ensuring their safety on the road. Similarly, daily safety checks of vehicles and defect reports by drivers are key safety procedures. Ensuring that vehicles are safely loaded within their maximum payload and axle weight limits is also important for road safety.

Additionally, there are concerns about safe load handling and the use of loading aids (forklift trucks, for example) and with regard to vehicle manoeuvring in depots and works premises, which alone results in many workplace deaths and injuries annually – see Chapter 5.1.

It is important for the professional driver to remember that whether driving, loading, unloading, carrying out daily safety checks or even when washing or cleaning heavy vehicles, a moment of carelessness or a fleeting diversion of attention can result in an accident in which he, or other people, may be hurt or, even worse, killed. The safety message is clear: *take care and concentrate on the job in hand at all times*.

THE VEHICLE 'USER'

The law requires 'users' of goods vehicles to ensure they are maintained and operated safely and within the law at all times. In this context the 'user' of a vehicle is:

- the driver of a vehicle, driving on behalf of his employer;
- an owner-driver who uses his vehicle in connection with his own business;
- the owner of a vehicle who employs a driver to drive it for him;
- the hirer of a vehicle (ie, one that is borrowed, leased or hired without a driver) who drives it himself or pays the wages of a driver to drive it for him.

It is the 'user' who may be prosecuted in any circumstance where the law is broken. Even the driver is liable as the user of the vehicle, although only an employee, because he is driving it on the road in connection with his employment. Therefore, he too is responsible if it is not in a safe and legal condition, or is overloaded beyond legal limits. Thus, for example, if a vehicle is found with a defective tyre, or overloaded when stopped by the police or enforcement officials, both he and his employer would be prosecuted for the relevant offences. Only if one or other of them could show that they had no reasonable way of knowing of the defect or of the overload would there be any hope of escaping conviction.

C&U REQUIREMENTS

The C&U (construction and use) regulations (see also Chapter 4.1) require all vehicles and trailers, and all their parts and accessories, and the weight, distribution, packing and adjustment of their loads, to be such that no danger or nuisance is caused to any person on the vehicle or on the road. Also, they must not be used for any purpose for which they are so unsuited as to cause danger.

It is an offence if a bulk or loose load causes nuisance, as well as a danger to other road users – these loads must be properly secured, if necessary by physical restraint (ie, sheeted and roped), to stop them falling or being blown from a vehicle.

THE SAFETY OF LOADS ON VEHICLES

The way in which vehicles are loaded and loads are secured is essential for safe vehicle operation. Similarly, for safety reasons, loads should not exceed the maximum permitted in law for the vehicle as shown on its 'Ministry plate', nor should they be loaded so as to cause individual maximum axle weights to be exceeded.

THE DRIVER'S RESPONSIBILITIES

The driver is legally responsible for the safety of the load on his vehicle and for ensuring that all statutory requirements are met. In particular, he should have regard for:

- its overall safety;
- the safe use of load-securing equipment;
- the way the load is distributed on the vehicle and secured;
- the weight limits on individual axles and on the whole vehicle.

With specialized loads such as those that are exceptionally large or heavy, those comprising dangerous substances (whether in bulk or in packages) and when animals are carried, for example, further specific requirements must be strictly observed. It is important for the driver to be fully aware of the appropriate regulations and understand how they apply to him. He can be prosecuted, as well as his employer, for using a vehicle on the road with an unsafe or insecure load, for failing to comply with specific load regulations or for having an overweight vehicle. The penalties are severe and the driver risks losing his driving licence.

SAFETY OF LOADS

The C&U (Road Vehicles [Construction and Use] Regulations 1986 as amended) regulations make it a specific legal requirement for all vehicles and trailers, and all their parts, to be safe and not likely to cause danger to any person. This also applies to the weight of the vehicle, the way it is loaded and how the load is distributed, packed and adjusted. Furthermore, vehicles and trailers must not be used for any unsuitable purpose that may cause or be likely to cause danger or nuisance. It is illegal for bulk and loose loads to cause a nuisance or danger to other road users and they must be prevented from falling or being blown from the vehicle.

The DfT Code of Practice called *The Safety of Loads on Vehicles* was used to provide the following list of DOs and DON'Ts for drivers and others concerned with the loading of vehicles. While these points remain valid, they are not specifically included in the latest version of the Code published in 2002:

DO

1. Make sure your vehicle's load space and the condition of its load platform are suitable for the type and size of your load.
2. Do make use of load anchorage points.
3. Do make sure you have enough lashings and that they are in good condition and strong enough to secure your load.
4. Do tighten up the lashings or other restraining devices.
5. Do make sure that the front of the load is abutted against the headboard, or other fixed restraint.
6. Do use wedges, scotches etc, so that your load cannot move.
7. Do make sure that loose bulk loads cannot fall or be blown off your vehicle.

DON'T

1. Don't overload your vehicle or its axles.
2. Don't load your vehicle too high.
3. Don't use rope hooks to restrain heavy loads.
4. Don't forget that the size, nature and position of your load will affect the handling of your vehicle.
5. Don't forget to check your load:
   - before moving off;
   - after you have travelled a few miles;
   - if you remove or add items to your load during the journey.
6. Don't take risks.

DISTRIBUTION AND STABILITY OF LOADS

It is the driver's responsibility to ensure that at all times the load on his vehicle is correctly distributed according to the maximum permissible axle loadings (see the Ministry plate in the cab) and that it is well secured and safe. As mentioned above, this is a vital aspect of safe operation – loads that fall from vehicles can cause serious injury (or even a fatality) to other persons on the road or the pavement, or result in a vehicle accident with similar consequences. Insecure or unsafe loads can result in prosecution and may incur heavy fines as well as potential loss of the operator's 'O' licence and the driver's LGV vocational entitlement to drive such vehicles.

When loading a vehicle, care must be taken that the load is evenly distributed to ensure stability of the vehicle and to comply with the legal limits on axle weights and gross weight. On multi-delivery work the driver must make sure that when part of the load has been off-loaded during delivery, none of the axles has become overloaded due to the transfer of weight. This can happen even though the vehicle gross weight is still within legal limits. All loads should be securely and safely fixed and roped and sheeted if necessary. It is an offence to have an insecure load or a load that causes danger to other road users and both the driver and his employer can be prosecuted, fined heavily (up to £5,000 per offence) and have their respective LGV driving entitlement and 'O' licence penalized.

Gross weight calculation

The gross weight of a goods vehicle is the unladen weight of that vehicle plus the weight of its driver, any passengers carried and fuel (ie the tare weight), plus the load and load-securing devices – in other words, the weight of the vehicle when it is laden and ready for the road. The permissible maximum weight is that shown on the VOSA (Ministry) plate and plating certificate.

Vehicles may only be operated up to the maximum legal limit as shown on this plate, which is not necessarily that which is shown on the manufacturer's plate.

Axle weight calculation

In order to calculate front or rear axle weights for vehicles, the following formula is used:

1. Determine the vehicle wheelbase.
2. Determine payload.
3. Calculate the front loadbase (ie the centreline of the front axle to the centre of gravity of the load); or calculate the rear loadbase (i.e. centreline of rear axle to the centre of gravity of the load).
4. Apply the formula as follows:

$$\frac{\text{Payload (P)} \times \text{Loadbase Distance (D)}}{\text{Wheelbase}}$$

NB:
1. If *front* loadbase distance is used, the answer will be the weight on the *rear* axle.
2. If *rear* loadbase distance is used, the answer will be the weight on the *front* axle.

LOADING UNITS AND LOAD SECURING

Loads carried by goods vehicles vary considerably in the way they are presented for loading, how they are packed and stacked and how they have to be handled on to and off the vehicle. Many are bulk loads (such as sand and gravel, grain and loose fertilizer, and chemicals in liquid, granule or powder form) carried in tipper and tanker vehicles. Other loads comprise large units, from ISO shipping containers to individual items of plant or machinery which have to be craned on and off vehicles.

However, there are many everyday types of load that are loaded by hand directly on to the vehicle loading area (commonly referred to as 'hand balled'). This slow, inefficient and dangerous practice tends to be shunned wherever possible, being replaced by unitization in the form of pallets, stillages or roll-cages into or on to which packages are stacked ready for loading by fork-lift truck or via a vehicle tailboard lift.

These simple devices eliminate much of the manual labour associated with vehicle loading and considerably reduce the health risks for drivers and loaders.

Drivers can also learn a great deal about loading techniques, load securing and load safety from the following excellent publications:

1. Department of Transport (DfT) Code of Practice *Safety of Loads on Vehicles*.
2. Driving Standards Agency (DSA) publication *The Official Guide to Driving Goods Vehicles*.

Both of these are available from The Stationery Office (online from www.tso.co.uk) or from retail bookshops.

Overloading and weighing of loads

It is an offence to drive or operate an overloaded goods vehicle on a road and both the driver and operator may be prosecuted. Where a vehicle is suspected by the enforcement authorities to be overloaded, the driver may be instructed to drive for up to 5 miles (8 kilometres) for a weight check. The maximum fine for overloading is £5,000 per offence – note; one overload could result in more than one offence. Convictions for overloading offences also jeopardize the operator's licence.

Defence

It is a defence against an overloading prosecution to prove that at the time the contravention was detected the vehicle was proceeding to the nearest available weighbridge or was returning from such weighbridge to the nearest point at which it was reasonably practicable to remove the excess load. It is a further defence, where the weight exceeds maximum limits by not more than 5 per cent, to prove that the weight was within legal limits at the time of loading the vehicle and that nobody had since added anything to the load.

Securing loads

Load security is extremely important; it affects the stability of the vehicle and can lead to prosecution if a load is unsafe or, worse, falls from a vehicle. The following key points should be observed:

- the type of load;
- the suitability of the vehicle for carrying that load;
- whether the load is stable;
- the most suitable type of load restraint;
- the need for protection from the weather;
- the need to secure the load against theft;
- how stable and safe the load will be under emergency braking;
- how stable the load would be if one of the vehicle tyres were to blow out (especially with high loads such as pallets, hay and straw etc).

Loads must not cause danger to other road users. They should:

- be securely stowed using suitable devices;
- not be too large for the capacity of the vehicle (ie, within load length and width limits);
- be within the vehicle's legal weight limits.

Load restraints must be correctly used depending on the type of load being carried.

Use of ropes
Ropes are totally unsuitable for some loads, such as steel plates, scrap metal and ISO steel containers etc. They should only be used where they can actually get a purchase on the load and will not be cut or damaged by sharp edges. When ropes are used, they should be secured with the aid of 'dollies', which are a form of knot traditionally used in haulage on sheeted and loose loads to ensure correct tension and prevent slippage, and which can only be released when required.

Straps
Load-securing straps, usually made from strong webbing, are widely used in place of ropes both for loads on open vehicles and for securing loads inside curtain-sided and closed-body vehicles.

Chocks and battens
Large and particularly heavy objects such as metal ingots, castings, fabrications, should be chocked with timber or old rail sleepers etc. Generally, these should be nailed to the load platform to stop movement of the load.

Chains
Chains, with tensioners, are the best form of security where there is any danger of the weight of the load being too great for ropes or where its sharp edges would shear ropes or straps.

Twist locks
When ISO cargo (shipping) containers are carried on road vehicles they should be secured with twist locks, which are designed to lock the container securely to the load platform or skeletal frame. For maximum safety, if the vehicle does not have twist locks, containers should not be carried. It is a misconception that containers can be held in place by their own weight or by ropes – too many fatal accidents caused by containers moving or falling from vehicles are proof of this.

Your own life and the lives of others may depend upon the security of your load.

VEHICLE BATTERIES

Drivers of modern vehicles are fortunate in, generally, not having to deal with batteries, unlike their predecessors whose life used to be blighted by underpowered and defective – to say nothing of regularly flat – batteries. However, there still are drivers who have to work with poor batteries and they may not realize the dangers inherent in recharging and the use of 'jump leads' for emergency starting, for example.

A high level of injuries occur annually from exploding batteries through mishandling and improper use, generally causing acid burns to the face, eyes and hands, as well as other injuries. For this reason, the HSE warns of the dangers of charging batteries, particularly those described as maintenance-free, but which still give off flammable hydrogen gas, which, on contact with a naked flame, burns and causes the battery to explode.

General precautions

- Always wear goggles or a visor when working on batteries.
- Wherever possible, always use a properly designated and well-ventilated area for battery charging.
- Remove any metallic objects from hands, wrists and around the neck (eg, rings, chains and watches) before working on a battery.

Disconnecting and reconnecting batteries

- Turn off the vehicle ignition switch and all other switches or otherwise isolate the battery from the electrical circuit.
- Always disconnect the earthed terminal first (often the negative terminal, but not always – CHECK) and reconnect it last using insulated tools.
- Do not rest tools or metallic objects on top of a battery.

Battery charging

- Always observe the manufacturer's instructions for charging batteries.
- Charge in a well-ventilated area. Do not smoke or bring naked flames into the charging area.
- Make sure the battery is topped up to the correct level.
- Make sure the charger is switched off or disconnected from the power supply before connecting the charging leads, which should be connected positive-to-positive, negative-to-negative.
- Vent plugs may need to be adjusted before charging. Carefully follow the manufacturer's instructions.
- Do not exceed the recommended rate of charging.
- When charging is complete, switch off the charger before disconnecting the charging leads.

Jump starting precautions

While jump starting is an accepted practice, it is a dangerous one for anyone who is unwary or inexperienced. For this reason it is always safest to follow the HSE guidelines below.

Preparation
- Always ensure that both batteries have the same voltage rating.
- If starting by using a battery on another vehicle, check the earth polarity on both vehicles.
- Ensure the vehicles are not touching.
- Turn off the ignition of both vehicles.
- Always use purpose-made, colour-coded jump leads with insulated handles – red for the positive cable and black for the negative cable.

Connection for vehicles with the same earth polarity
- First connect the non-earthed terminal of the good battery to the non-earthed terminal of the flat battery.
- Connect one end of the second lead to the earthed terminal of the good battery.
- Connect the other end of the second lead to a suitable, substantial, unpainted point on the chassis or engine of the other vehicle, away from the battery, carburettor, fuel lines or brake pipes.

Connection for vehicles with different earth polarity
In view of the potential for confusion only skilled and experienced personnel should attempt this:

- First connect the earthed terminal of the good battery to the non-earthed terminal of the flat battery.
- Connect one end of the second lead to the non-earthed terminal of the good battery.
- Connect the other end of the second lead to a suitable, substantial, unpainted point on the chassis or engine of the other vehicle, away from the battery, carburettor, fuel lines or brake pipes.

Starting
- Ensure the leads are well clear of moving parts.
- Start the engine of the 'good' vehicle and allow it to run for about one minute.
- Start the engine of the 'dead' vehicle and allow it to run for about one minute.

Disconnection

- Stop the engine of the 'good' vehicle.
- Disconnect the leads in the reverse order to that in which they were connected.
- Take great care in handling jump leads; do not allow the exposed metal parts to touch each other or the vehicle body.

5.3

Stowaways and smuggling

International drivers have much to concern themselves with when returning to the United Kingdom from journeys abroad. Besides all the official paperwork that has to be dealt with, these days there are worries as to whether any stowaways (ie, illegal immigrants or, as they are officially called, 'clandestine entrants') may be hidden in the load. To help stowaways enter this country is an offence that, if detected, can have serious consequences for the driver and his employer. Similarly, it is illegal to smuggle prohibited goods into the country, eg, drugs, pornographic literature and films, weapons and ammunition and illegal quantities of cigarettes, tobacco and alcoholic drink.

STOWAWAYS

Concern about the numbers of illegal immigrants entering this country stowed away in goods vehicles has resulted in severe penalties being imposed on drivers and operators under the Nationality, Immigration and Asylum Act 2002 (as amended). A penalty of £2,000 is imposed for each illegal immigrant found, with confiscation of the vehicle should the fine not be paid. Anybody aiding illegal immigrants to enter Great Britain could be imprisoned for up to seven years. Proof of 'due diligence' may be accepted in defence of any charges under the legislation, but it is important for an accused driver to clearly show that he followed the Home Office Civil Penalty Code of Practice.

Home Office Civil Penalty Code of Practice

Where it is alleged that a person is liable to a penalty under the Immigration Act for bringing a clandestine entrant into the United Kingdom it is a defence to show:

- he did not know and had no reasonable grounds for suspecting that a clandestine entrant was, or might be, concealed in the transporter;

- that there was an effective system in operation in relation to the transporter to prevent the carriage of clandestine entrants; and
- that on the occasion concerned, the person or persons responsible for operating that system did so properly.

Measures to be taken to secure vehicles against unauthorized entry

- Before final loading takes place, all existing cuts or tears in the outer shell or fabric of the vehicle that exceed 25 centimetres in length must be repaired and sealed so as to prevent unauthorized entry.
- If present at the time of final loading, the driver must check to ensure that no persons have gained entry to the vehicle and are concealed inside. It must then be locked, sealed, or otherwise made secure to prevent unauthorized entry. If not present at the time of final loading the driver must, where possible, ensure that such checks are conducted at that point by reputable persons and then obtain written confirmation that these checks were properly conducted and that the vehicle did not contain concealed persons at the time of final loading and securing.
- When the final loading has been completed, the load space must be secured immediately by lock, seal or other security device, preventing unauthorized entry.
- Tilt cords and straps, where used, must be undamaged, pass through all fastening points, be made taut and be secured by lock, seal or other security device.
- There must be no means of entry to the load space, other than via access points that have been secured by lock, tilt cord/strap and seal, or other security device.
- Locks, tilt cords, straps and other devices used to secure the load space must be of robust quality and effective.
- Seals other than Customs' seals must be distinguished by a number from a series that is unique to the owner, hirer or driver. This must be recorded in documentation accompanying the vehicle.
- Where a sealed container (except a container sealed by Customs) is loaded on to a vehicle, the owner, hirer or driver must, where possible, check to ensure that it does not contain unauthorized persons. It must then be resealed and made secure in accordance with the above requirements. These actions and the number of the new seal used must be recorded in documentation accompanying the vehicle.
- The same checking, securing and recording procedure detailed above must be followed where the load space in the vehicle has been opened by the owner, hirer, driver, or any other person before the final checks detailed below are carried out.

- Where a new driver becomes responsible for the vehicle *en route* to the United Kingdom, he should ensure that it does not contain unauthorized persons and that the requirements detailed above have all been met.
- The foregoing paragraphs will not apply to any vehicle that cannot be secured by means of lock, seal or other security device. However, in these cases, the owner, hirer or driver will need to establish alternative arrangements to prevent unauthorized entry; and to be able to demonstrate that such arrangements have been made and complied with.

Measures to be taken immediately prior to the vehicle boarding the ship, aircraft or train to the United Kingdom, or before arrival at the UK immigration control at Coquelles [ie, the Channel Tunnel terminal]

- Where used, check tilt cords and straps for evidence of tampering, damage or repair.
- Where used, check that seals, locks or other security devices have not been removed, damaged or replaced. In order to ensure that there has been no substitution, numbers on seals must be checked to confirm that they correspond with those recorded on the documentation accompanying the vehicle.
- Check the outer shell/fabric of the vehicle for signs of damage or unauthorized entry, paying particular attention to the roof, which may be checked from either inside or outside the vehicle.
- Check any external storage compartments, toolboxes, wind deflectors and beneath the vehicle.
- Check inside the vehicle. Effective detection devices may be used for this purpose at the discretion of the owner, hirer or driver, but this will not obviate the requirement that the other checks detailed above be carried out. Where it is not possible to secure a vehicle lock, seal or other security device, a thorough manual check of the load and load space must be conducted.

General principles

- Vehicles should be checked regularly *en route* to the United Kingdom to ensure that they have not been entered, particularly after stops when left unattended.
- A document detailing the system operated to prevent unauthorized entry must be carried with the vehicle, so that it may be produced immediately to an immigration officer on demand in the event of possible liability to a penalty.
- A report detailing the checks that were carried out must be carried with the vehicle. If it is possible to arrange, the report should be endorsed by a third party who has either witnessed or carried out the checks himself by arrange-

ment with the owner, hirer or driver, as the report will then be of greater evidential value.

- Whilst owners, hirers or drivers may contract with other persons to carry out the required checks on their behalf, they will nevertheless remain liable to any penalty incurred in the event of failure to have an effective system in place or to operate it properly on the occasion in question.
- Where the checks conducted suggest that the security of the vehicle may have been breached, or the owner, hirer or driver otherwise has grounds to suspect that unauthorized persons have gained entry to the vehicle, it must not be taken on to the ship, aircraft or train embarking for the United Kingdom, or to the UK immigration control at Coquelles. Any such circumstances must be reported to the police in the country concerned at the earliest opportunity, or, at the latest, to the passport control authorities at the port of embarkation. In the event of difficulties arising, owners, hirers or drivers should contact the UK Immigration Service at the proposed port of arrival for advice.

SMUGGLING

Customs are concerned about the volume of smuggled goods, particularly tobacco products, being brought into the United Kingdom. It is estimated that tobacco smuggling amounts to some £2.5 billion annually, costing each British taxpayer £50.

Besides new measures to detect smuggling, such as sophisticated X-ray equipment, tougher penalties have been introduced that could result in convicted offenders losing their vehicle (all goods vehicles found to be carrying contraband goods are seized – 300 LGVs were impounded in just one year) and their driving licence and facing up to seven years in prison.

Drivers (and others) returning to the United Kingdom from EU countries may bring back, duty free, an unrestricted amount of goods (other than prohibited articles) provided they are for their own personal use (or for gifts) and are not for resale. However, anybody who brings back more than 3,200 cigarettes or more than 110 litres of beer, 90 litres of wine or 10 litres of spirits may be asked by Customs to justify the reason why.

If the permitted limits for personal imports are exceeded, or a satisfactory explanation cannot be given for the goods carried, or if the Customs officer suspects the goods are to be sold, they will be seized and may not be returned. Furthermore, the vehicle in which they are found may also be impounded and disposed of. The offender may be fined heavily on conviction, or even sent to prison, and they may lose their driving licence.

When returning from *outside* the European Union, the maximum legal limits for personal importation of dutiable goods are as follows:

- wine – 2 litres;
- spirits – 1 litre;
- fortified wine – 2 litres;
- cigarettes – 200;
- cigarillos – 100;
- cigars – 50;
- tobacco – 250 grams;
- perfume – 60 cubic centimetres/millilitres;
- toilet water – 250 cubic centimetres/millilitres;
- other goods – £145.

Customs hotline
Customs has a special 24-hour confidential telephone number for reporting suspected cases of smuggling. Names do not have to be given and calls will not be traced. Customs Confidential: 0800 59 5000.

5.4

Driver health and lifestyle

Health and safety, as we have already seen in Chapter 5.1, is an important topic affecting both the LGV driver and his employer. Similarly, these days, there are concerns about drivers' personal health and lifestyle. An increasing awareness in recent years of the adverse effects of certain work occupations and lifestyles has resulted in the publication of many newspaper and magazine articles and television programmes on the need for and the ways and means of achieving healthier ways of living.

Lorry driving is renowned for being one of the worst possible occupations health-wise. The public perception of the average trucker is of an overweight frequenter of greasy-spoon transport cafes. And no wonder: many drivers are large and, in most cases, the only place they can get food on the road is at a traditional transport cafe or motorway service area where the all-day fry-up has been obligatory for decades.

But there is, increasingly, recognition among drivers themselves, their employers, health counsellors and the medical profession at large that the LGV driver needs special attention because, by its very nature, his job is an unhealthy one. Sitting in a lorry cab for eight or nine hours a day is itself a health risk; it leads to both posture and weight problems. An unsuitable diet occasioned by a lack of eating establishments offering healthy meal options leads also to weight problems and to other medical conditions (not least heart disease). Additionally, the need to negotiate overcrowded motorways and urban traffic congestion day in and day out in all weathers, with delivery deadlines to meet, is a sure cause of undue tiredness, stress and anxiety, which are the cause of many related ailments and 'lost' working days.

ERGONOMICS AND DRIVER POSTURE

What is ergonomics? Most people have heard of the word and relate it to the design of something, a car for instance or a kitchen. In fact, it is more than just a way of designing things, it is to do with people's efficiency in their workplace. Basically, this means understanding the nature of the work and the way that people need to do that work. The cook, for instance, needs a kitchen where the fitted appliances (cooker, sink, refrigerator, storage cupboards etc) and the cooking and other utensils are located in an ideal relationship to each other so he is not crossing from one side of the kitchen to the other while preparing food, cooking and clearing up afterwards and not having to stretch for items that are almost out of reach. An ergonomically efficient kitchen will be comfortable and a pleasure to work in, not one where the cook is exhausted from to-ing and fro-ing, reaching up and bending down all the time to accomplish simple tasks.

This is a good analogy that can be readily translated to the truck driver's working environment. He needs to have all the essential vehicle controls falling readily to hand, without having to stretch to reach them and especially so in an emergency. And whereas the cook is on his feet but does not want to have to move about too much, the truck driver, conversely, is sitting down for hours on end and does not want to finish his driving stint with a cricked back and aching arms and shoulders. He needs his seat to be ergonomically designed to provide adequate support and comfort and yet to allow him to move easily and reach all the vital vehicle controls, and other controls such as those for the heater/ventilation system, radio/CD player and cigarette lighter without undue strain.

A well-shaped and well-positioned driving seat will make all the difference to the stresses and strains on the driver's body and affect the rate at which fatigue sets in during a long journey. Similarly, how he organizes other aspects of the driving cab will play its part too – for example, where he places his clipboard of delivery notes, his newspaper, his flask and sandwiches, his sunglasses and so on. He might not (should not! one hopes) need his lunch pack while driving or indeed his newspaper, but he may need his sunglasses, so they should be close to hand, as should a road map if he needs to rely on one. But even when stopped, reaching across to get his newspaper or lunch can do untold harm to his back muscles. Far better that he carefully positions everything close to hand where it is readily accessible, but secure so he does not have to lunge across the cab to stop things falling to the floor or being jettisoned into the windscreen when he brakes hard.

This is understanding what ergonomics is about: achieving efficiency in the workplace – the so-called 'human factor'. This is easily appreciated when climbing into the latest heavy lorry cabs, especially top-of-the-range models, which are the epitome of ergonomic efficiency, veritable havens of comfort and convenience, with wraparound instrument panels and infinitely variable seat positioning so that all the controls and switches fall readily to the driver's hand. All clearly designed to make the driver's job as stress- and fatigue-free as possible.

Posture relates to the position of the body and the way in which a person holds their body, upright or slouched, for example. Bad posture derived from a poor seating position is common among truck drivers, leading to the inevitable back troubles, which are one of the greatest causes of lost working time in this country, but worse, it could lead to permanent disability. There is not much the driver can do if his truck has a badly shaped or positioned seat, apart from complaining to the boss. It is well known that some truck seats are worse than others in this regard, but regular stops to get out of the cab and have a stretch and a walk can help considerably, as can undertaking structured exercise to strengthen back muscles – but this needs the advice of a physiotherapist or experienced fitness trainer. This is something the employer should be persuaded to arrange and fund where appropriate. After all, he does have a statutory duty to safeguard the health and safety of his employees and must take steps to eliminate any risk of injury arising from work situations.

TIREDNESS WHILE DRIVING

There is considerable concern these days about an apparently increasing trend in road accidents resulting from driver tiredness and fatigue. According to the DfT, the main points for drivers to observe are that they should:

- Make sure they are fit to drive, particularly before undertaking any long journeys (over an hour) – avoid such journeys in the morning without a good night's sleep or in the evening after a full day's work.
- Avoid undertaking long journeys between midnight and 6 am, when natural alertness is at a minimum.
- Plan their journey to take sufficient breaks. A minimum break of at least 15 minutes after every two hours' driving is advised.
- If they feel at all sleepy, stop in a safe place and either take a nap for around 15 minutes, or drink two cups of strong coffee.

WORK-RELATED STRESS AND FATIGUE

It is well known that working situations can cause stress, which may manifest itself in the health of employees and consequently in the risk of accidents in the workplace. In fact, work-related stress is becoming recognized as a major cause of employee illness and absenteeism, as indeed is fatigue (not necessarily to be confused with tiredness while driving).

All employers have a duty in law to ensure that their employees are not made ill by their work. Transport employers particularly need to recognize that the stress or undue fatigue created in driving situations can make their employees ill.

Stress is a person's natural reaction to excessive pressure – it is not a disease. However, excessive and long-term stress can lead to mental and physical ill health causing, for example, depression, nervous breakdown and even heart disease. Stress in one person can lead to stress in other people who have to cover their work. Fatigue, which, as stated above, should not necessarily be confused with falling asleep while driving, is a longer-term ailment generally caused by extreme tiredness or through excessive mental or physical exertion. Constant worry over personal problems or work situations will gradually wear a person down to the point where they become exhausted or fatigued and then become incapable of carrying out their work properly. In the case of LGV drivers this can lead to a worrying lack of concentration and attention while driving, or the inability to remember things.

DRIVING AND DRUG TAKING

We have seen in previous sections the adverse effect that drugs have on drivers, but it is useful to consider them here in the context of lifestyle. Many reasons may explain why an individual turns to drugs. Peer group, social and lifestyle pressures may be a major influence, but there is no doubt that pressure at work and the strain of long-distance driving and having to meet tight delivery schedules are important contributory factors in the case of transport industry workers. Whatever the cause, the resultant consequences can be very grave, with, as we have seen, the risk of a fatal road accident as the ultimate penalty.

Taking illegal drugs such as cannabis, which is a very common practice, has an adverse effect on a person's reaction times, while other drugs may have the opposite effect. Both cocaine and Ecstasy, for example, may increase reaction times, but severely affect accuracy and judgement, while amphetamines may increase reaction times in the short term, but again severely affect accuracy and judgement. These, of course, are the vital faculties needed for driving and it is clearly irresponsible for a driver to jeopardize his ability to judge and react sharply by indulging in such substances.

A similar reproof could also be made about the use of prescribed tranquillizers, sedatives and anti-depressants, as well as diabetes and epilepsy drugs. Although legally prescribed for use by the individual, invariably they have a potentially adverse effect on a driver's judgement and reactions and therefore increase the risk of an accident. Obvious signs of drug abuse include:

- hangover;
- repeated late arrival for work;
- mood changes;
- an inability to concentrate;
- irritability and aggression with workmates;
- impaired job performance;
- an obvious shortage of money (eg, typified by borrowing);
- a tendency to criminal activities such as theft to pay for drugs.

Generally, individuals suffering the effects of drug abuse fail to recognize any or all of the above symptoms in themselves – and this too is a further indicator of the situation and why such people are a great danger to themselves and to others.

In the case of truck drivers, if they feel drowsy, dizzy, confused, or suffer other side-effects that could affect their reaction times or judgement, they should not drive, or, if already on a journey, they should stop and rest and/or seek help. Continuing to drive could lead to an accident in which they and other innocent people could be injured or even killed.

EATING HABITS AND HEALTHY DIETS

Healthy eating is an important part of everyone's life. A truck driver is no different. It's not compulsory or even necessary to exist on a diet of 'greasy spoon' breakfasts, midday fry-ups or burgers and chips and Coke with everything. This is a lifestyle, but not the right one. Newspapers, magazines and TV programmes constantly highlight good, healthy eating habits and lifestyle diets – even the transport trade press increasingly features articles on good eating and fitness for LGV drivers. There are important messages here because, while a sylph-like on-the-go young woman, for example, may find it interesting and desirable to follow such regimes, her need to do so may not be so great as that of a typical middle-aged, overweight truck driver who spends eight or nine hours a day sitting (dare I say slumped) in a lorry cab. He'll be dying of a heart attack while she's still out dancing!

The message in all this is clear: the combination of a largely sedentary occupation and the eating habits that it tends to engender is unhealthy, leading to the real possibility of serious – life-threatening – illness such as heart disease and strokes. Add to this the risks associated with smoking and you have a real time bomb waiting to go off. One of the major aspects of the problem is the build-up of cholesterol in the bloodstream – especially LDL cholesterol, which sticks to artery walls and is absorbed by eating 'fatty' (ie, saturated fat) foods such as those containing animal fats (eg, mainly meat, especially red meat, but also other animal products such as dairy foods).

The right foods

An ideal diet would contain skimmed (or semi-skimmed) milk, chicken and fish rather than one incorporating full-fat milk and lots of red meat. Starchy foods, such as bread (especially wholemeal), cereals, rice, pasta or potatoes (but not potato crisps), should form the main part of a daily meal. These foods provide a sustained energy release. They should be combined with at least five portions of various fruit and vegetables every day, which may include fresh, frozen or canned fruit and vegetables and dried fruit.

Note: a one-portion measure is equivalent to a medium-sized apple or three spoonfuls of vegetables or beans.

It is important to avoid eating too much fat, especially saturated fat. Dairy foods and meat dishes can be high in fat, so it's better to choose lower- or reduced-fat versions whenever possible. There are hidden fats in biscuits, cakes, chocolate, crisps and chips so these should be avoided as much as possible. Cutting down on salt is another key aid to good health, or at least a healthy heart – they (ie, doctors and others) say that most of us eat far too much salt. The advice generally given is to get out of the habit of adding salt to food at the table and always taste food before adding salt.

Eating regularly through the day without skipping meals is the best way to achieve a good eating regime, starting with a good (not fried) breakfast, which will set you up for the day and help towards a healthier diet.

Blood pressure and cholesterol tests

Any driver concerned about his overall health is strongly advised to contact his doctor to arrange blood pressure and cholesterol checks. The former takes mere minutes and the latter only requires a quick blood test in a morning after fasting from the previous evening – no great hardship at all and pain-free! It is surprising how many men (particularly) in their 50s and 60s have not had their blood pressure taken in years and never had cholesterol tests (the author hadn't either, until hit with the sudden and unexpected need for a heart by-pass operation). But these simple tests are so important and can highlight problems that can readily be dealt with by medication.

Well-known road haulier Eddie Stobart has been reported as having his cholesterol measured and being surprised by the result, which reputedly shocked him. In consequence, he employed a nutritionist to tell his 1,200 drivers how to eat healthily.

Cholesterol levels, determined by blood test, should be at around a maximum of 5.0 (the medical profession has been gradually reducing this arbitrary benchmark over recent years in an effort to improve cardiac health). Anything above this level demands attention, initially by following a structured diet to reduce fat in the bloodstream, but if the result shows a much higher level (eg, over 6 or 7) then medication would most likely be prescribed.

FITNESS AND EXERCISE

The average middle-aged and overweight truck driver (and many seem to fit this description) is not going to take kindly to any suggestion that he should get out of the cab and start exercising. Better that he starts on a good eating regime first. However, good eating or diet alone will not reduce the effects of years of 'gut-busting' breakfasts; it does need exercise as well.

Walking is a good alternative to gymnasium workouts. A brisk walk of some 20 or 30 minutes daily (combined with a healthy eating plan) will, over time, do wonders for that portly figure and, more importantly, will stave off the potential risk of heart attack. It will drive away many of the stresses of work, lift the burden of depression and fatigue and engender an improved sense of well-being.

HEALTH CHECKS

Health and safety legislation places legal duties on employers, either by direct requirement or by implication, to provide health checks and/or health surveillance for employees. For instance, employees who use computer screens regularly must be provided with eye and eyesight tests, while drivers involved with the carriage of live animals must be regularly screened to ensure they do not, or are not, developing animal-related diseases that transmit to humans. Under the COSHH regulations, employers must carry out monitoring and surveillance of employees' health where risk assessments carried out under the legislation indicate that this is necessary and appropriate. Night-shift workers subject to the Working Time Directive must be provided with health assessments. Large goods vehicle drivers have to undertake a strict medical examination before first obtaining their vocational driving entitlement, and five-yearly after the age of 45 years.

Fitness of employees to carry out their particular job safely and efficiently is, therefore, a key factor for any employer. Nobody wants to be made ill, or sustain injury through their work and employers certainly do not want to see trucks standing idle, productivity falling and customers left wanting through avoidable staff absences. Clearly, therefore, it is in employees' best interests to comply with their employer in agreeing to undertake health surveillance or be party to a monitoring system or attend for specific medical checks where this is deemed necessary or advisable.

Truck drivers are no different from other employees in this regard. Their work can be hazardous, they can be subject to a variety of occupational ailments and injuries and they can face long-term infirmity in some instances. They therefore have a duty to safeguard their own health and to take appropriate steps to seek advice or medical help if they feel unwell or unduly stressed, especially if the condition appears to be related to their work situation. Such conditions should be reported to the employer either directly, via the company's doctor or nurse, or perhaps through a union representative if this is appropriate.

Medical conditions left unattended and unreported generally do not get better of their own accord. Seeking help is not wimpish, it is a responsible course of action in everybody's best interests.

Many firms these days offer their employees free periodic health screening and, indeed, fitness training and dietary and lifestyle advice – for example, TNT UK, which endeavours to encourage its employees to adopt a healthy lifestyle. Some employees may baulk at such offers, but it has to be said that they are usually made as much in the best interests of the individual employee as those of the employer. A wise employee would take every opportunity to grasp such opportunities when they are offered.

PERSONAL PROTECTION

All drivers should be constantly aware of the need for personal protection irrespective of the loads they carry, whether these are valuable or not, or whether they present particular dangers.

This personal protection should be considered in three ways as follows:

- the need to wear protective clothing, headwear and footwear, such as high visibility vests/jackets/belts, hard hats where necessary and protective (ie steel toe-cap) boots;
- the need to note the proximity of other vehicles (parked and moving), the walls, pillars and posts of the premises' infrastructure, nearby fork-lift truck operations and most importantly the presence or likely presence of people, whether other drivers, loaders or office staff or even visitors to the premises;
- the need to be spatially aware of what is going on around them and who is nearby or watching what they are doing. Such people may be checking out the possibilities for stealing goods off the vehicle tailboard or even hijacking the whole vehicle with or without its load.

Suffering personal injury or harm as result of inadequate personal protection will result in pain and stress for the LGV driver, most of which could have been avoided by use of the proper equipment. Similarly, damaging other vehicles and property can cause a lot of hassle, delay and disruption to work schedules, but injuring or, worse still, killing somebody on work premises will prove to be a psychological nightmare for the driver from which recovery will not come easily.

Part 6

Transport operations, service and logistics

6.1

The road haulage economic environment

The UK road haulage industry faces many difficult economic challenges, not least those of:

- exorbitant fuel prices, especially when compared with those in other EU member states;
- poor haulage rates in a market place where the true worth of the industry is not fully recognized; and
- unfair competition from both domestic operators who have no compunction about breaking the law to gain an advantage, and from foreign hauliers who enter the United Kingdom and compete unfairly with UK firms while using cheaper fuel, employing cheaper labour (eg, drivers from Eastern European countries) and paying dubious regard to legal requirements.

In due course there will also be the drastic impact on haulage costs of the Working Time Directive, the revised drivers' hours rules, the digital tachograph and the EU's proposed driver training directive.

Key issues such as the importance of fuel consumption on vehicle operating costs and the effects of unfair competition on his employer's business are important matters for the professional LGV driver to understand. Matters relating to working time and digital tachographs, for example, have already been discussed elsewhere in this *Handbook*.

FUEL CONSUMPTION

Next to wage costs, fuel is the most expensive cost item for a vehicle operator, accounting for up to one-third of operating costs. Fuel is subject to occasional and dramatic shortages as a result of political unrest in some of the major oil-producing countries, while scientists predict total extinction as world supplies of crude oil are consumed ever more rapidly by developed nations, which have become increasingly dependent on transportation systems powered by oil-based (ie, fossil) fuels.

While the search for and research into acceptable alternative fuels and power units goes on, it is important to take steps to minimize consumption of our present fuel supplies. As well as being a problem for nations, this is a problem that concerns all fleet operators, whatever their size. Besides any conscience they may have about energy conservation they will readily appreciate that fuel consumption must be reduced in the campaign to keep vehicle operating costs down.

Fuel and the vehicle

Fuel consumption is substantially related to the type of vehicle, its power unit and driveline, its mechanical condition, the use to which it is put and how it is driven. Manufacturers offer fuel economy models within their ranges so the cost-conscious operator can choose between economy and outright performance. The fuel-conscious operator who is in a position to buy new vehicles will undoubtedly choose fuel economy models where these are suited to his particular needs. However, for the most part, fleet operators have to stick with the vehicles they already have in their fleets and are faced with the need to consider how improved fuel economy can be achieved with existing vehicles.

Three principal areas exist for fuel consumption improvement in the vehicle itself:

● mechanical condition;
● efficient use;
● addition of fuel economy aids.

Mechanical condition

A poorly maintained vehicle inevitably consumes more fuel and for this reason particular attention should be paid to efficient maintenance of the following components:

● *Fuel system* (fuel tank, pipe lines, filters, pump and injectors). There should be no leaks and the vehicle should not emit black smoke. Both of these are causes or consequences of excessive consumption as well as potentially resulting in test failure and prosecution. Fuel pumps and injectors should be properly serviced as recommended by the manufacturers.
● *Wheels and brakes*. Wheels should turn freely and without any brake binding. Front wheels should be correctly aligned. Brake binding and

misalignment cause unnecessary friction, leading to the use of more fuel. Axles on bogies should be correctly aligned because tyres running at slip angles have a high rolling resistance and therefore are a source of increased fuel consumption.

- *Driving controls.* Throttle cables, clutch and brake pedals should be correctly adjusted so the driver has efficient control over the vehicle. In particular, engine tickover should be accurately adjusted to save throttle 'blipping' to keep it running when the vehicle is stationary.

Efficient use

Inefficient use of vehicles constitutes the greatest waste of fuel. The following activities should be avoided by careful route planning, scheduling and prior thought about the cost consequences:

- vehicles running long distances when only partially loaded;
- vehicles covering excessive distances to reach their destination;
- large vehicles being used for running errands or making small-item deliveries, which could be accomplished more efficiently, and certainly more economically, by other means;
- vehicles running empty.

It is frequently argued that traffic office staff have little control over these matters, since customer demands for orders and the need to give drivers freedom to choose routes are dictates that overrule efficient planning. Nevertheless, attempts should be made to persuade those concerned about the need for restraint in the quest for saving fuel and thereby reducing costs.

Fuel economy aids

The quest for fuel saving has led to a market for economy aids that can be added to existing vehicles. These aids fall into three general categories:

- streamlining devices such as cab-top air deflectors, under-bumper air dams, front-corner deflectors for high trailers and box vans, in-fill pieces for lorry and trailer combinations and shaped cones for addition to the front of van bodies;
- road speed governors, which restrict maximum speed – one of the greatest causes of excessive fuel consumption (speed limiters are a mandatory requirement on certain heavy vehicles);
- engine fans and radiator shutters designed to ensure that diesel engines are always operating at the correct temperature to give the most efficient performance and fuel economy.

All these devices can be economically justified to a varying degree, but it is important to note that fitting streamlining devices in isolation only reduces fuel consumption if vehicle speeds are kept down. If the driver is able to use the few extra miles per hour that these devices provide – which he will do unless otherwise restricted – then there will be little fuel saving and the cost of fitting would not be wholly justified.

Fuel and tyres

The type and condition of tyres on a vehicle play a significant part in its fuel consumption. It is a proven fact that the lower rolling resistance inherent in radial ply tyres adds considerably to the fuel economy of the vehicle compared to the greater resistance of cross-ply tyres.

Improvements in fuel consumption of 5 to 10 per cent can be expected from the use of radial ply tyres. Low-profile tyres, which offer a number of operational benefits over conventional radial tyres – such as reduced platform height and reduced overall height – offer further possibilities for fuel saving.

These savings will only be achieved if the tyres are in good condition, are correctly inflated to the manufacturer's recommended pressures and are properly matched, especially when used in twin-wheel combinations. Neglect of tyre pressures is common in fleets and under-inflation is one of the major causes of tyre failure, besides being a major contributor to excessive fuel consumption.

Fuel and the driver

Driving techniques, above all else, influence the overall fuel consumption of vehicles. A driver with a heavy right foot will negate all fuel-saving measures and devices and destroy any expectations of acceptable fuel consumption. Poor driving that has these consequences falls into two categories: high-speed driving and erratic, stop–go driving.

Fast driving consumes excessive fuel: this fact is beyond question but the extent of the extra consumption is difficult to assess accurately. However, tests carried out with a heavy articulated vehicle on motorway operation indicated that fuel consumption increased quite dramatically when the vehicle was travelling at over 40 mph (64 kph). In the tests, at 40 mph (64 kph) the fuel consumption was 10.5 mpg, at 50 mph (80 kph) this reduced by 2.6 mpg to 7.9 mpg and at 60 mph (96 kph) a further reduction of 1.5 mpg was experienced, making a 3.75mpg difference between 40mph and 60mph travelling speeds. This represents a 35.7 per cent increase in fuel consumption. The real significance of these figures will be fully appreciated when annual motorway travel is calculated and this is multiplied by the increase in consumption, by the number of vehicles in the fleet and by the cost per litre of diesel fuel.

The effects of erratic driving are more difficult to determine, but it is safe to say that it results in abnormally high fuel consumption as well as causing excessive wear and tear on vehicle components. Impatience behind the wheel and an inability to assess in time what is happening on the road ahead lead the driver to seesaw between fierce acceleration to keep up with the traffic and violent braking to avoid running into the vehicle in front. Hence the excessive use of fuel.

More economical driving is achieved by greater concentration on the road and traffic conditions ahead, anticipating well in advance how the traffic flow will move, and what is happening in front so that acceleration and braking can be more progressive and a smooth passage assured.

Another fuel-saving practice that drivers can adopt is to stop the engine while the vehicle is stationary rather than letting it tick over for unnecessarily long periods. If he feels this is necessary because his battery is in poor condition, then it is much cheaper to deal with the battery and charging problems than pay for the extra fuel to compensate.

FUEL ECONOMY CHECKLIST

Check:

- fuel systems free from leaks;
- fuel pump and injectors serviced and correctly adjusted;
- exhaust not emitting black smoke;
- air cleaners not blocked;
- engine operating at correct temperature;
- wheels turning freely;
- controls properly adjusted and lubricated.

Tyres:

- condition and inflation pressures;
- possibility of changing to radials on all vehicles.

Drivers:

- speed limits not being exceeded;
- driving methods smooth and gentle;
- engines stopped when vehicle standing.

Gas-powered heavy trucks

Increasingly, environmentally conscious transport operators are looking to natural gas for powering heavy vehicles. Among the key players is Somerfield, the supermarket firm, which has a number of compressed natural gas-powered vehicles in service. Besides the savings in fuel costs, these vehicles are much quieter than conventional diesel-powered vehicles – quieter even than a saloon car, it is said, thus allowing night-time deliveries to stores without upsetting local residents.

There are three main types of gaseous fuels in use in the United Kingdom:

- liquefied petroleum gas (LPG);
- compressed natural gas (CNG);
- liquefied natural gas (LNG).

All these three types of gas are used by both van and truck operators due to their environmental benefits, particularly:

- clean exhaust emissions;
- reduced engine noise;
- favourable duty treatment.

COMPETITION

One of the key tenets of EU policy is that all businesses must be allowed to compete fairly – on the so-called 'level playing field'. In the United Kingdom this principle is enshrined in the Competition Act, which applies to all businesses irrespective of their trade and size – even sole traders such as owner-driver hauliers. Principally, the Act prohibits anti-competitive agreements and abuse of a dominant position in the market.

6.2

The road haulage business environment

To be a professional LGV driver today, unlike his predecessors of a decade or so ago, involves a great deal more than just knowing how to drive and load a heavy vehicle correctly. These days, for example, the broad scope of knowledge demanded by the forthcoming EU driver-training directive for those choosing this profession for a career also includes the need to understand the nature of a road haulage business, how it is structured and how it conducts its activities in a commercial environment.

This is particularly true for those who are, or who aspire to be, owner-driver road hauliers – of which we may expect to see many more in the future as a result of the favourable treatment given to this category of operator under the Working Time Directive rules for mobile workers: namely, a deferment of the stringent rules to be imposed on employee drivers until at least 2009. This is likely to encourage some own-account firms to avoid the restricting effects of the reduced working time by employing more sub-contract owner-drivers or by hiving off their existing employed drivers and creating a new force of contracted owner-drivers.

In recognition of these EU demands, this chapter examines the basic types of business organization into which most haulage businesses are formed, how contracts play a part in business dealings, why road hauliers should protect their liabilities by adopting specific conditions of carriage and the implications of quality management.

TYPES OF BUSINESS ORGANIZATION

Business is conducted in many forms, the simplest organizational structure being the person working on his own account as a sole trader or sole proprietor. Larger businesses are usually formed into partnerships or into limited liability companies (many of the largest national and international firms – but not many hauliers – are formed into public limited companies). Each of these various forms of commercial organization differs in the nature of the legal obligations to be met and each has relative advantages and disadvantages depending on size, the nature of the trade or commercial activity in which they are engaged, their financial needs and the wishes of the owners. The main legal differences and requirements and the relative advantages and disadvantages of each as they affect a haulage business are briefly described here.

Sole traders

The simplest form of business is the sole trader. Any person can start a business in this way, very cheaply and with the minimum of fuss. Setting-up costs are negligible, legal requirements are minimal and the owner is mainly only responsible to himself and to his customers.

The advantage of operating as a sole trader is freedom from the need to comply with Companies Act legislation, which requires legal registration and other complex formalities to be followed, including the need for accounts to be kept in a proper form and audited annually, and completed returns of directors and shareholders to be sent to Companies House. The disadvantage is that the proprietor (ie, owner) has no legal protection against his personal liabilities for meeting creditor (ie, those to whom he owes money) demands for payment if the business should fail. In this event, his belongings and even his house may have to be sold to help pay off what he owes.

If the business succeeds it will need capital for expansion and consequently assistance from the bank, for which security has to be provided. Usually the bank will want to take a second charge on the proprietor's home (if he owns it, or is buying it on mortgage). Thus if repayments cannot be made, the bank holds the house, which it could sell to recover any outstanding balance on the loan.

All profits made by the business become the proprietor's income (ie, rewards for the risks taken and the effort put into the business), from which he both derives his livelihood and builds up capital resources for future asset (eg, vehicle) replacement or expansion. He must, of course, declare these profits for taxation purposes and pay any tax due.

Partnerships

This form of business is an expansion of the sole trader structure. Instead of one person owning the business two or more people own it, sharing the ownership, the work and the profits either equally or in unequal proportions. The partners are, however, personally liable for any debts incurred by the partnership business.

Individual partners are agents for the partnership (usually referred to as a 'firm' – as opposed to a company as described below) and as such can bind the other partners in contracts whether specifically authorized to do so or not. The partnership firm can be sued in its business names or by separate writ to each of the partners individually. Should a partner be sued individually, he may be entitled to a contribution towards any damages awarded against him from the other partners whether they have been individually sued in the same action or not.

A partnership business cannot buy and have land conveyed to it as such, only to one or more of the partners as individuals who can *declare a trust for sale* for all the partners in equity (ie, who own equity in the business).

While most partnerships are constituted as general partnerships, with all partners being equally liable for the business debts as mentioned above, the Partnership Act 1907 allows a form of limited partnership under which individual partners' liabilities for the debts may be limited to the amount of capital they invested in the business. However, in such cases there must still be at least one general partner with unlimited liability.

Usually (ideally!) the partners in a business have a legal agreement setting out their responsibilities and liabilities (ie, for the partnership debts) in proportion to their share of the ownership of the business, and any profits made that are not retained for future use in the business are shared proportionately in accord-ance with the terms of the agreement.

In the absence of a partnership agreement, the law, in the form of the Partnership Act, will imply terms under which it (and HM Revenue & Customs) will look upon the partners as all having equal shares but with each person 'jointly and severally' liable for any debts of the partnership. In other words, if the other partners have no personal assets, one partner with assets could be left to meet the tax liabilities and all the other debts of the partnership should the business fail.

Many professional firms such as accountants, solicitors, surveyors, estate agents and consulting engineers operate as legally constituted partnerships (solicitors and accountants, for example, cannot by law limit their liabilities, so they have no choice but to operate as partnerships). In contrast, the road haulage industry comprises many partnerships based on little more than friendship, mutual trust or family relationships (eg, father and son, husband and wife, etc).

The advantage of a partnership is that there are more people to contribute initial finance and more people to share the work, the decision-making and the worries. The burden of providing security is also shared. The disadvantage is that people do not always agree, and argument and distrust can lead eventually to the failure of a business. Another major aspect of contention is that profits have to be shared in proportion to ownership rather than in proportion to the work and effort put into making the business a success.

On dissolution of a partnership, which may be due to business failure or perhaps as a result of irreconcilable differences of opinion among the partners, the assets of the business must be sold and the funds used to pay off outstanding commercial debts and loans and to meet other liabilities such as the tax and National Insurance contributions of the partners and employees (a priority) and other employment liabilities. Should there be a shortfall of funds from the realization of assets, the partners will have to personally meet any outstanding amounts from their own resources (ie, sale of their own personal assets including, if necessary, their car or even their home). Conversely, if there is a surplus after the disposal of assets, this may be shared among the partners either equally or in proportion to their individual share of the partnership business.

On the death of a partner, which may in itself be a reason for dissolution as described above, the remaining partner/s must account to that late partner's personal representative (ie, the executors to his estate) for the amount of his interest in the firm (ie, the value of his share of the business). In these circumstances, all tax due under the old partnership (ie, up to the time of the death) will normally become due immediately, except where special arrangements are made with HM Revenue & Customs about continuation of the partnership with the remaining partners.

Recognizing that such an event may occur, it is usual for partnerships to be advised to take out appropriate insurance cover to provide sufficient funds to meet payments due to HM Revenue & Customs and to the deceased partner's estate should the eventuality arise.

Limited liability companies

If a person (or persons) forming a business wishes to remove the risk of loss of personal property and possessions in the event of the business failure, he can form a private limited liability company. This is a legally constituted corporate body (ie, a 'company') formally registered with the Registrar of Companies in which the parties to the business hold shares in equal or unequal proportions. The owners of the business are therefore the shareholders (or members) of the company. The company has a registered name approved by the Registrar of Companies, but not one that may be confused with any other registered company or that is either sensitive (eg, implying royal connections or suggesting that the company is a national body or authority) or offensive. The word 'limited' must be added as the last word of the name.

There must be at least two shareholders. One person must be appointed as a director of the company and another as the Company Secretary (neither of whom need be shareholders, but usually they are). The Company Secretary is the legal officer of the company upon whom all legal notices are served. For example, if the company is prosecuted for offences committed by the company, its directors as individuals or its employees, this is done through the Company Secretary, who may not be personally liable, but it is he who is answerable to the court on behalf of the company (the company may, of course, be legally represented in such cases). He also has responsibility under the Companies Act for ensuring that all statutory requirements are met, for recording the minutes of board meetings, ensuring that annual accounts and a balance sheet are produced, and making the necessary annual returns to Companies House.

In forming the business or in raising capital for expansion, friends or relatives may be asked to invest funds in return for shares in the company *but it is not permitted to advertise for the public to invest in or buy the shares of a private limited company.* Some or all of the shareholders may be elected to be directors of the company (ie, the people who control the business and make the important decisions). The directors can choose a Chairperson from among themselves for the purpose of conducting meetings of the Board of Directors. The Chairperson usually has a casting vote, which is intended to resolve any 'stalemate' situations in voting decisions.

When a company is formed, the subscribers (the founders) decide on the amount of shares that will form the legally constituted 'share capital' of the business. For example, this may be 100 shares at £1 each to make it a £100 share-capital company. These shares are divided among the subscribers according to their contribution and according to the decision on who is to have the controlling interest. One shareholder may have 51 shares and the second one 49 shares, or they may have 50 each, which means neither has a controlling interest.

Once the share capital and the holdings of each of the subscribers are determined, this becomes the maximum limit of their personal liability if the business goes into liquidation. So, if their shares are fully paid up, the shareholders do not have to make any other contribution towards the debts of the company.

Often the share capital of a company is not fully paid up. For example, two people could form a £100 company, of which only two £1 shares are 'issued' or 'paid up' (one each). In the event of liquidation, they become liable to pay the balance of their allocation of shares (say, another £49 each if they have equal shares).

Company directors carry considerable legal responsibilities and can be held liable for a whole range of offences against company law (some 200 in all). They have a fiduciary duty to the company (ie, duty of trust to safeguard the property and assets of the company). They must act in good faith and must not allow their personal interests to conflict with those of the company. Besides this duty to the company (not necessarily to the shareholders of the company) they also have a duty to the employees. If they fail in their duties the directors can be held personally liable for any loss that is attributable to their negligence, or to any act outside their authority or in breach of duty or trust – in other words, they could be forced to pay compensation out of their own pockets.

Public limited companies

When a company becomes very large and needs to raise more capital for expansion by investment rather than by borrowing, it seeks to become quoted on the stock market so that its shares can be sold on the market to all and sundry and it can become 'public' and put the letters 'PLC' (public limited company) after its name.

CONTRACTS

Whether the road haulier or the owner-driver realizes it or not, it is a fact that the business of road haulage is conducted by means of contracts between hauliers and their customers who request them to carry, and sometimes store, goods on their behalf. These contracts are not always formally constituted in writing, more often being the consequence of a telephone call in which the customer asks the haulier to pick up and deliver a load of goods. Nevertheless, no matter how casual the arrangement, a legal contract does exist as described below.

Legally enforceable contracts

An enforceable contract must contain the following essential points:

- an offer and an acceptance (ie, the customer asks and the haulier agrees to do a haulage job);
- details of a consideration (ie, a benefit or payment is to be made);
- an intention for the parties to be legally bound by the contract (this is always assumed by the courts unless there is a written provision to the contrary – in other words, the parties do intend to do what they have said they would do).

It is important to note that a contract exists when an offer has been made and accepted – there is no requirement for it to be in writing.

Capacity to contract

Contracts may be made only between those persons and parties who have a legal capacity to contract. In other words, this generally means that contracts may be made between adults, but a minor (ie, a person under 18 years of age) does not have capacity to contract, neither do mental patients and those persons afflicted by drunkenness. Limited companies (ie, corporate bodies) have capacity to contract so long as authority is given in the company's Memorandum of Association.

Performance of contracts

Contracts may be discharged by 'performance' – legal parlance that basically means completing the job. However, in general terms there are four classes of performance:

- Entire performance is when both parties have fully performed the obligations placed on them by the contract (eg, the haulier to carry and deliver the load, the customer to have paid the haulier's account for the job).

- Substantial performance is a term used when a dispute over non-completion of a contract is referred to court and the court determines that one party is not required to perform every term of the contract for the other party to be made liable. For example, the defendant may be required to pay for work done but may counterclaim against the contractor for 'defect in performance' (ie, for work not done or work badly done).
- Partial performance is where one party is prepared to accept and pay for something less than full (ie, entire) performance of the contract (ie, where the job is not completed, but the customer agrees to pay anyway).
- Frustration is where a contract proves impossible to fulfil from the outset and is therefore void (ie, impossible of performance).

Discharge of contracts

Discharge of a contract is when the parties to it are freed from their mutual obligations under the contract. This may be either lawfully by agreement, by performance (see above), by frustration, or unlawfully by breach of the contract.

Compensation for loss through damage

Where there is a breach of contract for the reasons given above, damages may be claimed by the plaintiff (ie, the party who suffered the loss and who sues the defendant for compensation). These damages, if awarded by the court, will normally fall into one of the following categories:

- Ordinary damages. These arise naturally from the breach of contract for losses that cannot be positively proved or ascertained. The amount of damages awarded will depend on the court's view of the nature of the plaintiff's injury (ie, loss).
- Special damages. These are losses that do not arise naturally from the breach of contract and are awarded for losses that can be positively proved or ascertained (ie, where specific amounts of loss can be stated).
- Exemplary and aggravated damages. These are additional damages above those awarded for actual loss and intended to punish the defendant and to deter him, and others, from similar conduct in the future. Hence the reason why they are invariably referred to as punitive damages.

Carriers' liability for goods – private/common carriers

In road haulage operations the operator enters into a contract each time goods are accepted from a customer to be carried to a specified destination. In most cases he accepts these goods in the role of *private* carrier, whereby his liability is limited to the terms specified in his conditions of carriage, which are either printed on the back of his business paper or quotation sheets or are posted up in the office. If he has no conditions of carriage and holds himself out to carry for all and sundry without reserving the right to refuse to carry goods tendered, he undertakes the role of *common* carrier (ie, under the Carriers Act 1830) and his liability for loss of or damage to the goods, irrespective of the degree of negligence, is unlimited.

CONDITIONS OF CARRIAGE

When goods are carried under a specific contract between the owner of the goods and the haulier (in the role of private carrier as opposed to common carrier), the haulier limits his liability by applying conditions of carriage, which are the terms on which a contract is made with the owner of the goods. By contracting to carry goods in accordance with specified conditions of carriage, the haulier limits his liability under the terms of those conditions. All road hauliers should protect their liability by adopting conditions of carriage, either their own or, if they are a member of the Road Haulage Association, those of the Association.

Road hauliers' power to restrict legal liability

The road haulier may include in his conditions of carriage appropriate and easily understood terms and clauses that define the limits of his liability. If he does this, the haulier then remains liable only for his own negligence and that of his servants (ie, employees).

The haulier is also liable for loss or damage that the consignor (sender) suffers as a result of unreasonable delay of the goods in transit where such loss was reasonably foreseeable (eg, if fresh fruit was consigned to a market it would be known beforehand that delay might result in the market being missed and the fruit becoming worthless). The haulier is not liable if a delay is caused by the consignor stopping delivery of the goods while in transit, for example, because he does not wish the buyer to receive them due to the buyer's possible inability to pay (for example, because of his insolvency). Similarly, the haulier is liable for wrongful delivery of goods if this is due to wilful misconduct by his servants, but not if it is merely a negligent mis-delivery. The haulier is not liable in respect of dangerous goods where he did not know that the goods were dangerous; had he known, he could have either refused to carry them or imposed special conditions or charges.

In making an offer to consign goods via the haulier, the owner implies acceptance of the conditions where they have been drawn to his attention, directly or otherwise (they may be printed on the back of the quotation or they may be referred to on the haulier's letter heading, literature or consignment notes) prior to the movement taking place. The conditions of carriage limit the haulier's responsibility for loss or damage to the goods as a result of his own or his servants' negligence, up to a maximum limit of value (usually £800/£1,300 or more per tonne). He is not liable for loss or damage to the goods in excess of this value unless he has been informed of their value and undertakes to carry them and become the insurer of the excess amount over the standard conditions. If the haulier is advised that goods to be carried exceed this value, extra insurance cover should be arranged with the Goods in Transit insurers.

Breach of contract

While the haulier can limit his liability as described previously, he cannot include in the contract a clause that exempts him from liability for a *fundamental breach of contract*. In other words, he cannot fail to do what he has contracted to do and then avoid liability for this failure (eg, by failing to deliver goods that he has contracted to deliver, although he could avoid liability for failure to deliver them at, say, a specific time).

Rights to lien and bailment

The road haulier has a right to lien (ie, possession) over goods entrusted to him for carriage until the carriage charges are paid. Lien falls into two categories: particular lien means that a specific consignment of goods may be held until the carriage charges in respect of that particular consignment are paid, and general lien means that any goods may be held until charges for previous consignments have been paid.

Particular lien is a standing right in law but the right to general lien is only applicable if specified in the haulier's conditions of carriage. The rights to lien only confer a right to detain goods, not to charge for their storage to enforce the lien and not to dispose of them in order to recover lost carriage charges unless such actions are specifically forewarned in the conditions of carriage.

A haulier may detain goods that are consigned for carriage but that cannot be delivered for some reason (eg, because the customer's delivery address is closed when he gets there) – known as 'bailment'. He then becomes a 'bailer' of the goods and as such has a duty to avoid them becoming lost or damaged through negligence. The goods may be held until the carriage charges are paid, either on his vehicle or in his yard, and if his conditions of carriage include the necessary provision, demurrage (ie, delay) charges may be raised.

QUALITY MANAGEMENT

Increasingly, road hauliers are facing demands from customers, and from principal contractors, to meet recognized standards of quality assurance in the form of certification to international standard ISO 9001:2000.

A great deal has been written about the subject of 'quality', and many myths have been spread, but it is quite simply the concept of doing things right first time, and right every time. This saves having to repeat operations at extra cost and to the annoyance of the customer, whether in production of goods or the provision of a service – road haulage, for example. It means supplying customers with the service they need, not what the supplier thinks he can best provide. In haulage, it means, particularly, providing cost-effective deliveries – on time, to the right address with the load intact and undamaged and delivered by a courteous driver in a presentable vehicle.

Achieving quality assurance (QA) certification involves many complex steps, changed ideas, new thinking and acceptance that 'old ways' must be replaced by new methods, plus extra paperwork, form filling, writing of manuals, checking and rechecking of standards, and visits from inspectors.

What are quality systems and quality management? A quality system is one where problems, queries, faults, and anything that could give rise to customer dissatisfaction or complaint, are identified and eliminated. Every aspect of operating procedure is critically examined to ensure that nothing unexpected (short of pure accident – and contingencies can even be established for these) can arise to jeopardize service to the customer. Quality management is the management of quality systems – a totally new way of doing business, hence the expression 'total quality management' (TQM).

Assessment and accreditation

Quality assessment and accreditation is the process by which a firm demonstrates to an accredited certification body that its services meet pre-established quality standards, followed by certification of this fact.

Firms whose quality systems meet specified standards may register with an approved body and, on satisfactory completion of the formalities, receive 'Registered Firm' status, when they may use the accreditation body's symbol of approval on the company literature (ie, letterheads, brochures) and on vehicles.

Standards

The essence of a quality haulage service is that every step in fulfilling customer orders is undertaken in accordance with a documented standard – a set of rules governing the best way to operate and against which day-to-day operations are compared. Thus, performing to standard means performing as set out in the rules. ISO 9001:2000 is a standard for quality systems, which identifies the basic disciplines and specifies the procedures and criteria to be applied to ensure that services are of a quality that will always meet specified customer requirements.

6.3

The road haulage market and image

Road haulage accounts for approximately 80 per cent of all freight traffic carried in the United Kingdom while rail freighting amounts to only some 8 per cent. The rest, in relatively small percentages, is carried by sea, air and inland waterways and by pipeline. Industry figures show that, in fact, while rail freight accounts for only 8 per cent as stated above, over the past eight years the volumes carried by rail have risen by some 50 per cent. Currently, government emphasis is on encouraging the switch of as much freight as possible from road to rail, and where feasible to inland waterway, in the interests of reducing traffic congestion, road traffic accidents and air pollution from vehicle exhaust emissions – the so-called 'green challenge'.

MARKET SEGMENTATION AND SPECIALIZATIONS

Road haulage covers a very broad spectrum of freighting activities that differ widely in specializations and operating methods, and consequently in the equipment used and the particular skills of the people employed. The principal segmentation is that between own-account operations and professional haulage, as reflected in the different types of operator licence required, namely restricted 'O' licences for the former where they carry only goods in connection with their own trade or business (eg, as a manufacturer or supplier of goods) and standard licences for the latter that carry goods for others for hire or reward. Further divisions apply between road hauliers carrying goods only within the United Kingdom (requiring only a standard national 'O' licence) and those carrying goods internationally (requiring an international 'O' licence).

There is a third important segment comprising contract haulage or logistics operators that are essentially professional hauliers from a licensing point of view, but which are contractually tied to customers, in whose name, colours and logos they run vehicles on an exclusive basis – these are often termed third-party logistics providers.

Further segmentation occurs by virtue of the nature of the goods carried and this results in a very wide variety of specializations from the general haulier carrying virtually any goods, usually on a flat-sided or tilt-sided vehicle, at one end of the scale to, for example, the specialist dangerous goods bulk tanker operator, the temperature-controlled (ie, refrigerated) transport operator or the car-transporter specialist.

Here is an indication of some of the many specializations in road haulage:

- express parcels (eg, same-day, next-day services);
- road tanker operations (ie, chemicals/foodstuffs, etc);
- carriage of abnormal loads;
- furniture removals (domestic and industrial and new furniture);
- machinery carriage (often including an installation or removal service for such items);
- livestock carriage;
- timber haulage;
- steel haulage (including rolled steel, billets and ingots);
- boat haulage;
- contract hire operations;
- distribution and storage;
- refrigerated transport (ie, temperature-controlled);
- international haulage (specialized or general);
- groupage operations (ie, the assembly of many small consignments into full vehicle or container loads);
- pallet network operators;
- bulk tipping (minerals/fuels/aggregates/cement/grain/animal feeds);
- ready-mixed cement (ie, using truck-mixers);
- container haulage;
- vehicle/trailer hire/spot rental;
- distribution of motor vehicles (ie, car transporters);
- motor parts distribution;
- lorry-mounted crane hire.

Within these specializations there are many sub-specializations: for example, hauliers who provide only local or only long-distance services, those who cover only certain geographical regions, those who follow only particular routes (eg, Glasgow–London–Glasgow) and those who serve only particular countries (eg, United Kingdom–Eire, United Kingdom–Spain).

ANCILLARY ACTIVITIES AND DIVERSIFICATION

Not surprisingly, many hauliers seek to expand their trading activities by venturing into a variety of ancillary activities such as storage, redistribution, motor vehicle repair and machinery installation and removal, for example. In some cases these activities arise because existing haulage customers have requested them, while in others it is the haulier himself endeavouring to add value to his basic services as a means of gaining new or retaining existing customers and adding further revenue streams to his business.

FREIGHT FORWARDING AND GROUPAGE

The role of freight forwarders is to provide a complete transport service for the export or import of goods (as well as for inland movements) covering some or all of the following aspects:

- advice on the best method of movement (ie, road, sea, air);
- advice on legal/commercial requirements;
- advice on the best services;
- making necessary bookings with appropriate transport services;
- completing all documentation;
- advising on and arranging packing and labelling;
- arranging insurance cover as necessary;
- arranging for collection and following through until delivery is effected;
- arranging Customs clearance for export/import consignments;
- ensuring that all charges are reasonable and presenting a comprehensive final account.

Groupage

This is the practice of collecting small consignments together (in industry terminology, less than container loads – LCLs) and consolidating them into bulk loads for onward shipment (ie, the trunk haul) in a large vehicle or an ISO shipping container. Break-bulk is a term used to describe the unloading of consolidated loads ready for delivery of individual consignments to their respective destinations. In the case of import/export groupage, much of this work is carried out at inland clearance depots (ICDs) where HM Customs and Excise have a presence for clearing the necessary import/export documentation for such loads.

INTERMODAL FREIGHTING

Intermodal freight transport is a means of delivering goods, particularly over longer distances and across international boundaries, using two or more individual transport modes (eg, road haulage and rail freight) to provide the most economic and efficient method of delivering goods to their destination. Typically, such operations involve the movement of:

- complete, driver-accompanied road vehicles conveyed on rail for the long-haul leg of the journey (eg, via Eurotunnel's Freight Shuttle service through the Channel Tunnel);
- unaccompanied articulated semi-trailers carried piggyback on rail, ISO shipping containers or intermodal swap bodies transferred from road to rail and vice versa to complete a journey;
- road vehicles carrying ISO containers or swap-bodies from the point of loading to a rail terminal for transfer to rail for onward transit;
- road vehicles delivering ISO containers to a rail terminal for rail-haul to a port for short-sea or deep-sea shipping;
- freight (invariably in bulk loads) deep-sea shipped then transferred to barge for onward movement on rivers/inland waterways by barge or lighter (eg, the LASH system).

Combined road–rail transport, the most prominent form of intermodalism, is a specialized sector within the broader concept of intermodal transportation. This concept combines the best attributes of road and rail where road haulage provides an infinitely flexible local collection and delivery service to premises with no rail connection while rail freighting provides the long-haul facility for whole trainloads of freight between terminals, quickly, economically and, importantly too, relieving our crowded, noisy and polluted road network of many individual heavy lorry loads.

Note: ISO containers are those which meet international standards for shipping and for transfer between transport modes.

ROAD HAULAGE MARKETING

Road hauliers are dependent on marketing skills to win business from their competitors and from other transport modes. Marketing is basically the task of promoting a company and its services to customers (existing and potential) in such a way that the customer wants to use the services offered because the rates are set at the levels he is prepared to pay (ie, the right price), because the service level offered is what he wants for the delivery of his goods, because he is convinced of the reliability and integrity of the haulier, because the vehicles are right for his work, because the haulage drivers are professional in their approach and for many other reasons. It can be summed up as the function of identifying, anticipating and satisfying customer requirements with profit for his business.

PUBLIC RELATIONS AND BRAND IMAGE

Public relations is simply the matter of ensuring that everybody who comes into contact with the firm (customers, the public, the authorities – ie, police, enforcement staff, local authority etc – neighbours, employees, trade and professional people with whom it has dealings and so on) gains a good impression of it. The concept is for the haulier to make them think that his firm is good, professional and reliable among other qualities, not just in its services to customers, but in every other way; for example, being seen as concerned for the local environment by not creating undue air pollution, noise, fumes or obstruction by scruffy lorries parked where they should not be and suchlike.

Brand image

Brand image is about having a good name in the industry. It is easy to name the high-profile hauliers that everybody looks up to like Eddie Stobart, but there are many others who have created their own brand image by the smartness of their vehicles and drivers, and by their reputation for good service to customers.

This is where the role of the LGV driver is important – helping to create the brand image, not necessarily through wearing a collar and tie (which in Eddie Stobart's case is a company rule), but in efficiently carrying out instructions regarding deliveries, working within the law, not being a bully on the road and representing the best interests of his employer when face to face with customers.

How a driver conducts himself, when out on the road in full public view, and when delivering to customer premises, says a great deal both about himself and about his employer's business. A non-aggressive driving style, courtesy to other road users, a smart appearance and polite manner to customers and others all go a long way towards creating a good image for his firm. His role is that of an ambassador and very often the only representative of his firm that the customer sees on a regular basis.

GOOD ENVIRONMENTALISM

One of the most important and topical issues in transport is the impact that the haulage industry has on the environment. Green issues feature in every aspect of transport from the siting of vehicle depots, to the routeing of heavy goods traffic and the disposal of certain loads, especially waste. One of the ways that a haulier can significantly enhance his brand image is by establishing sound environmental credentials. He can do this by considering the following essential factors:

Vehicle depots:

- where they are sited;
- the noise, fumes, vibration and light emitted; and
- the disposal of waste.

Vehicle operations:

- engine, exhaust, tyre, body and load noise;
- smoke, fumes and gases emitted;
- fuel/oil consumption;
- visual impact;
- the routes and schedules selected; and
- load utilization (ie, to avoid wasted journeys).

Besides these more controllable aspects of transport, there are other aspects that have a powerful impact, but over which the transport manager has virtually no control, namely vehicle design and manufacture, road planning and building, legislative controls that are not necessarily environmentally oriented, and customer demand, which is influenced more by commercial pressure and financial consideration than by the vehicle operator's quest to, among other things, reduce fuel consumption, deliver during non-congested times, or combine loads to improve vehicle efficiency.

Drivers and owner-driver hauliers are undoubtedly limited in the steps they can individually take towards improving the environment, but this does not mean they should take no steps at all. Simple measures are available that will make a valuable contribution and the LGV driver can make his contribution to some of these. The following are just a few examples of the environmentally friendly measures that a road haulier could adopt:

In the depot:

- Examine how waste material is stored and disposed of.
- Ensure that controlled waste is correctly and safely stored on site and removed only by licensed disposal contractors.
- Avoid burning waste.
- Ensure that recyclable material is identified and saved for proper disposal – including waste paper and packing materials from office and stores.
- Ensure that vehicle washing does not result in dirty (ie, grease-laden) water draining on to neighbouring properties or into sewage systems.
- Ensure that oil and fuel spillages do not pollute drains.
- Use recycled products, such as paper, for administrative uses and packing.

- Undertake regular depot clean-up campaigns (in particular, ensuring that the outside appearance of the depot is 'environmentally friendly' to local residents, business visitors and others).

On the vehicle:

- Ensure legal requirements regarding noise, smoke, exhaust emissions and spray suppression are complied with.
- Economize on fuel consumption.
- Train drivers to ensure courtesy and consideration on the road and the use of defensive driving methods.
- Ensure that drivers obey parking and obstruction rules, and are aware of the problem of visual intrusion, noise and vibration on neighbouring domestic properties (contravention of these matters can jeopardize 'O' licences).
- Route vehicles and plan journeys to avoid congestion – ensure full utilization of vehicles to avoid extra or unnecessary journeys (which add to congestion, air pollution and the operator's own costs).
- Consider the visual impact of vehicles in terms of their general appearance and livery (change aggressive liveries to present a 'softer' image).

In the community:

- Consider the sponsorship of local community efforts to improve the environment and encourage staff to undertake environmental protection projects.

6.4

Principles of logistics and the supply chain

Present-day professional LGV drivers may well be driving vehicles emblazoned not with the old logos of 'Road Haulage' or even 'Distribution', but more likely with such terms as 'Logistics' or 'Supply Chain'. Not only do these terms represent a new era in buzzwords, but they indicate new concepts in the way that firms organize their businesses, taking what is known as the 'global' approach. In other words, they don't see transport as being separate from warehousing, or any of the other individual functions as being separate from each other. All are seen as being joined up and having a cost and/or operational bearing on each other under the logistics or supply chain banner. Here we look briefly at the accepted definitions of these two concepts merely to give the LGV driver an understanding of what they mean.

Logistics is defined in many different ways but, principally, it is a 'total' concept covering the planning and organizing of the supply and movement of materials or goods from their original source through various stages of production, assembly, packing, storage, handling and distribution and delivery to the final consumer. Supply chain, like logistics, is also variously defined, but is broadly recognized as being the continuous link between the supply of raw materials through production to delivery of the finished product to the final consumer.

These are key functions within most firms these days, invariably commanding board-level appointments for those in charge. Transport, or road haulage, which at one time was the key element of goods delivery, is just one aspect of the whole logistics concept. Now, with the broader concept of logistics taking hold in firms, all the individual functions, from raw materials inwards to outward delivery of finished product to the customer, are rolled up together under a single logistics or supply chain management function. This ensures a continuous flow line of materials and goods through all their various stages and importantly, too, ensures smooth flows of key information and documentation from the beginning to the end of the process so there are no undue bottlenecks where, for example, a delivery of goods is held up because somebody has failed to produce the accompanying paperwork.

This all-encompassing vision has many readily definable advantages, not least, at its most simplistic, the concept that lorries delivering finished goods to customers could call to pick up raw materials or components on the way back to provide two-way loading – one of the principal objectives in achieving efficient transport operations. Such integration permits a global view of total logistics costs within firms, presenting greater opportunities to achieve cost savings. It is a well-established fact that an integrated approach to logistics can lead to both efficiency improvements and cost savings.

These days, information technology (ie, IT – the use of computers) allows management to examine the efficiencies and costs of the various elements that make up an integrated logistics system and the system as a whole, a task that previously was laborious and long-winded if not completely impossible.

The logistics industry looks at integration in a variety of ways and spanning a number of functions. For example, where the customer demands just-in-time (JiT) deliveries the supplier needs to ensure that an integrated materials management system is in place to provide a flow of stock into and through the production and packaging phases so that sufficient finished product is available in time for delivery to meet the customer's schedule. Or put another way, the customer will not receive his/her JiT deliveries if the supplier does not have the stock of goods to meet the demand. And the supplier will not have that stock of finished goods if the flows of material through the production and packing processes are not adequate to produce the necessary stock back-up. Integrated systems will ensure that these vital flows of materials, components and finished products are ready on time, to specification and at an acceptable cost.

The LGV driver may feel that his job hardly impacts on these functions but, in fact, it does. An efficient logistics or supply chain operation relies as heavily on the final delivery being made correctly – namely, efficiently and promptly – as it does on the correct materials being taken in for production of the goods. If the driver does his job well – meeting schedules, delivering to the right address, dealing with the paperwork, getting a clear signature for the goods – then he too contributes to an efficient logistics operation.

6.5

Training for transport

Driving large goods vehicles (LGVs) requires a variety of personal skills, not least the ability to pass the theory, hazard perception and practical driving tests to gain a licence, and from September 2009 meeting the new Driver CPC requirements. However, depending on the nature of the work they are employed on, drivers may need further specialist training; for example, to obtain their Dangerous Goods Vocational Training Certificate (VTC) – commonly referred to as the ADR certificate. Similarly, if they need to operate lorry-mounted cranes or forklift trucks for loading and unloading purposes, this too requires specialist training to meet safety standards.

In road haulage, Skills for Logistics has responsibility for establishing the industry's occupational training standards. It provides a range of training opportunities for people entering the industry, as well as the Young LGV Driver Scheme (described in Chapter 3.5). Foundation and Advanced Modern Apprenticeships offer training linked to recognized national qualifications across all sectors of the freight transport industry. Apprentices typically gain their initial experience and Level 2 qualifications by driving, working in the warehouse or working in the office and can go on to achieve a Level 3 NVQ/SVQ.

NVQ/SVQ QUALIFICATIONS

National and Scottish Vocational Qualifications are work-based qualifications awarded to employees who have demonstrated their ability to do their job to an agreed industry standard. They enable competence to perform tasks that are assessed by observation in the workplace, with any relevant previous experience counting towards their assessment. They can also be used either as a way of structuring training and assessment of new recruits, or as a tool to recognize the skills of existing staff, perhaps as an adjunct to routine assessment. A number of

S/NVQs have been developed for use within the road transport and distribution industry as follows:

NVQ/SVQ Driving Goods Vehicles (Levels 2 and 3)

The Level 2 Qualification is for goods vehicle drivers who can show the minimum level of occupational competence required for a goods vehicle driver. The Level 3 Qualification is for drivers who can show broader driving competencies and be considered as professional goods vehicle drivers. The two qualifications 'Driving Goods Vehicles' are made up of the following units and elements of competence:

Level 2
Mandatory units:

- monitoring the loading of the vehicle by others;
- completing predriving preparations;
- maintaining the safety and the security of the load, self and property;
- awareness of driving conditions;
- operating the vehicle systems;
- driving the vehicle on public roads;
- driving the vehicle in restricted spaces.

Additional units:

- unloading the vehicle;
- coupling and uncoupling the vehicle.

Candidates must get all the mandatory units for a full award. The additional units do not form part of the qualification, but are available for candidates who have the opportunity to demonstrate competence in these areas.

Level 3
Mandatory units:

- monitoring the loading of the vehicle by others;
- unloading the vehicle;
- completing predriving preparations;
- maintaining the safety and security of the load, self and property;
- awareness of driving conditions;
- operating the vehicle systems;
- driving the vehicle in restricted spaces;
- driving the vehicle safely and efficiently on public roads.

Optional units:

- obtaining information on the delivery and collection of loads;
- planning the route and timings for the delivery and collection of loads;
- loading the vehicle;
- coupling and uncoupling the vehicle.

Candidates must get all mandatory units, plus at least any two optional units, for a full award.

NVQ/SVQ Transporting Goods by Road (Level 2)

The qualification 'Transporting Goods by Road' is made up of the following units and elements of competence. Candidates must achieve all seven units:

Unit 1 – Contribute to the maintenance of health and safety in the workplace
1.1 Contribute to maintaining a healthy and safe workplace
1.2 Implement procedures to deal with risks to health and safety
1.3 Maintain the cleanliness of the working environment
1.4 Manually lift and handle goods safely
Unit 2 – Contribute to the security of the workplace
2.1 Maintain the security of people, stock and premises
2.2 Implement procedures to deal with risks to security
Unit 3 – Contribute to effective working relationships
3.1 Maintain own performance in achieving quality standards
3.2 Work with colleagues to optimize productivity
Unit 4 – Contribute to the provision of customer services
4.1 Develop and maintain effective relationships with customers
4.2 Provide service related information to customers
4.3 Assist in resolving customer complaints
Unit 5 – Prepare for the transport of goods and materials
5.1 Prepare vehicle for use
5.2 Organize your own work
Unit 6 – Transport goods and materials
6.1 Operate and control a laden vehicle
6.2 Monitor and review progress
Unit 7 – Collect and deliver goods and materials
7.1 Prepare for the transfer of goods and materials
7.2 Transfer goods and materials

NVQ/SVQ Performing Road Haulage and Distribution Operations (Level 3)

Unit 1 – Contribute to improving customer service

1.1 Identify opportunities for improving customer service
1.2 Make recommendations for improving customer service
Unit 2 – Manage information for action
2.1 Gather required information
2.2 Inform and advise others
2.3 Hold meetings
Unit 3 – Manage yourself
3.1 Develop your own skills to improve your performance
3.2 Manage your time to meet your objectives
Unit 4 – Create good working relationships
4.1 Create good working relationships with colleagues
4.2 Create good working relationships with your manager
Unit 5 – Contribute to a safe and healthy working environment
5.1 Access and control risks to health and safety
5.2 Implement procedures to deal with threats to security, health and safety
Unit 6 – Coordinate activities with others
6.1 Organize work activities
6.2 Provide technical leadership on engineering activities
Unit 7 – Monitor and maintain the storage of goods
7.1 Monitor and maintain the condition of goods and materials in storage
7.2 Monitor and maintain the systems and facilities for the storage of goods and materials
Unit 8 – Assist in the generation and retention of business
8.1 Contribute to the generation of business
8.2 Contribute to the retention of business
Unit 9 – Maintain the movement of goods and materials
9.1 Plan the movement of goods and materials
9.2 Monitor the movement of goods and materials
Unit 10 – Contribute to auditing against specified standards
10.1 Contribute to undertaking audits
10.2 Make recommendations and implement required actions
Unit 11 – Facilitate individual learning through coaching
11.1 Coach individual learners
11.2 Assist individual learners to apply their learning

Mandatory units:

- contribute to improving customer service;
- manage information for action;
- manage yourself;
- create good working relationships;
- contribute to a safe and healthy working environment.

Optional units:

- coordinate activities with others;
- monitor and maintain the storage of goods;
- assist in the generation and retention of business;
- maintain the movement of goods and materials;
- contribute to auditing against specified standards;
- facilitate individual learning through coaching.

In order to gain a full N/SVQ, candidates will have to achieve all the mandatory units plus any two optional units

LIFTING EQUIPMENT TRAINING

It is a requirement that all forklift truck (FLT) operators should be properly trained or have taken a formal course of FLT instruction and have been tested and awarded a FLT Certificate of Competence. Many road transport courses include FLT training taking the trainee step by step through the basic operations. Normally, these courses are of one week's duration and involve truck maintenance, practical and theoretical training. On completion of this training the trainee will be subjected to a written practical and oral test. Successful trainees will be awarded a certificate of competence for the appropriate truck – counterbalance or reach. The minimum age requirement for this training is 17 years.

DRIVER TRAINING FOR DANGEROUS GOODS

Drivers of dangerous goods-carrying road tanker and tank container-carrying vehicles and those carrying dangerous goods in packages must hold Vocational Training Certificates gained by attending an approved course and passing a written examination set by the City and Guilds of London Institute (C&G). In common parlance these VTCs are referred to as ADR certificates since the need for driver training and certification was originally derived from the European Agreement on the Carriage of Dangerous Goods by Road (ADR). This legal requirement applies broadly where the carriage of specified dangerous goods is in:

- road tankers with a capacity exceeding 1,000 litres; or
- vehicles carrying tank containers with a capacity greater than 3,000 litres (with certain exceptions); or
- vehicles exceeding 3.5 tonnes permissible maximum weight carrying specified dangerous goods in packages.

Vocational training certificates are valid for a period of five years and are renewable, subject to the holder attending an approved refresher course and taking a further examination within the 12 months prior to the expiry date of an existing certificate.

Drivers must carry their certificate with them when driving relevant vehicles and must produce it on request by police or a goods vehicle examiner. It is an offence to drive a dangerous goods vehicle without being the holder of a certificate, or to fail to produce such a certificate on request.

Employer responsibilities

It is the responsibility of the employer to ensure that dangerous goods drivers receive training so they understand the dangers arising from the products they are carrying and what to do in an emergency situation, and that they hold relevant certificates covering the vehicle being driven and the products carried. Employers must retain records of all instruction and training given to drivers.

Approved training and the SQA examination

Dangerous goods driver training is carried out at approved establishments where the Scottish Qualifications Authority (SQA) examination can be taken. The syllabus for the examination involves both theoretical sessions and practical exercises. The examination itself comprises a core element designed to assess the candidate's practical and legal knowledge plus a specialist element for either road tanker and tank container drivers or packaged goods drivers (or both if required). Additionally, candidates have to pass individual 'dangerous substance' examination papers covering each of nine classes of dangerous goods, to test their specialist knowledge of the products they carry in their work.

Candidates who pass the examination by achieving a pass mark of at least 75 per cent in each element – ie, core, tanker/package and substance – will receive their vocational training certificate. Those who fail can apply to resit the examination without further training within a period of 16 weeks from receipt of the notification of failure. Further information on the training and examinations may be obtained from the SQA on its website: www.sqa.org.uk.

TRAINING FOR LORRY LOADER OPERATORS

There are no mandatory requirements at the present time for goods vehicle drivers to hold certificates of competence to operate lorry-mounted cranes (often referred to by the generic term Hiabs). However, under the Health and Safety at Work Act employers have a statutory duty to provide adequate instruction and safety training on this type of equipment for all employees who may be required to operate it.

Voluntary scheme

A voluntary certification scheme is run by the Construction Industry Training Board (CITB) to improve safety on construction sites. This scheme is strongly supported by those in the construction industry, who may refuse entry to their own sites to non-certified lorry drivers. Mainly, the Board's scheme is concerned with ensuring a sound understanding of safety procedures for the use of a wide range of equipment including lorry-mounted cranes and skip loaders. Under the scheme, the Board provided certification of existing lorry-loader and skip-loader operators who could show by means of employer confirmation that they were experienced in the use of such equipment.

Existing operatives prior to June 1993 who could produce an employer declaration could obtain the Board's safety certificate under a grandfather rights arrangement and a similar arrangement applied to skip-loader operatives until the end of 1994. However, since then newcomers seeking first-time certification and drivers renewing grandfather rights certificates have had to undergo (re-) training and site-based assessment to show that they can operate such equipment with complete safety. CITB safety certificates are renewable at five-yearly intervals.

FIRST AID TRAINING AND CERTIFICATION

Because of the high-risk nature of most jobs within the transport industry it is good sense to have had first aid training – you never know when it may come in useful at work, on the road, or even at home or while on holiday. Certification courses are usually available from, or are run in conjunction with, St John Ambulance and the British Red Cross and last one week. At the end of the course, the trainee is tested both practically and verbally with successful trainees being awarded either a First Aid Essentials Certificate or a First Aid at Work Certificate or its equivalent.

6.6

Mobile communications and ITS

Increasing use of both mobile communications and Intelligent Transport Systems (ITS) have been shown to be cost-effective and efficient aids to transport operations where these days it is essential:

- for vehicle drivers to be in contact with their base, colleagues, customers and other key contacts (eg, vehicle breakdown services and repair agencies);
- for firms to know where their vehicles are at any given time and able to contact drivers to exchange vital data;
- for drivers to have on-board route and traffic information; and
- eventually, in connection with electronic road charging systems.

It is widely accepted that once a driver drives off in his vehicle he is totally cut off from his workplace until he arrives at a known destination where a message can be relayed to him, or he manages to find an operational roadside telephone. If he is an owner-driver it makes life particularly difficult, being out of touch with what is going on in his business.

In these days of high costs, competitive market places and a fast pace of business life, and taking account of technological developments, this is an unacceptable penalty of having people travelling by road during working hours. The inability to contact a business executive could result in missed business opportunities. The inability to contact delivery drivers could mean wasted journeys because of cancelled orders or changed plans arising after they have left the depot. It could mean a driver getting back to base and then having to revisit a customer visited earlier in the day because he could not be contacted *en route* to be warned of late, or forgotten, order items.

It is a common experience in transport operations for considerable cost to be wasted through late, changed, redirected, cancelled orders and instructions. Try as he might, the transport or fleet manager can rarely avoid his share of these annoying frustrations and there is nothing that he can do unless he can contact the driver on the road.

Vehicle-based mobile communications change all this and the wasted costs of the past can be turned into savings and even into profit quite simply by being able to contact the driver, relay details of the changed plans and generally divert vehicles to meet the current needs of the business. The savings in wasted time and miles, the avoidance of heavy vehicles returning home empty because they can be directed to pick up return loads, and the response to last-minute customer demands are significant benefits, which in themselves, or with other benefits, add up to offset the capital costs of buying and installing communications equipment and the on-going costs of rentals and call charges.

COMMUNICATIONS SYSTEMS

Mobile communications can be reviewed under five broad headings as follows:

- CB radio;
- radio pagers;
- private mobile radio (PMR);
- cellular (mobile) telephones;
- satellite-based systems.

CB radio

Citizens' Band (ie, CB) radio was officially inaugurated in Britain in 1982 when the law made it permissible to operate such systems, which had hitherto been illegal and had caused difficulty because their use interfered with the radio links of the emergency services and other official networks. Initially, it was enthusiasts who used CB as a means of 'friendly' communication, to chat to other users and generally communicate non-business information. In time, however, it proved capable of serving more important needs such as the reporting of accidents and other emergencies, breakdowns, road blockages, diversions and so on. Similarly, it proved to have some use in providing communication between vehicle drivers and their base – within limited range – for the purposes of passing information about loads, schedules and changed instructions, for example.

Despite its obvious use for these purposes, CB has significant disadvantages: the frequencies are cluttered with undisciplined, long, sometimes foul and frequently frivolous conversation and chatter, which can be heard by all users due to lack of privacy. This in itself is another disadvantage, along with the general interference experienced and the congestion on channels. Furthermore, the equipment itself has its limitations in terms of power and range, and in some areas there is less than satisfactory reception.

CB use has declined over recent years from a peak of around 300,000 licences in 1980, and now there seems to be little enthusiasm for its use. The former legal requirement for CB use to be licensed was abolished by the government from 8 December 2006.

Radio pagers

Radio pagers (commonly called bleepers) are a portable means of contact but only on a one-way basis from the sender to the receiver. Pagers fall into two main categories, tone pagers and voice pagers. With either type a person can be alerted to the fact that he is required and with more sophisticated equipment can be advised by varying tones to follow specific predetermined instructions – for example, to ring one telephone number or another. Voice pagers or 'talking bleepers' convey a spoken message that is usually repeated twice, thereby alerting the user to follow specific courses of action. Some pagers are capable of alerting the user by vibration (silent pagers) so that outsiders are not aware of the sound or so that the user is not interrupted in mid-conversation by an audible 'bleep'. Others have the ability to display messages on a liquid crystal screen from a text memory of up to some 800 characters.

While the cost of pagers is relatively low (usually only a few pence per day) and the unit itself is small and unobtrusive to carry around in the pocket (some are no bigger than credit cards), there are disadvantages to their use. The first is the limited range (generally not more than about 15 miles (24 kilometres)) and the second is the need for the receiver to find a working telephone in order to make the call for which he has been alerted.

Private mobile radio (PMR)

Portable radios are used for private two-way communication, usually between a base station and a number of mobiles (ie, radio-equipped vehicles), with the added facility in some cases of the mobile units being able to talk to each other. Generally, mobile radio operates over a limited range of some 10 to 20 miles (about 15 to 30 kilometres), depending on location and the height of the base station aerial. Much depends on the type of terrain between the base station and the mobile unit. In open country, far greater range may be obtained than in a city with built-up areas and many tall buildings.

Many systems have the disadvantage that anybody in the vehicle or within earshot can hear the message being relayed and that all mobile units hear a message intended for one only. However, some equipment has a facility for selective calling so that only one unit need be contacted at a time.

In the main, mobile radio is restricted to a closed system but there are facilities whereby this can be extended by linking into one of the national relay networks that have many base stations throughout the country. The Securicor 'Relayfone' system is a good example. Developments are in hand to allow, in the future, interconnection of private mobile radio systems into the public switched telephone network (PSTN).

Typical of PMR systems are those used by local taxi services where the driver has a hand-held microphone with an 'ON/OFF' switch. This PTT (press to talk) switch must be depressed to enable the driver to talk to the base station and then released while he listens to the returning message. The disadvantage of this is the road safety risk created by a driver trying to control his vehicle and operate the microphone switch (the Highway Code warns against such practices, and the police are alert to this habit and will take action against offending drivers).

Mobile radio operates on a number of alternative radio frequencies as follows:

- Low-band VHF (25–50 MHz) provides the greatest range but it suffers from high noise levels and heavy channel loadings (used by police and emergency services).
- High-band VHF (150–174 MHz) provides good coverage in built-up areas with less noise but there is still heavy usage of the channels.
- UHF (450–512 MHz) has a much shorter range than VHF but there is much less congestion on the channels and it provides good penetration in urban areas where there are many buildings and tall structures.

Within these radio frequencies equipment may be obtained for AM or FM operation.

Band 3

Increased demand for mobile communication led to the allocation by the government of the VHF slot left vacant by the old 405-line black and white TV network for use in providing communications services. This is now called Band 3 PMR and is operated by the two official franchise holders, GEC and Band Three Radio, each with 200 channels.

This system will be of interest to those requiring only brief communication (ie, not full conversation) between base station and vehicle (mobile unit), but with little need for communication outside and who wish to avoid the relatively high call costs of cell phones and the rather higher capital costs of the cellular telephone units themselves.

Cellular (mobile) telephones

The advent of the cellular telephone system has revolutionized mobile communications. Today it is possible to have a telephone interconnected to the national and international telephone networks from a vehicle-based (ie, mobile) installation or from a set carried neatly in a handbag or jacket pocket. Such systems provide the user with the facility to dial direct to almost any telephone number in the United Kingdom or to reach such numbers via the British Telecom operator, and to make international calls and calls to any other cellular telephone. Similarly, any telephone user can dial direct to a mobile cell phone number.

The principle of the Total Access Communications System (TACS) cellular telephone system is that instead of a connection by wire as with the conventional telephone, the link is made by radio airwaves in the 900MHz radio band frequency using only 50MHz bandwidth. The United Kingdom is now divided into a number of individual cells like a honeycomb. Each cell is anything from 2 kilometres to 30 kilometres across with a transceiver that relays cellular calls to and from the normal public switched telephone network (PSTN), as well as from one cellular telephone to another.

A central computer (the brains of the system) monitors all traffic in the system and switches calls from one transceiver to another as the mobile cell phone user travels from one cell into another. Calls go through both the cellular network and the British Telecom network, which is why call charges are higher than with the normal PSTN system and especially in the London area.

The government has licensed two operators to provide the network, namely British Telecom (Cellnet) and Racal (Vodafone), and currently some 90 per cent of the UK population is covered by both systems.

Equipment for operation within the cellular telephone system can be divided into three groups:

- mobile units (eg, installed in vehicles);
- transportable units (for use in vehicles or can be carried in a briefcase, for example);
- portable units (small units, which can be readily carried around and even fitted into a jacket pocket).

Voice activation

A relatively new development in vehicle-based mobile units is voice activation to overcome the problems (and illegalities) of answering the telephone and dialling numbers for outward calls while actually driving the vehicle. This equipment is programmed to recognize a voice signal (usually just a single word) spoken into the handset, which sets off the dialling of a predetermined number (eg, base, office, home). Other equipment is dashboard mounted so calls can be received and made 'hands off' to avoid the road safety risks and contravention of the advice given in the new *Highway Code* against using 'phones' while on the move.

Warning

It is useful to caution users and potential users of cellular telephones about three particular matters as follows:

- Proper installation of equipment in vehicles is essential both for efficient operation and for safety reasons. Special care is needed in the case of installation in heavy vehicles with 24-volt electrical systems to avoid wiring faults and other electrical problems.
- Insurance of equipment in vehicles is important; it is highly attractive to thieves. If stolen or lost in a vehicle accident or fire, an insurer may decline to accept a claim if the installation of the equipment had not been notified beforehand. In general, motor insurance does not cover a cellular phone. It is relatively easy for the subscriber to prevent fraudulent use of a stolen set by notifying the airtime retailer. The retailer can disconnect the stolen unit remotely, thus preventing further use. Mobile cell phones are not easy to steal because the handset, transceiver and wiring loom have to be removed.
- Users should be aware that foreign customs officials may impound mobile communications handsets when entering certain countries because use of the equipment is not compatible with overseas telecommunications networks and might interfere with emergency services.

SAFETY

The *Highway Code* includes a section (new edition 2007 – paragraph 149) on the use of microphones and in-car (ie, including lorry) technology. It warns against using a hand-held mobile phone or microphone while driving, and even against using hands-free equipment, which will distract the driver's attention from the road. It advises drivers to find a safe place to stop to use such equipment. However, drivers should not stop on the hard shoulder of a motorway to answer or make a call, no matter how urgent – this is illegal.

SATELLITE-BASED COMMUNICATIONS SYSTEMS

Technological developments in satellite-based communication systems provide facilities for long-range telephone, fax and paging links between base and vehicle, as well as positive vehicle tracking systems. Such systems are now widely used in North America and are of increasing interest to UK and European transport fleet operators. Using the same basic technology that puts instantaneous live pictures from sporting events and news reports on our television screens, the precise location of vehicles can be pinpointed and messages passed, but on a one-way basis only from base to vehicle, not vice versa, so drivers cannot abuse the system by calling friends and relatives worldwide.

It is not likely that satellite communications will completely replace other two-way mobile communications systems but with the proliferation of Euro-wide transport operations since the opening of the Single European Market in 1993, it has provided operators with a reliable and spontaneous means of contacting their drivers thousands of miles from base and at a price that, in terms relative to the cost of the driver constantly telephoning home to see if he is wanted, would be considered cheap.

A number of systems are in current use including those of British Telecom Mobile Communications (BTMC) via the Inmarsat satellite system, a consortium in which DAF Trucks has an interest (Roadacom), Locstar (a French company backed by Daimler-Benz and British Aerospace), and a joint US/French operation called Qualcomm-Alcatel in conjunction with Eutelsat (the European satellite consortium).

THE GLOBAL POSITIONING SYSTEM (GPS)

The Global Positioning System, originally devised by the US military to assist navigation of both ground and air crew, incorporates over 24 satellites orbiting the Earth in outer space. As the system developed, it has been utilized for civilian purposes, in particular the marine, leisure and commercial markets.

The nature of the satellite signal enables the GPS receiver, ranging in size from a standard mobile phone to a small television set, to track it accurately and efficiently. At least three satellites are in view of the receiver at any one time, and this decodes the information to display global position in longitude and latitude, and a number of different coordinate formats. Because it does not rely on radio signals, GPS can be used anywhere in the world.

A relatively new use for GPS is for 'in-vehicle systems', which now are capable of incorporating CD, radio and GPS in a single unit. For navigation purposes, it is just a case of entering a destination (eg, the name of a road) and within seconds the distance, route and travel time are calculated and displayed. A voice gives commands for turning at the correct junctions and a map on the screen is a useful navigation aid.

The Blaupunkt system, for example, gives accurate information for navigation in the United Kingdom, but the system also incorporates CD ROMs that can be downloaded in seconds to allow navigation on almost any road in Europe. Many such systems are in use by ambulance services, couriers and haulage firms.

SIEMENS VDO SYSTEM

Siemens VDO Automotive was the first company in the United Kingdom to incorporate the Traffic Message Channel service (TNIC) into its after-market satellite navigation systems, enabling it to combine satellite navigation with real-time traffic information. TMC provides up-to-the-minute information on current traffic conditions, which is relayed to vehicles equipped with any VDO Dayton or Philips CARiN navigation systems (the two brands are owned by Siemens VDO) using RDS TMC, a digital data stream carried by radio broadcaster Classic FM. Data are gathered from a wide variety of sources, including real-time information from vehicles actually out on the road. The system is also 'intelligent', being capable of differentiating between different types of delays, for example slow-moving traffic, accidents, fog or roadworks. TMC data can also be used by the navigation system to automatically plan alternative routes around incidents or congested areas and to predict arrival times. This form of real-time traffic information significantly adds to the usefulness of on-board navigation, turning it into a driving aid that can assist in reducing journey times, even for drivers travelling on routes they use regularly.

INTELLIGENT TRANSPORT SYSTEMS

Intelligent Transport Systems (ITS), using telematics (ie, the combination of information technology and telecommunications), provide online (electronic) information and control systems for all modes of transport, including vehicle-based systems. Typical of such systems used in road transport are those that operate:

- variable message signs (VMS) for (eg, on motorways) on-board route and traffic information (eg, Trafficmaster);
- traffic control and enforcement signs (eg, the latest-type digital speed cameras);
- electronic road charging;
- traffic monitoring;
- vehicle-to-base communications; and
- electronic ticketing.

Appendix I

APPROVED DRIVER CPC TRAINING CENTRES

Accrington & Rossendale – Accrington, Lancashire. PCV

Alan Moffat Training Services – Carlisle, Cumbria. PCV/LGV

Automotive Transport Training – Hinckley, Leicestershire. LGV

Baker Hammond – Stowmarket, Suffolk. PCV/LGV

Birds Transport Training – Oldbury, West Midlands. PCV/LGV

Blackpool Transport Services – Blackpool, Lancashire. PCV

Bournemouth Transport – Dorset. PCV

Carntyne Transport Ltd – Glasgow. LGV

Ceva Logistics Ltd – Nuneaton, Warwickshire. LGV

Chevron Training – Flint, North Wales. LGV/ PCV

Chris Blyth Training Services – Towcester, Northamptonshire. PCV

Community Transport Association – Hyde, Cheshire. PCV

Crosshands Training Ltd – Llanelli, Carmarthenshire. PCV/LGV

CTTS Management Ltd – West Lothian. PCV/LGV

DATS – Torquay, South Devon. PCV

Driver Training Centre Ltd – Hastings, East Sussex. PCV/LGV

Driving Services UK Ltd – Ledsham, Cheshire. PCV/LGV

Durham County Council – Durham. PCV/LGV

East London Bus Group – Ilford, London. PCV

EPIC Training and Consulting Services Ltd – St Albans, Hertfordshire. LGV

EYMS Bus & Coach Training – Hull. PCV

First Group plc – Weston-Super-Mare, North Somerset. PCV

Freight Transport Association – Tunbridge Wells, Kent. LGV/ PCV

Gap Training – Driffield, Yorkshire. PCV/LGV

Go-Ahead Group – Camberwell, London. LGV/ PCV

GoAhead Training – Dundee. LGV/ PCV

Guild of British Coach Operators Ltd – Southend-on-Sea, Essex. PCV

Hargreaves Training – Leeds. LGV
Ipswich Buses – Ipswich, Suffolk. PCV
JB Hamill @ Teamtrain Ltd – Gateshead, Tyne and Wear. LGV
Jeff's Coaches Ltd – Helmdon, Northamptonshire. PCV
Kent Metro Ltd – Maidstone. LGV/ PCV
Lothian Buses plc – Edinburgh. PCV
Melmerby Training Services – Ripon, North Yorkshire. PCV/LGV
Mercedes Benz UK Ltd – Barnsley, South Yorkshire. LGV
Metroline Travel Ltd – Wembley, London. PCV
Minimise Your Risk – Telscombe Cliffs, East Sussex. PCV
Morris Travel Ltd – Carmarthen, Wales. PCV/LGV
Motts Travel – Aylesbury, Buckinghamshire. LGV/ PCV
National Express – Birmingham. PCV
Newport Transport Ltd – Newport, Gwent. PCV/LGV
NFT Distribution Driving Academy – Somercotes, Derbyshire. LGV
North Birmingham Training – Birmingham, West Midlands. PCV
North Tyneside Council – Newcastle, Tyne & Wear. PCV/LGV
Nottingham City Transport – Nottingham. PCV
Novadata TAB Ltd – Braintree, Essex. PCV/LGV
Omnibus Training Ltd – Wimbledon. PCV
Oran Ltd – Alloa, Scotland. LGV
Oxford Bus Company – Oxford. PCV
Peter Smythe Training – Mansfield, Nottinghamshire. PCV/LGV
Phoenix Training – Llansannan, North Wales. PCV
Pride Training UK Ltd – Long Eaton, Nottingham. PCV
Red Rose Training – Manchester, Lancashire. PCV/LGV
Road Haulage Association – Peterborough, Cambridgeshire. PCV/LGV
Robert Wiseman Dairies – East Kilbride. LGV
RTITB Ltd – Telford, Shropshire. PCV/LGV
Scotguide – Glasgow. PCV
Simon Management Ltd – Redhill, Surrey. LGV
Somax Ltd – Bristol – North Somerset. PCV/LGV
South Birmingham College – Birmingham, West Midlands. PCV/LGV
Specialist Training and Consultancy Services Ltd – Accrington, Lancashire. PCV/LGV
Stiller Academy – Newton Aycliffe, Co. Durham. LGV
System Group Ltd – Carlisle, Cumbria. PCV/LGV.
Tangerine Transport Solutions Ltd – Wembley, London. PCV
THB Risk Management Ltd – Peterborough, Cambridgeshire. PCV/LGV
Training Force – Bristol, North Somerset. LGV
Transdev Blazefield – Starbeck, Harrogate. PCV
Translink – Belfast, Northern Ireland. PCV
Transtech Training Services at MANCAT – Openshaw, Manchester. PCV
Travel West Midlands – Walsall, West Midlands. PCV

Tyneside Training Services – Newcastle-upon-Tyne. PCV/LGV
Wakefield College – Wakefield, Yorkshire. PCV/LGV
Ward International Consulting Ltd – Fareham. LGV/ PCV
Warrington Borough Transport Ltd – Warrington, Cheshire. PCV
Welwyn LGV – Beverley, East Yorkshire. LGV/ PCV
West Nottinghamshire College – Mansfield, Nottinghamshire. LGV/ PCV
Zenith Driver Training – Lee-on-Solent, Hampshire. PCV/LGV

Appendix II

DRIVING LICENCE AND DRIVING TEST FEES

DRIVING LICENCE FEES

(As at April 2008)

- **First provisional licence** (car, motorcycle, moped) — **£45.00**
- **First provisional licence** (lorry or bus) — **FREE**
- **Changing provisional for first full** — **FREE**
- **Duplicate** – If your licence is lost, stolen, destroyed or defaced — **£22.00**
- **Replacement** – change of name and/or address — **FREE**
- **Exchange** – This includes adding a test pass to a full licence, adding or surrendering provisional motorcycle entitlement, removing expired endorsements — **FREE**
- **Exchanging** an old-style pink or green licence for a new-style one — **£10.00**
- **After revocation under the New Drivers Act** — **£45.00**
- **Renewing your licence**
  Car licence (at age 70 and over) — **FREE**
  Full – medium/large vehicle, minibus/bus — **FREE**
  Provisional – medium/large vehicle, minibus/bus — **FREE**
  For medical reasons — **FREE**
- **Exchanging licences from other countries**
  Full Northern Ireland car licence — **FREE**
  Full Northern Ireland for medium/large vehicle, minibus/bus — **FREE**
  Full EC/EEA or other foreign licence (including Channel Islands and Isle of Man) — **FREE**
- **New licence after disqualification**
  Car licence, motorcycle, medium/large vehicle, minibus/bus — **£60.00**
  If disqualified for some drink/driving offences — **£85.00**

DRIVING TEST FEES

Test fees as at April 2008

Theory Test

Standard fee for bus and lorry drivers including a Hazard Perception test.	£32.00

Practical Test – Weekdays

Car	£48.50
Tractor	£48.50
Motorcycle	£60.00
Lorry/Bus	£89.00
Car and Trailer	£89.00

Practical Test – Saturday and Weekday Evenings

Car	£58.00
Tractor	£58.00
Motorcycle	£70.00
Lorry/Bus	£107.00
Car and Trailer	£107.00

Extended Test Weekday – after disqualification

Car	£97.00
Motorcycle	£120.00

Extended Test Saturday – after disqualification

Car	£116.00
Motorcycle	£140.00

Index